LATER LANGUAGE DEVELOPMENT

Later Language Development

The School-Age and Adolescent Years

Second Edition

Marilyn A. Nippold

pro·ed
An International Publisher

8700 Shoal Creek Boulevard
Austin, Texas 78757-6897
800/897-3202   Fax 800/397-7633
www.proedinc.com

An International Publisher

© 1998 by PRO-ED, Inc.
8700 Shoal Creek Boulevard
Austin, Texas 78757-6897
800/897-3202   Fax 800/397-7633
www.proedinc.com

Library of Congress Cataloging-in-Publication Data

Nippold, Marilyn A.
    Later language development : the school-age and adolescent years /
Marilyn A. Nippold. — 2nd ed.
        p.   cm.
    Rev. ed. of : Later language development / edited by Marilyn A.
Nippold.   1988.
    Includes bibliographical references and index.
    ISBN 0-89079-725-0 (alk. paper)
    1. Language acquisition.   I. Later language development.
    II. Title.
P118.L3895   1998
401'.93'—dc21
                                                                97-20020
                                                                CIP

This book is designed in Goudy.

Printed in the United States of America

    4   5   6   7   8   9   10   07   06   05   04   03

This book is dedicated to my students—
past, present, and future.

About the Cover

The title of this painting is "Prometheus," by Northwest artist Allen Cox. Greek mythology credits Prometheus with bringing the gift of fire to mankind against the wishes of the gods. With fire comes light and knowledge ... and the foundations of civilization. The painting "Prometheus" represents a flame-like burst of light exploding upward, illuminating the surrounding darkness – a visual metaphor regarding this titanic act of enlightenment by a single individual.

The work of Allen Cox often addresses aspects of myth, metaphor, and language from a visual perspective. Cox, who holds an MFA in painting from the University of Oregon, has been creating and exhibiting his abstract paintings since 1982. His creations can be found in public, private, and corporate collections throughout the United States.

CONTENTS

FOREWORD

Marilyn Nippold has done a huge favor for all of us who strive to cover the more advanced language abilities of upper-grade youth and adolescents in our courses on language development. In this second edition of *Later Language Development*, she has compiled, integrated, and interpreted the extensive research on this population for a number of important topics. There is also a welcome expansion of the age range involved—downward to include elementary children and upward to include young adults.

Since she, herself, has made substantial contributions to the relevant literature, Dr. Nippold is able to write about it with great familiarity. Consequently, this text is rich with examples of the actual research tasks so that the reader quickly understands each study or structured observation. Her lucid comments on factors to keep in mind when constructing tests of adolescent language abilities stem from her wide knowledge base in this area and are singularly helpful to test constructors.

Dr. Nippold wisely concentrates on a selected number of topics, and these are covered in depth. These topics include lexical acquisition and use, the language associated with formal reasoning, aspects of figurative language, syntactic growth, and (my favorite) the development of persuasion and negotiation. Other topics receive a unique treatment. For example, the chapter on conversation and narration focuses on the interface of these two important uses of language.

This book will be useful to anyone seeking an increased understanding of the relationships among cognitive development, language acquisition, and academic performance. This certainly includes speech–language pathologists, developmental psychologists, and teachers of upper-grade youth.

In conclusion, I would like to proffer the following example of analogical reasoning: "Eating Godiva chocolate" is to "A pleasant taste experience" as "Reading this book" is to "A meaningful learning experience."

M. Irene Stephens
Northern Illinois University

PREFACE

This book is a revision of *Later Language Development: Ages Nine through Nineteen* (Nippold, 1988), which was a multi-authored text for which I served as editor. The second edition is now a single-authored work, a modification that was made in response to readers' requests for greater consistency in style and focus throughout the book. I wish to thank each of the authors who contributed chapters to the first edition for their encouragement as I worked on the revision, and for their significant contributions to the study of later language development.

Another modification is that the age range of the revised edition has been extended downward, to include information about language development in young elementary school-age children, in addition to older children and adolescents. This change was also made in response to readers' requests to provide a more comprehensive coverage of language development in youth. Similarly, where information was available, language as it continues to develop into adulthood has been discussed in more detail, a change that reflects a growing interest among researchers in studying language as it evolves throughout the life span. For example, chapters in this book describe how the ability to define words and to explain proverbs continues to grow throughout childhood, adolescence, and well into adulthood.

Since 1988, when the first edition was published, numerous studies have been conducted on the topic of later language development, information that covers school-age children, adolescents, and adults. In revising the book, I have attempted to incorporate much of this newer research into the chapters while also uncovering older research that was not included in the first edition. It is gratifying to see that interest in later language development is continuing to grow.

It is expected that this book, as it attempts to pull together a large body of research on a diverse set of topics, will serve as a reference for students, researchers, teachers, clinicians, and others who are interested in language development through the life span. This topic should occupy the minds of individuals well into the future as the realization proliferates that language development has no clear point of completion. I hope to be able to update the book more frequently in an effort to keep up with the many exciting discoveries that lie ahead.

C H A P T E R

LATER LANGUAGE DEVELOPMENT: AN OVERVIEW

"As long as one talks, one must keep on learning how to talk."

—Mildred Berry (1969, p. 185)

This book is about language development during the school-age and adolescent years. *School-age children* are defined as those who range in age from 6 through 12 years and who attend elementary or middle school (Grades 1 through 6). *Adolescents*, ranging in age from 13 through 18 years, are students who attend middle school or high school (Grades 7 through 12). Information reported in this book indicates that significant growth occurs in many aspects of language during the 6 through 18 age range, and that language continues to develop even into adulthood. In fact, it is difficult to identify any point in the life span when the process of language development is truly complete. Given the protracted and continuous nature of this process, "language through the life span" is a reasonable perspective to hold on this topic.

During the 1960s, researchers began to examine with intensity a broad range of linguistic attainments that occur during infancy and early childhood, a pattern that continues to the present. Many studies of language development in school-age children and adolescents have also been conducted since that time. Interest in studying older children even seems to have escalated in recent years, particularly since the linguistic bases of reading and writing have become more widely recognized (Kamhi & Catts, 1989). However, compared to early language development, studies of later language development traditionally have received much less emphasis in books, journals, conferences, and workshops devoted to the topic of language development. Perhaps this situation will improve as more is said about the close connection between

1

continued growth in language and the academic and social success of school-age children and adolescents.

Years ago, pioneers in the field, such as Mildred Berry (1969), recognized that language continued to develop well beyond the preschool years. However, detailed descriptions of the linguistic attainments of school-age children and adolescents were not widely available, and no cohesive or integrated review of the literature on this topic had been published. Because of the traditional emphasis on early language development, some readers may question the possibility of significant growth in language during the school-age and adolescent years. They also may argue that language development is basically complete by the time a child begins school, because their ears tell them this.

For example, upon listening to the audiotaped language samples of two children, ages 6 and 8 years, it may be difficult for individuals to determine which child is older, because even the 6-year-old already speaks in long and complex utterances, produces clear articulation, uses a wide variety of words, and actively contributes to the conversation, much like the 8-year-old. When linguistic developmental markers are identified in the spoken mode, there is no doubt that by age 6 most children are performing very well. However, when those markers are broadened to include written forms in addition to spoken forms of language, it becomes clear that the 8-year-old, who reads fables to her younger sister and writes imaginative stories on her word processor (see Figure 1.1), is far ahead of the 6-year-old in her language development.

Even if some readers concede that language continues to develop during the school-age years, they still may subscribe to the notion that this process is complete by the time a child reaches adolescence. The roots of this notion run deep. Thirty years ago, Lenneberg (1967) set forth his influential theory concerning the "critical period for language acquisition." The theory stated that children are maximally ready to acquire language between the ages of 2 and 12 years because of biological maturational processes that regulate the onset and timing of language learning. With the onset of puberty, according to the theory, the capacity for language acquisition is diminished.

There is ample evidence to support the existence of a critical period of language acquisition, particularly in studies of bilingualism. Most young children can easily learn a second language, particularly if they are immersed in a foreign culture where their native language is not spoken. After puberty, it becomes more difficult to become bilingual (Fromkin & Rodman, 1988; Obler, 1993). As Pinker (1994) explained, adolescents and adults can learn a foreign language with adequate motivation, instruction, and practice, but most will not attain *mastery* of that language. Hence, there are limits in the human capacity to become fully bilingual. However, this should not be interpreted to mean that growth in language cannot occur beyond puberty. In fact, Lenneberg (1967) himself pointed out that certain aspects of language, such as vocabulary, continue to expand throughout the life span. The important point is that the existence of a critical period of language acquisition, a time when children are maximally ready to learn language, does not negate the fact that further growth in lan-

One day my friend Lindsey and I went up Mount St. Helens and then back down just because we wanted to. Then when we were just about to leave we heard this loud BOOM!!

All this dusty gas like a big big huge cloud came down after us. Luckily we were in our car, so we zoomed out of the park and we zoomed as fast as we could.

Suddenly we were trapped between Mount St. Helens and ten police cars. All ten police got out of their car to give me a ticket but they soon were running back to their cars. They turned up their engines and roared off like a herd of buffalo charging at something.

Lindsey and I followed to my house and hid under the beds. But we forgot to close the windows so the gas found us and our whole room was filled up with smoke. So we raced to Lindsey's house and hid under the bed. This time we remembered to close the doors and the windows.

But it must have crept in from the wall because the room we were in was filled with ash. So off we were again. We went to my mom's house and my dad's house but the smoke came in through the drain pipe, and it brought a lot of icky water. It brought it to where we were hiding so we ran out of the house and basically traveled all around the city of Washington. It chased us all the way to Brazil. Someone offered us a hamburger but we couldn't stop for anything unless the gas and dust stopped.

We traveled all the way to Russia and Madagascar, and back to the United States and back to Washington. Do you know where it went next? It went back through my mom and dad's house, back out the drain pipe, back to Lindsey's house, out the cracks in the walls and back to my house through the windows. And then do you know where it went? It went back to Mount St. Helens and it was still chasing us. So guess where we are? In the volcano waiting for it to blow again. So we can get away.

By Emily

Figure 1.1. Story written at school by an 8-year-old girl using a word processor and printer.

guage can and does occur beyond that period in typically developing youth. Lenneberg described the years before puberty as the period of *primary* language acquisition, and, given what is known about the nature of language development beyond puberty, that perspective is well taken. As is later discussed, language development in adolescents compared to that which occurs in younger children differs markedly in terms of its speed, salience, and substance.

Language development in adolescents is a gradual and protracted process, and change can be difficult to observe. To document language growth in adolescents, it is often necessary to compare widely separated age groups (e.g., 13-year-olds versus 18-year-olds) and to examine the use of low-frequency syntactic structures and intersentential linguistic phenomena in spoken and written contexts (Nelson, 1988; Nippold, Schwarz, & Undlin, 1992; Scott, 1988). Additional tasks that can reveal language growth in adolescents include defining abstract nouns (McGhee-Bidlack, 1991), explaining the meanings of idioms and proverbs (Nippold & Rudzinski, 1993; Nippold, Uhden, & Schwarz, 1997), and solving third-order verbal analogy problems (Nippold, 1994). The use of language in diverse social situations should also be examined (Cooper & Anderson-Inman, 1988). For example, observing how adolescents modify the content and style of their speech to persuade or negotiate with different listeners for a variety of purposes can reveal important developments in language (Flavell, Botkin, Fry, Wright, & Jarvis, 1968; Selman, Beardslee, Schultz, Krupa, & Podorefsky, 1986).

Early Versus Later Language Development: Critical Processes

When processes thought to be important for language development are considered, some interesting contrasts become apparent. This is especially true when young children are compared with school-age children and adolescents.

One important contrast concerns the sources of input for language learning. For most infants, toddlers, and preschool children, spoken communication is the primary source of input for language stimulation. For most school-age children and adolescents, in addition to spoken communication, written communication plays an increasingly important role. Around the third or fourth grade (ages 8 through 10 years), a major transition occurs and students begin to use their reading skills to learn advanced vocabulary, figurative meanings, and complex syntax. The ability to read fluently and accurately frees the child to acquire a great deal of linguistic and world knowledge independently and to pursue personal interests more readily (Reed, 1986).

As a result, children become increasingly individualistic in their language development during the school-age and adolescent years (Gallatin, 1975; Kamhi, 1987). For example, a fourth grader's special interest in dinosaurs may inspire her to read many books on the subject. As her interest expands, she may gradually acquire a specialized "dinosaur lexicon" that contains words such as *theropod*, *cretaceous*, and *triassic*, terms that may be unfamiliar to her peers, not to mention her parents. As her interest in dinosaurs continues to grow, it may eventually expand into related topics such as archaeology or volcanology, which she may study more formally in high school or college.

As children progress through school, the greater freedom afforded to them in the selection of course work, extracurricular activities, and social contacts also promotes the development of linguistic individualism (Kamhi, 1987). Thus, it is not uncommon to find adolescents who show average performance in algebra class but outstanding performance in theater arts. This phenomenon of increasing individualism makes it difficult to establish firm guidelines for "normal" language development in school-age children, adolescents, and young adults. In semantics, for example, this is apparent in the different types of words students acquire as a result of their academic pursuits. A high school student who elects to study advanced biology soon learns the terms *centromere*, *chromatid*, and *nucleoplasm*, whereas a peer who enrolls in auto mechanics gains an understanding of *pneumatic suspension, catalytic converters,* and *hydraulic valves.* Both students are acquiring new concepts in a similar way, through meaningful exposure in context, but the products that result from that process differ.

Another contrast in processes between early and later language development concerns the role of *metalinguistic competence;* that is, the ability to reflect upon and to analyze language as an entity itself. Gombert (1992) reported that around age 6 or 7, a time when children typically begin first grade, they show an increasing tendency to employ their metalinguistic competence to enhance their own understanding and use of language in all domains—phonological, morphological, syntactic, semantic, and pragmatic. Language development in school-age children and adolescents heavily depends upon metalinguistic competence (Grunwell, 1986; van Kleeck, 1984, 1994). For example, learning to read and write requires the active analysis of certain aspects of language that were largely ignored during the preschool years or were experienced more passively. In first grade, students are asked to perform such tasks as identifying the words in a sentence that sound the same but look different (e.g., "He saw the man's son standing in the sun"), or identifying the word in a sentence that tells how an agent performed some action (e.g., "The pig walked away slowly") (Fay, Ross, & LaPray, 1981). By seventh grade (ages 12 through 13 years), they routinely determine the meanings of unfamiliar compound words (e.g., *yachtsman, landfall, breadstuffs*) by analyzing the component words and the surrounding context for more clues to meaning (Welch & Bennett, 1981b).

Metalinguistic competence also enables the school-age child or adolescent to determine the meanings of unfamiliar figurative expressions such as metaphors, proverbs, and idioms. This is accomplished by analyzing the words contained in the expression, scrutinizing the linguistic context in which it occurs, and generating a temporary interpretation of the expression that can later be accepted or rejected as more clues become available.

An additional contrast between early and later language development concerns the child's increasing ability to think abstractly. As children move from preschool to elementary school, their reasoning evidences a gradual transition from concrete to abstract. For example, a 4-year-old girl may believe that Santa Claus is a man in a red suit with a white beard who brings toys at Christmas. In contrast, her 9-year-old sister thinks of him as a symbol of the Christmas spirit, having gone through a complex process of weighing the evidence concerning his literal existence several years earlier (Scheibe & Condry, 1987).

This increasing ability to think abstractly is reflected in children's language development. For example, a difference in abstractness is evident in the types of words children acquire at different ages. For the 4-year-old, a large number of words having concrete referents will be added to her lexicon (e.g., *futon, Dalmatian, tofu*). In contrast, as her 9-year-old sister acquires new words, many of them will represent abstract concepts (e.g., *welfare, relevance, democracy*). Whereas young children are often quite literal in their interpretations of language, older children show an increasing ability to appreciate nonliteral meanings. For example, upon hearing Mom and Dad talk about "skeletons in the closet," the 4-year-old might think about Halloween and feel frightened. In contrast, the 9-year-old will be able to determine from the situation and from past exposure to this idiom in spoken contexts that their parents are talking about old family secrets. This contrast in abstractness is also evident in children's understanding and appreciation of linguistic ambiguity. Around second grade (ages 7 through 8 years), children begin to tell and laugh at jokes and riddles whose humor stems from phonological, lexical, or syntactic ambiguity (Q: "What animal can jump as high as a tree?" A: "All animals. Trees cannot jump") (McGhee, 1979). By eighth grade (ages 13 through 14 years), they can understand and appreciate the more sophisticated ambiguity that occurs in magazine advertisements ("Introducing the Upper Crusts. Two sensational new entrees from Stouffer's"), bumper stickers ("Midwives hold the future"), and handbills ("Oregon can't afford a U.S. senator who doesn't know the price of bread") (Nippold, Cuyler, & Braunbeck-Price, 1988). Most preschool children have little understanding or appreciation of such uses of language.

Related to abstractness is the child's ability to take the social perspective of other persons. This is another important contrast between early and later language development, and one that is critical to all aspects of pragmatic development. Compared to younger children, school-age children and adolescents are more aware of the thoughts, feelings, and needs of their co-conversationalists and of the consequences of their own communicative behaviors. As a result, they show greater ability to adjust the content and style of their speech accordingly. For example, adolescents demonstrate code-switching through the selective use of certain slang terms with their peers but not with their parents, teachers, or younger siblings. Moreover, older adolescents are more likely to resolve interpersonal conflicts by compromising and showing concern for the feelings of others compared to their younger counterparts.

Content of the Book

This book covers selected topics in later language development. Chapters 2, 3, and 4 each address a different aspect of the lexicon: word knowledge (Chapter 2), word finding (Chapter 3), and word definition (Chapter 4). The information reported in those chapters reflects a large and growing database, and one that actually began many years ago. Although presented as separate chapters, there is substantial interdependency among the topics. For example, without having a clear understanding of the meaning of a particular word, it would be difficult to retrieve that word during purposeful communication, or to provide a proper definition of it when giving a lecture or writing a technical report. The act of defining a word, which requires reflection on the lexical knowledge base (Watson, 1985), may cause a person to think more carefully about subtle aspects of meaning that help distinguish that word from others that denote similar but importantly different messages. As a result of this metalexical process, knowledge of the target word may become more elaborate and more firmly established in memory (Bjork & Bjork, 1992).

Investigations of word knowledge, word finding, and word definition are consistent in demonstrating that competence in each area is related to cognitive and linguistic development and to academic achievement (Astington & Olson, 1987; Kail & Hall, 1994; Nagy & Herman, 1987; Snow, Cancini, Gonzalez, & Shriberg, 1989; Thorndike, Hagen, & Sattler, 1986; Wechsler, 1991; Wolf & Goodglass, 1986; Wolf & Segal, 1992). Studies have also shown that quantitative and qualitative changes occur in all aspects of lexical development during the school-age and adolescent years. New words are added to the lexicon, old words take on new and subtle meanings, and it becomes easier to organize and to reflect upon the content of the lexicon (Nagy & Herman, 1987; Schecter & Broughton, 1991; Watson, 1985). The ability to articulate one's lexical knowledge also improves (Feifel & Lorge, 1950; Markowitz & Franz, 1988; McGhee-Bidlack, 1991), as does speed and accuracy in calling up words (e.g., German, 1986, 1990; Wiegel-Crump & Dennis, 1986).

As the reader progresses through the book, it will become apparent that lexical attainments are intricately related to many other aspects of later language development, such as verbal reasoning (Chapters 5 and 6), the understanding of figurative expressions (Chapters 7, 8, 9, and 10), the production of complex syntax (Chapter 11), and the use of language in social settings (Chapters 12 and 13). For example, solving a verbal analogy problem (e.g., "*philatelist* is to *stamps* as *entomologist* is to _?_") or interpreting a proverb (e.g., "Of idleness comes no goodness") requires knowledge of word meanings, as does the production of cohesive discourse using subordinating conjunctions (e.g., *although, unless, whenever*) or adverbial conjuncts (e.g., *moreover, conversely, similarly*). Moreover, when talking with others socially, speakers must be able to call up the appropriate words to express themselves quickly, accurately, and tactfully.

Chapters 5 and 6 focus specifically on the development of *verbal reasoning*, a mental construct where language and cognition converge. This symbiotic relationship is evidenced in the following mathematics problem for eighth-grade students:

> To make spaghetti sauce, add one can of tomato paste and two cans of water to one package of mix. Add a spoonful of salad oil. How many cans of water would you use with three packages of mix? How many cans of tomato paste would you use with eight cans of water? (*Growth in Mathematics, Level 8,* 1978, p. 132)

To solve this problem, students must read and comprehend the sentences, set up the proportions, and perform the operations of multiplication and division. Competence in verbal reasoning reflects one's level of linguistic and cognitive development, and it is predictive of academic success (Achenbach, 1969, 1970; Armour-Thomas & Allen, 1990; Feuerstein, 1979; Keating & Caramazza, 1975; Lorge & Thorndike, 1957; Sternberg, 1979, 1982).

Problems in verbal reasoning are either inductive or deductive. Inductive problems include analogies (e.g., "*Bear* is to *cub* as *cow* is to _?_"), proportions (e.g., "One package is to two cans as three packages is to *n* cans"), series completions (e.g., "June, August, October, _?_"), and classifications (e.g., "Which of the following words does not go with the others? aunt, cousin, sister, friend"). Understanding figurative expressions such as metaphors (e.g., "The house was a box with no lid") and proverbs (e.g., "The plump pig gets all the pears") also involves inductive reasoning. Deductive problems include syllogisms (e.g., "All blocks are green. This is a block. Therefore, _?_"), probability (e.g., "You toss a coin. It can land heads or tails. Toss it 100 times. How many times can you expect it to land heads?"), and combinations (e.g., "Here are three different shapes—triangle, circle, and square. Show me all the different ways you can combine them").

Inductive and deductive problems differ in the extent to which the information they contain is logically sufficient evidence for the solution (Sternberg, 1982). With inductive problems, the information supports the solution but is not sufficient evidence for it. For example, to solve the "Bear" analogy given earlier, one must draw on outside information concerning the relationship between *bear* and *cub* in order to generate an item that goes with *cow* in the same way that *cub* goes with *bear*. With deductive problems, however, the information presented is logically sufficient evidence for the solution. For example, the conclusion to the "Block" syllogism also given earlier is based entirely on the two premises.

Students are called upon to reason inductively and deductively during the elementary, middle, and high school years, particularly during the formal study of mathematics, science, and debate. Given the contribution of verbal reasoning to students' academic success, it is important to examine the findings from developmental studies in the areas of inductive and deductive reasoning. Space limitations preclude a review of all types of inductive and deductive problems. Therefore, analogies and syllogisms are the focus for examining inductive and deductive reasoning, respectively. Those two types of problems have been studied extensively in school-age children and adolescents.

Chapters 7, 8, 9, and 10 address the development of figurative language. Major types of figurative language include metaphors, similes, idioms, slang terms, proverbs, ambiguity, and sarcasm. Figurative expressions of all types pervade the English language. For example, they often occur in spoken form during conversations, lectures, and news reports, and in written form in novels, poems, textbooks, newspapers, and magazines. Gaining competence with figurative language is an important part of becoming a culturally literate and linguistically facile person.

The development of figurative language has been studied for over 70 years. Much of the interest in this topic stems from the belief that figurative competence reflects a person's cognitive level (Arlin, 1978; Billow, 1975; Cometa & Eson, 1978; Piaget, 1926; Smith, 1976), creativity (Gardner, Kircher, Winner, & Perkins, 1975; Paivio, 1979; Schaefer, 1975), and abstract reasoning ability (Brown, 1965; Hoffman

& Honeck, 1980; Kogan, Connor, Gross, & Fava, 1980; Ortony, 1979). Although figurative language is first understood during the preschool years (Boynton & Kossan, 1981; Dent, 1984; Gardner, 1974; Gentner, 1977; Vosniadou & Ortony, 1983), comprehension steadily improves throughout childhood and adolescence, and into adulthood (Boswell, 1979; Gorham, 1956; Lodge & Leach, 1975; Nippold, Uhden, & Schwarz, 1997b; Richardson & Church, 1959; Watts, 1944). Students whose home and school environments place a high value on spoken and written communication may acquire competence with figurative expressions more rapidly than those whose environments place less emphasis on those areas, a position which is consistent with the language experience hypothesis of figurative development (Ortony, Turner, & Larson Shapiro, 1985). Less is known about how figurative language develops in terms of production. However, it has been suggested that production follows a U-shaped behavioral curve such that novel, imaginative expressions are commonly produced by preschoolers, decrease during the elementary school years, but again show an increase during adolescence (Gardner et al., 1975; Gardner, Winner, Bechhofer, & Wolf, 1978). Further research is necessary to explore this interesting hypothesis.

Improvements that occur in spoken and written syntax are discussed in Chapter 11, a topic that epitomizes the gradual, subtle, and protracted nature of later language development. To see growth in syntax beyond the preschool years, one must examine the use of low-frequency syntactic structures and look beyond the isolated sentence for evidence of complex and cohesive discourse (Scott, 1988). In addition, one must examine the older student's use of syntax in formal academic settings. It is not unusual for high school students to use the simpler syntax of their younger years when talking with their peers at lunch, but then to produce long and complex sentences, coherently linked, when writing a persuasive essay for school on a controversial topic.

Finally, the development of conversation, narration, persuasion, and negotiation is discussed in Chapters 12 and 13. It is fitting that these topics conclude the book, as proficiency with all types of discourse depends, to a large extent, upon attainments in all other aspects of language. These include the understanding and use of appropriate words, the ability to engage in verbal reasoning, knowledge of figurative expressions that might be employed to tell a story or to convince a person to accept a particular position or to perform a desired action, and syntactic sophistication sufficient to produce clear, logical, and coherent conversation.

The Science of Later Language Development

If there is a constant theme throughout this book, it is that scientific inquiry should be the basis for learning about language development in youth. Hence, the information in each chapter was derived largely from data-based empirical research.

Ideally, in research, interesting questions are posed and answers are sought in an organized and systematic fashion that involves an unwavering respect for scientific integrity—the patient, accurate, and objective observation of behavior; careful reflection on the data obtained; and an attitude of openness and flexibility in interpreting the results, which includes a willingness to accept the possibility that one's own theories are not supported by the data (Feynman, 1985). A certain amount of subjectivity in research is inevitable due to factors such as the investigator's knowledge base, experiences, interests, and expectations (Prutting, 1983). However, the effort to strive continuously for scientific integrity is critical, because it produces research that ultimately leads to more valid, reliable, and socially beneficial information.

It is also important to note that most of the research discussed in this book was conducted in the United States, Canada, or Great Britain and primarily involved the participation of individuals who spoke standard English (an exception is Chapter 11, which includes information on Dutch-speaking children). This situation reflects the availability of information on later language development at this time. It is hoped that more information will become available on youth who speak languages and dialects other than standard English.

Implications

The major goal in writing this book was to assemble a large body of relevant literature on later language development and to attempt to present it in a cohesive and integrated fashion. The information contained herein has important implications for educational planning and curriculum development for typical learners during the school-age and adolescent years. It also has implications for youth with language disorders, particularly if one subscribes to the notion that language intervention based on the developmental model is a viable approach, as this author believes (also see Nelson, 1993). This is not a book on language disorders and no efforts were made within the book to apply the information to youth with language disorders. However, it is important to mention some potential applications for such youth. During the past 20 years, school-age children and adolescents with language disorders in the United States have received more attention than previously from teachers, speech–language pathologists, and other professionals in public school settings. With the passage of Public Law 94–142, the Education for All Handicapped Children Act of 1975, all students with disabilities were guaranteed the right to a free, appropriate education in the least restrictive environment. As a result of this federal law, it was no longer excusable to ignore the older child or adolescent who was experiencing language-based academic difficulties. The effort to assist these older students resulted in the production of a large number of standardized tests designed to identify language disorders in school-age children and adolescents. However, many of those tests reflected the "cart before the horse" syndrome: Because no solid frame of reference was available for later language development, tests were produced largely under the guidance of clinical intuition and guesswork. A major problem with many of the tests is that they contained sections that evaluate aspects of language that normally develop by much younger ages. For example, the *Adolescent Language Screening Test* (Morgan & Guilford, 1984) was designed for students ages 11 through 17. However, this test evaluates the production of consonant clusters and Brown's (1973) grammatical morphemes. As another example, the *Fullerton Language Test for Adolescents* (Thorum, 1980) contains sections that evaluate sound blending, syllable counting, and basic morphology. Standardized tests that examine aspects of early language acquisition are likely to identify students having the more severe and obvious problems while bypassing those having more elusive but still troublesome linguistic deficits.

This problem can be addressed by designing adequate standardized and nonstandardized measures that evaluate important aspects of later language development, such as the use and understanding of advanced connectives (e.g., *whereas, moreover, likewise*), figurative expressions (e.g., proverbs, metaphors, and idioms), and low-frequency syntactic structures (e.g., adverbial clauses, appositive constructions). With older children and adolescents, both spoken and written forms of language should be evaluated, and, when deficits in any of these areas are identified, an intervention plan should be initiated.

On the positive side, test developers have begun to incorporate research in later language development into their products. For example, the *Test of Language Competence: Expanded Edition* (Wiig & Secord, 1989), for ages 5 through 18 years, contains subtests that assess the understanding of linguistic ambiguity and figurative expressions. Additionally, the *Test of Word Knowledge* (Wiig & Secord, 1991), for ages 5 through 17 years, examines sophisticated aspects of language such as knowledge and use of abstract words, the ability to define words, and the understanding of adverbial conjuncts. This trend should continue as additional research is conducted on language development during the school-age and adolescent years, and as the results become available to a wider audience of consumers.

There is much to be gained from an exploration of the literature on later language development, particularly for those who possess a keen interest in children and adolescents and a deep concern for their welfare. As the reader embarks on this journey, encouragement may be derived from the words of Confucius (551–479 B.C.), who explained that "Wisdom is rooted in watching with affection the way people grow" (Sawyer, 1982, p. 7).

Acknowledgments

Portions of this chapter appeared in the following publications:

Nippold, M. A. (1988). Figurative language. In M. A. Nippold (Ed.), *Later language development: Ages nine through nineteen* (pp. 179–210). Austin, TX: PRO-ED.

Nippold, M. A. (1988). Introduction. In M. A. Nippold (Ed.), *Later language development: Ages nine through nineteen* (pp. 1–10). Austin, TX: PRO-ED.

Nippold, M. A. (1988). Verbal reasoning. In M. A. Nippold (Ed.), *Later language development: Ages nine through nineteen* (pp. 159–177). Austin, TX: PRO-ED.

Nippold, M. A. (1993). Developmental markers in adolescent language: Syntax, semantics, and pragmatics. *Language, Speech, and Hearing Services in Schools, 24,* 21–28.

Nippold, M. A. (1995). Language norms in school-age children and adolescents: An introduction. *Language, Speech, and Hearing Services in Schools, 26,* 307–308.

C H A P T E R

THE LITERATE LEXICON

"Successful people in all walks of life . . . have in common a mastery of words."

—Flexner (1987, p. 1)

Reports have indicated that a typical school-age child acquires between 3,000 and 5,000 new words each year, or about 10 to 13 words per day (Miller & Gildea, 1987; Nagy & Herman, 1987). Continuing at that rate, the youth will know at least 80,000 different words upon graduating from high school (Miller & Gildea, 1987). Literacy, the ability to read and write proficiently, is closely related to the development of word knowledge during the school-age and adolescent years and continuing throughout the life span. Whereas literacy requires knowledge and use of a wide variety of words, the process of word learning itself is greatly facilitated by the literate activities of reading and writing (Carnine, Kameenui, & Coyle, 1984; Nagy, Herman, & Anderson, 1985; Perera, 1986).

During early childhood and continuing into the first few years of elementary school, spoken language serves as the primary source of input for word learning. At about the fourth-grade level, written language becomes a significant, additional source of learning. Students who are active and proficient readers, interested in a wide variety of topics, develop substantially larger vocabularies than their peers who read with less skill, interest, and motivation (Carnine et al., 1984; Miller & Gildea, 1987; Nagy et al., 1985). It is not surprising, then, that students who know more words display higher levels of reading comprehension than their peers with less extensive word knowledge (Nagy & Herman, 1987; Nagy et al., 1985; Sternberg, 1987).

Table 2.1
Examples of Words Understood by 75% of Students in Various Grade Levels

Grade 4:	bulldog, camper, cigar, crocodile, distance, dizzy, dodge, locket, sheriff, sniff, tangle, thirst, weedy, widow, wives
Grade 6:	adhesive, alto, appetite, bacteria, berth, bridal, campus, davenport, fatherless, fishery, gadget, grit, midst, pardon
Grade 8:	amend, archeology, byway, dimension, fluorescent, horoscope, inefficient, laughingstock, lingerie, officialdom, salutation
Grade 10:	circumstantial, deface, diversion, enshrine, gallows, hinder, implication, negligent, orthodox, pollination, proton, refrain
Grade 12:	acetylene, aft, buxom, condone, curlew, fascism, heresy, indicative, opportune, oppression, prophetic, secretariat

Note. Adapted from *Children's Knowledge of Words: An Interim Report* by E. Dale and G. Eichholz, 1960, Columbus, OH: Bureau of Educational Research and Service, Ohio State University.

As students progress through school, the types of words they encounter become increasingly rare and abstract, and they occur more often in formal written contexts than in casual spoken contexts (Nagy, Diakidoy, & Anderson, 1993). Hence, words that are learned as students grow older are more likely to express unusual and less tangible concepts than those they learned earlier. This qualitative shift in word learning is apparent from Table 2.1, which contains examples of words that were understood by 75% of students at Grades 4, 6, 8, 10, and 12 (Dale & Eichholz, 1960).

Word learning continues well beyond the high school years; indeed, new words may be learned throughout the life span, particularly by persons who are active and proficient readers (Miller & Gildea, 1987; Palermo & Molfese, 1972; Riegel, Riegel, Quarterman, & Smith, 1968). The vocabulary of a language constantly changes because of cultural, historical, and regional influences in addition to scientific and technological advances (Langacker, 1973). For example, *concede, assert*, and *remark* are words that entered the English language during the early part of the seventeenth century (Olson & Astington, 1986a), whereas *byte, fax*, and *mainframe* were introduced more recently as products of the computer age. Therefore, word learning that occurs in school-age children, adolescents, and adults must include not only the acquisition of long-standing words but also of those that are new to the language. The fact that words often change their meanings over time also adds complexity to the process of acquiring word knowledge through the life span. For example, at one time, *notorious* meant 'widely known,' but today it means 'widely and unfavorably known.' Also, during the 1950s, *hospitalize, finalize*, and *publicize* were viewed as substandard by authorities of the English language and their use was discouraged (Crystal, 1988). More recently, those words have become common and acceptable.

Growth in word knowledge involves more than the addition of words to the lexicon. Growth also occurs through the development of an organized network where semantically related words become more closely associated (Entwisle, Forsyth, & Muuss, 1964; Nelson, 1977; Riegel et al., 1968). The syntagmatic–paradigmatic shift, which occurs most dramatically between the ages of 5 and 9 years (Lippman, 1971), seems to reflect this type of semantic reorganization. This can be observed during word association tasks where a word is presented (e.g., *dog*) and the individual is asked to say the first word that comes to mind. A 5-year-old is likely to respond *syntagmatically* with a word that might follow in a sentence (e.g., *barks*), but a 9-year-old is likely to respond *paradigmatically* with a semantically related word, which is often a coordinate (e.g., *cat*), subordinate (e.g., *collie*), or superordinate (e.g., *animal*) of the target word (Israel, 1984).

Growth in word knowledge also occurs through changes in the meanings of particular words for the individual (Palermo & Molfese, 1972). As McNeil (1970) pointed out, simple vocabulary counts give a misleading picture of lexical development because "words can be in a child's vocabulary but have different semantic properties from the same words in the vocabulary of an older child or an adult" (p. 116). For example, preschoolers often use the words *because* and *before* even though a complete understanding of those words as intrasentential connectives may not be reached until adolescence (Flores d'Arcais, 1978). Double-function terms such as *cold, bright, sweet,* and *crooked* also illustrate this phenomenon. Although their physical meanings may be understood by young children, the psychological meanings may not be understood until preadolescence, and the manner in which the two meanings overlap may not be fully grasped until adolescence or early adulthood (Asch & Nerlove, 1960; Nippold, Cuyler, & Braunbeck-Price, 1988; Schecter & Broughton, 1991).

Children's errors in word usage also illustrate the phenomenon of partial lexical knowledge. More than 20 years ago, researchers such as Bloom (1973) and Clark (1973) studied semantic development in young children, reporting that toddlers' overextensions (e.g., calling all small, furry animals *kitty*) were inconsistent with adults' usage of those same words until the child had developed a more complete understanding of the concepts involved. Researchers have also found that similar types of errors are made by older children as they attempt to use new and unfamiliar words, errors which offer insight into their notions of what a word means. For example, Miller and Gildea (1987) reported that students in Grades 5 and 6 (ages 10 through 12 years), having only partial knowledge of the words *meticulous, relegate,* and *redress,* wrote the following revealing sentences:

I was *meticulous* about falling off the cliff.

I *relegated* my pen pal's letter to her house.

The *redress* for getting well when you're sick is to stay in bed. (p. 99)

As with young children, the errors of older children indicate that acquiring a full understanding of a word is a gradual rather than an "all or none" process (Nagy et al.,

1985). In fact, the phenomenon of partial lexical knowledge occurs throughout the life span. This can be seen, for example, in an adult who knows that *calceolaria* and *delphinium* are types of flowering plants but cannot distinguish them on sight or explain how they differ (Miller & Gildea, 1987).

How Are Words Learned?

Given the amazing capacity that individuals display for acquiring new words, it is interesting to consider various methods by which this process occurs during the school-age and adolescent years. Three primary methods by which young people gain an understanding of words include direct instruction, contextual abstraction, and morphological analysis.

Direct Instruction

Direct instruction occurs when a knowledgeable person, such as a teacher, parent, or peer provides a definition of a word or labels an unfamiliar stimulus (Nagy et al., 1985; Wysocki & Jenkins, 1987). For example, a seventh-grade biology teacher may define the words *tundra, deciduous,* and *coniferous* before using those words during a lecture on terrestrial biomes of North America. Similarly, when a Boy Scout picks up an unfamiliar rock during a nature hike, a scout leader might inform the youth that he has just discovered an *agate*, thereby teaching him a new word.

The use of dictionaries to learn the meanings of new words also constitutes direct instruction (Carnine et al., 1984). At about the second grade (ages 7 through 8 years), dictionary usage is introduced in school, a sophisticated and scholarly method of lexical learning (Coon, Cramer, Fillmer, Lefcourt, Martin, & Thompson, 1980; Miller & Gildea, 1987). An important study skill, the use of a dictionary is encouraged throughout the elementary, middle, and high school years (Bennett, 1981; Coon et al., 1980; McDonnell, Nakadate, Pfordresher, & Shoemate, 1979; Welch & Bennett, 1981a).

Despite the commonness of dictionaries, however, their use does not necessarily translate into immediate and complete understanding (Carnine et al., 1984). Miller and Gildea (1987) reported that students in Grades 5 and 6 (ages 10 through 12 years), when asked to consult a dictionary to learn the meanings of unfamiliar words such as *stimulate, usurp,* and *erode*, subsequently wrote the sentences:

> Mrs. Morrow *stimulated* the soup.
>
> The thief tried to *usurp* the money from the safe.
>
> Our family *erodes* a lot.

Notably, those examples reflect literal interpretations of certain key phrases contained in the dictionary definitions (e.g., *stimulate* = 'to stir up'; *usurp* = 'to take';

erode = 'to eat out') (pp. 97–98) rather than the appropriate, but more abstract and less common meanings.

Contextual Abstraction

Contextual abstraction, or the use of context clues to determine the meanings of unfamiliar words that occur in spoken and written communication, is another primary method by which the lexicon expands during the school-age and adolescent years (Carnine et al., 1984; Nagy et al., 1985; Sternberg, 1987). Rich opportunities for learning new words in context include listening to lectures, news reports, and discussions, and reading a variety of books, magazines, and newspapers. The use of context clues to determine the meanings of unfamiliar words is encouraged in academic settings throughout the elementary, middle, and high school years (Bennett, 1981; Duffy & Roehler, 1981; Welch & Bennett, 1981a).

Learning in context begins with the initial exposure to a word, a process called *fast mapping* (Crais, 1990; Nagy et al., 1985). Upon exposure, the learner makes a prediction about the word's meaning based on clues available in the larger linguistic context. Table 2.2 contains examples of syntactic and semantic context clues that commonly occur in textbooks (Sinatra & Dowd, 1991). For further learning to occur, it is necessary for the student to encounter new words frequently and in multiple and diverse contexts (Nagy & Herman, 1987; Nagy et al., 1985). Because context clues do not always provide a sufficient amount of information in a clear and unambiguous manner, subsequent exposure to a word enables the learner to verify, expand, or otherwise modify initial hypotheses about its meaning. Written language often contains more complex vocabulary than spoken language. Therefore, word learning in older children and adolescents depends to a large extent upon the quantity and quality of reading they engage in, along with their ability to recognize clues that are relevant in determining the meanings of new words (Miller & Gildea, 1987; Nagy & Herman, 1987; Sinatra & Dowd, 1991; Sternberg, 1987).

The fact that students acquire a very large number of words each year (e.g., 3,000–5,000) precludes the possibility that they could rely solely on the more direct methods of word learning such as vocabulary lessons or dictionary usage in school (Miller & Gildea, 1987; Nagy & Herman, 1987; Sternberg, 1987; Wysocki & Jenkins, 1987). Despite the challenges involved in inferring the meanings of words from context, contextual abstraction is one of the most effective and efficient ways of increasing the breadth and depth of an individual's word knowledge (Nagy et al., 1985; Nagy & Herman, 1987).

Hence, in order to maximize students' ability to learn new words, teachers should provide direct instruction in the optimal use of context clues during independent reading activities (Nagy & Herman, 1987; Sinatra & Dowd, 1991; Sternberg, 1987). Teacher instruction followed by regular and systematic practice in applying the strategy is thought to be particularly beneficial (Carnine et al., 1984). Teachers should also encourage students to read widely, not only for pleasure and for gaining

Table 2.2

Examples of Syntactic and Semantic Context Clues that Occur in Textbooks

Syntactic Clues

1. Appositives: *Indigo*, a blue dye taken from plants, was sold by Southern plantation owners.
2. Relative clauses: The *apothecary*, who mixed the different drugs, placed his jars on the counter.
3. The conjunction "or": In 1953, Sir Edmund Hillary climbed to the *summit*, or highest point, of the world's tallest mountain.
4. Direct explanation: The transfer of pollen grains from one flower to another is known as *pollination*.
5. Linked synonyms: The student became very frightened by the noisy, disturbed, *tumultuous* crowd.
6. Participial phrases: The cat, drenched by the heavy rain, was *distressed*.
7. Categorical sequence: The fruits needed for this salad are apples, bananas, pears, *avocados*, and oranges.

Semantic Clues

1. Restatement: All instruments used during an operation must be *sterile*. They have to be free of germs so that none are introduced into the patient's body.
2. Illustrations or examples: Most office workers are encouraged to take short *respites* during the day. For example, they go to the water fountain, vending machine, a friend's office to chat, and the washroom.
   Rodents, such as rats and mice, are often dangerous to humans.
3. Similes: *Capillaries* are like tiny pipelines that connect veins and arteries.
4. Metaphors: The bean-shaped *mitochondria* are the cell's power plants.
5. Personification: The warming sun *caressed* the land, drying it gently after many days of rain.
6. Summary: The wealthy man enjoyed raising money for many charities. He gave large sums of his own money to homes for orphaned children, soup kitchens, and shelters for the homeless. He also turned one of his homes into a wonderful school for needy children. He was one of the most well-known *philanthropists* of our time.
7. Cause/effect: The pain was *alleviated* as a result of the drugs suggested by the doctor.
   Farmers lost many of their crops this year because rainfall was *meager*.

Note. Adapted from "Using Syntactic and Semantic Clues to Learn Vocabulary" by R. Sinatra and C. A. Dowd, 1991, *Journal of Reading*, 35, pp. 226–227.

The potentially unknown words are italicized.

new information, but also as a metalinguistic strategy for expanding their knowledge of words, and in turn, their ability to comprehend complex written language.

Morphological Analysis

Research has demonstrated that another important method of word learning is *morphological analysis* (Anglin, 1993; Nagy et al., 1993; White, Power, & White, 1989;

Wysocki & Jenkins, 1987). This occurs when an individual encounters an unfamiliar word (e.g., *serviced, seabound, talkativeness*), analyzes the components of the word, including its lexical (e.g., *service, sea, bound, talk*), inflectional (e.g.,*–ed*), and derivational (*–ive, –ness*) morphemes, and uses that information to infer the meaning of the entire word (Anglin, 1993). This strategy, commonly used when students encounter unfamiliar words when reading in school and beyond the classroom, makes a major contribution to vocabulary development (White et al., 1989).

Anglin (1993) reported that children in Grades 1, 3, and 5 (ages 6, 8, and 10 years) ($N = 96$) frequently used this metalinguistic strategy to decipher unfamiliar words, and that skill in using the strategy steadily improved during the elementary school years. He also reported that this method was especially effective in determining the meanings of compound words (e.g., *firesafe*) and words that contained derivational morphemes (e.g., *workable, explorational*). Wysocki and Jenkins (1987) reported that students in Grades 4, 6, and 8 (ages 9, 11, and 13 years) ($N = 135$) were able to derive the meanings of unfamiliar words through morphological analysis in combination with the use of context clues in written passages. Those researchers also found that older students (sixth and eighth graders) were more proficient at using and combining the two strategies than younger students (fourth graders). It is interesting to note that the understanding of certain derivational morphemes, particularly of suffixes (e.g., *–ette, –ize, –ify, –ful*), also increases during the school-age and adolescent years (Nagy et al., 1993; Windsor, 1994) and is closely related to reading ability (Nagy et al., 1993). Thus, as children expand and refine their knowledge of morphemes, they gain proficiency in applying that knowledge metalinguistically to broaden their understanding of words in general. As discussed later in this book, metalinguistic competence is a driving force in many other aspects of later language development as well, including the ability to define words (Chapter 4), to interpret figurative expressions such as metaphors, idioms, and proverbs (Chapters 7, 8, and 9), and to appreciate the ambiguity that occurs in jokes, riddles, and advertisements (Chapter 10).

In academic settings, students are encouraged to learn the meanings of lexical and derivational morphemes and to apply that knowledge to the process of vocabulary development (White et al., 1989). Tangible evidence of this can be found in curriculum guides, workbooks, and textbooks, particularly those that are used to teach reading and literature. For example, a lesson contained in a teacher's guide for a basal reading series (Durr, LePere, Pescosolido, Bean, & Glaser, 1981b) explained how to convey to students the idea that, "Knowledge of suffix meanings can be used to figure out the meanings of many unfamiliar words that contain known base words or word roots" (p. 88). To facilitate this process, the accompanying student workbook (Durr, Le Pere, Pescosolido, Bean, & Glaser, 1981a) contained a list of common suffixes with their definitions, shown in Table 2.3. Students were instructed to use the list to complete an exercise requiring them to demonstrate their understanding of the suffixes. As another example, an introductory literature textbook (Welch & Bennett,

1981a) provided explicit instruction in how to determine the meanings of unfamiliar compound words. After reading the steps outlined in the text, shown in Table 2.4, students completed a set of exercises that required them to apply the steps in relation to a story they had just read that contained numerous compound words (e.g., *flagship*, *millpond*, *yachtsman*, *breadstuffs*). Note that the fourth step encouraged the students to use context clues to confirm their hypotheses. Teaching students the meanings of common prefixes, suffixes, and root words; how to use that information to infer word meanings; and how to combine the two strategies of morphological analysis and attending to context clues while reading has been recommended as an effective way of enhancing vocabulary development, particularly in fourth-grade classrooms and beyond (White et al., 1989).

Table 2.3
Common Suffixes and Their Definitions Contained in a
Student Workbook Accompanying a Basal Reading Series

Suffix	Meaning
–able	'capable of being, worthy of,' as in *lovable*
–er	'one who performs an action,' as in *baker*
–ful	'full of, characterized by,' as in *painful*
–fy, –ify	'make or form into,' as in *simplify*
–ity, –ty	'having the quality of' or 'state of being,' as in *timidity*, *jollity*
–ous	'characterized by, full of,' as in *famous*
–ship	'condition of being' or 'character of being,' as in *apprenticeship*, *friendship*

Note. Adapted from *Practice Book: Awards* (p. 24) by W. K. Durr, J. M. LePere, J. Pescosolido, R. M. Bean, and N. A. Glaser, 1981a, Boston: Houghton Mifflin.

Table 2.4
Explicit Instruction Contained in an Introductory Literature Textbook on
How To Determine the Meanings of Unfamiliar Compound Words

Words that are made up of two or more small words are called *compound words*. Here are some of the compound words found in *First Crossing of the Atlantic*: breadstuffs, flagship, gulfweed, honeymoon, landfall, millpond, moonlight, nightfall, overestimate, seaworthiness, southwesterly, and yachtsman.

To figure out the meaning of a compound word which you do not know, follow these steps:

1. Separate the compound word into its parts. For example: rowboat = row/boat; snowstorm = snow/storm.
2. Define each part.
3. Put these definitions together to make a temporary definition for the whole word.
4. Look at the context clues in the sentence to see whether they support your temporary definition.

Note. From *Introduction to Literature* (p. 52) by B. Y. Welch and R. A. Bennett, 1981, Lexington, MA: Ginn. Copyright 1981 by Ginn. Reprinted with permission.

Summary

During the school-age and adolescent years, word knowledge develops through three primary methods: *direct instruction, contextual abstraction,* and *morphological analysis.* The extremely large number of words that are acquired during those stages of human development suggests that the latter two methods, which place significant demands upon metalinguistic competence, make the greatest contribution to this process. As students progress through school, they gain proficiency in using contextual abstraction and morphological analysis and in combining the two methods, where possible, to interpret new words with greater efficiency and accuracy. Even beyond adolescence, individuals who employ these methods and continue to read widely can acquire new knowledge of words throughout the life span.

What Words Are Learned?

The remainder of this chapter addresses the development of specific types of words that are important for the literate activities of reading, writing, listening to lectures, talking about language and thought, and mastering the school curriculum. These include polysemous and double-function terms, adverbs of likelihood and magnitude, metalinguistic and metacognitive verbs, and factive and nonfactive verbs. Knowledge of these and similar kinds of words constitutes an individual's "literate lexicon."

Polysemous Terms

Polysemous terms, pervasive in the English language, are words that have more than one meaning (Durkin, Crowther, Shire, Riem, & Nash, 1985). Very often these words have a primary meaning that is spatial and a secondary meaning that is abstract but semantically related to the primary meaning (Durkin, Crowther, & Shire, 1986). Knowing the secondary meanings of polysemous terms is often critical for acquiring an understanding of musical and mathematical concepts presented in school (Durkin et al., 1985). The related spatial, musical, and mathematical senses of the polysemous terms *up, above,* and *lower* are apparent from the following sentences:

▶ **Spatial:**

The boy ran *up* the hill.
The bird flew *above* the trees.
The desk is *lower* than the shelf.

▶ **Musical:**

The soloist went *up* an octave.
She sang *above* the noise.
Bill's voice is *lower* than Nan's.

▶ **Mathematical:**

We counted *up* by fives.
Jim's score was *above* the mean.
The sum is *lower* than the product.

Reports have indicated that the primary meanings of polysemous terms are often well-understood by preschool children, but that the secondary meanings are acquired much more slowly and are frequently a source of confusion to school-age children when used in reference to pitch, quantity, and comparative relationships (Durkin et al., 1985). In fact, difficulty in understanding the secondary meanings of polysemous terms may persist well into adolescence (Durkin et al., 1986). For example, Bell (1984) (cited by Durkin et al., 1986, p. 92) reported that when the terms *up* and *down* were used to ask questions concerning changes in rank (e.g., Question: "Norwich has gone up 6 places from 9th position. Where are they now?"), even high school students made many errors, revealing a belief that *up* always implies an increase in number by answering "15th."

Other researchers have also documented the difficulty that students often have in understanding polysemous terms. For example, Mason, Kniseley, and Kendall (1979) examined children's comprehension of 20 polysemous terms taken from upper-elementary grade textbooks. Many of the terms had secondary meanings that bore little or no relationship to their primary meanings (e.g., *strike, pitched, bored*). The primary meaning was simply the more common and concrete sense of the word, and the secondary meaning was the less common and more abstract sense. Students in Grades 3 and 4 (ages 8 through 10 years; $N = 80$) were administered a written multiple-choice task designed to assess their comprehension of the primary and secondary meanings of the words. Two forms of the task were constructed. The primary meaning of a word was tested on one form, and its secondary meaning was tested on the other. Each form was given to half the students in each grade level. Each problem consisted of a sentence that contained a polysemous term, followed by five answer choices. The sentence provided contextual support for either the primary or the secondary meaning of the word. For example, the problem below was used to test comprehension of the primary meaning of *strike*:

▶ Pete is going to *strike* the ball.
   (a) meet together   (d) hit
   (b) hide   (e) no answer (p. 58)
   (c) stop work

To test comprehension of the secondary meaning of *strike*, the same set of answer choices was used, but the following sentence was presented:

▶ The union is going to *strike* tomorrow (p. 58).

Students' comprehension of the terms also was examined in relation to their reading ability, as measured by performance on an informal reading task constructed by the researchers.

In terms of overall accuracy, mean scores of 49% and 63% were obtained by the students in Grades 3 and 4, respectively, indicating that comprehension of polysemous terms improved as a function of increasing grade level. It was also found that high-ability readers in both grade levels outperformed middle-ability and low-ability readers on the task. Moreover, for the two grade levels combined, accuracy scores were considerably higher on the primary (mean = 69%) than on the secondary (mean = 43%) meanings of the words, indicating that third and fourth graders had difficulty grasping the secondary meanings of polysemous terms, even when the sentential context supported those meanings. In view of their findings and the pervasiveness of polysemous terms in elementary-grade textbooks, the researchers recommended that students receive direct instruction in the secondary meanings of polysemous terms and that they be encouraged to attend more closely to potentially helpful contextual information.

Double-Function Terms

Double-function terms (e.g., *sweet, hard, cold*), a special type of polysemy, are words that have both a physical and a psychological meaning. Sometimes described as metaphoric, the physical meaning is said to be literal and the psychological meaning, which is derived from the physical meaning, is said to be nonliteral (Billow, 1977). A full understanding of double-function terms requires a person to be able to detect and explain how the physical and psychological meanings are related. As with other types of polysemous words, double-function terms are acquired gradually during the school-age and adolescent years.

Asch and Nerlove (1960) were the first researchers to examine children's understanding of double-function terms. They were interested in determining if the physical or the psychological meaning was learned first or if both meanings were learned simultaneously. Fifty children ranging in age from 3 to 12 years were interviewed individually about the meanings of some common double-function terms. For the youngest children, the 3- and 4-year-olds, objects representing each term were displayed. These included a sugar cube (*sweet*), a wooden block (*hard*), iced water (*cold*), a powder puff (*soft*), a gold disk (*bright*), a cylinder (*deep*), hot water (*warm*), and a twig (*crooked*). To assess comprehension of the physical meanings of the terms, the child was asked to find a certain item described by the examiner (e.g., "Show me something *sweet*"). The child then was questioned about the psychological meaning of the term (e.g., "Can people be *sweet* too?," "How do you know they are *sweet?*") (p. 50). If the child understood both the physical and the psychological meanings of a term, questions were asked concerning the relationship between the two meanings (e.g., "Why do we call sugar *sweet*, and kind, nice people *sweet?*") (p. 51). For children ages 5 years and older, no objects were displayed, and the children simply were asked to name an object that represented the physical meaning of the terms. All other procedures used with the youngest group were employed with each of the older groups.

The results indicated that most of the 3- and 4-year-olds understood the physical meanings of the terms but offered literal interpretations for the psychological meanings (e.g., "Poor people are *cold* because they have no clothes" p. 50). The 5- and 6-year-olds showed a beginning awareness of the psychological meanings, particularly of *sweet*, *hard*, and *soft* (e.g., "Debbie is a *sweet* girl because she is nice" p. 51), but they had no understanding of the relationship between the two meanings. Seven- and 8-year-olds showed a broader understanding of the psychological meanings (e.g., "*Soft* people are weak and don't fight" p. 52) but still could not relate those meanings to the physical. Nine- and 10-year-olds began to show some awareness of how the two meanings were related, and many of the 11- and 12-year-olds clearly understood the overlapping meanings (e.g., "*Bright* things and *bright* people are alike in that they are both outstanding, you notice them first" p. 53; "*Crooked* things and *crooked* people are roundabout and may be dangerous" p. 54).

Asch and Nerlove (1960) concluded that children understand the physical meanings of double-function terms several years before they understand the psychological meanings, and it is several more years before they grasp the relatedness of the two meanings.

Recently, the findings of Asch and Nerlove (1960) were replicated by Schecter and Broughton (1991) in a study that employed similar procedures but extended the age range of the subjects to early adolescence. Children who were ages 6, 8, 10, 12, and 14 years ($N = 35$) were questioned about the double-function terms *hard*, *warm*, *sweet*, *sharp*, *soft*, and *cold*. First they were asked to think of an object that could be described in that way (e.g., "Give me an example of a *hard* object" p. 123). Then they were questioned about the psychological meaning of that same term (e.g., "Can a person be a *hard* person, or not?" p. 123) and how the two meanings might overlap (e.g., "In what way are a [name of the subject's hard object] and a [subject's description of a hard person] alike?" p. 123).

In agreement with Asch and Nerlove (1960), Schecter and Broughton (1991) found that the ability to detect and explain the overlapping properties between the physical and the psychological meanings of double-function terms was a relatively late attainment, and that only the oldest children provided sophisticated responses. For example, when questioned about the term *sharp*, a 14-year-old responded in a way that evidenced clear and accurate analogical reasoning:

> It's kind of like a knife is sharp and it catches things quickly, and it's just kind of the same way—like a knife's supposed to have a keen edge, and you talk about keen

people and sharp people . . . A knife is physically sharp, and it cuts through things. And a person is mentally sharp and they see through things. (p. 127)

Other double-function terms that are less common than those presented in the studies conducted by Asch and Nerlove (1960) and Schecter and Broughton (1991) may remain difficult to explain throughout adolescence and even into adulthood, as when the terms *move* ("This car is designed to *move* you") and *absorbing* ("The *absorbing* facts about cornstarch") occur in advertisements for consumer products (Nippold, Cuyler, & Braunbeck-Price, 1988) (see Chapter 10). Although comprehension improves during adolescence, even young adults may have difficulty explaining just exactly how the physical and psychological meanings of those words overlap.

Adverbs of Likelihood and Magnitude

The development of adverb comprehension has also been investigated, and there is evidence that children's knowledge of subtle differences in the meanings of these types of words gradually increases. Two types of adverbs that have been studied include those that express likelihood (e.g., *possibly, probably, definitely*) and magnitude (e.g., *somewhat, rather, extremely*).

Adverbs of likelihood are used to indicate how probable it is that a particular event will occur. Such words often occur in spoken and written news reports and forecasts. For example: "According to recent news reports, seismologists believe that during the next 10 years, earthquakes *definitely* will occur in Oregon, and that some will *probably* cause widespread property damage and *possibly* loss of life." Children's knowledge of subtle differences in meaning expressed by these and other adverbs of likelihood is important for understanding a wide variety of topics discussed in academic and social contexts.

Hoffner, Cantor, and Badzinski (1990) examined children's understanding of the differences between the adverb pairs *possibly* vs. *definitely*, *probably* vs. *definitely*, and *possibly* vs. *probably*. For each pair of adverbs, four different stories were written that involved the use of both words. Each story concerned two children (two girls or two boys) who wanted to do a special activity. Children who were 5, 7, 9, and 10 years ($N = 78$), tested individually, listened to the stories and were asked to indicate which child got to do the activity. For example, the story below was used for the adverb pair *probably* vs. *definitely*:

▶ One day, Lori's uncle said, "We will *probably* go ice skating this afternoon." Robin's uncle said, "We will *definitely* go ice skating this afternoon." Only one of the girls went ice skating with her uncle. Do you think Lori or Robin went skating? (p. 221)

For each story, pictures of the main characters (e.g., Lori and Robin) were shown. Children indicated their response by pointing to the picture of the child they thought got to do the activity.

Performance on the task gradually improved as subject age increased. Overall accuracy scores of 53%, 65%, 80%, and 93%, respectively, were obtained by the groups of 5-, 7-, 9-, and 10-year-olds. Thus, while the 5-year-olds were performing at chance level, the 10-year-olds had nearly mastered the task. However, the three pairs of adverbs were not equal in difficulty. Children's accuracy was higher when answering questions that tapped an understanding of the differences between *definitely* and *possibly*, and *definitely* and *probably* than between *possibly* and *probably*. For example, the 10-year-olds correctly answered 98% of the questions for stories contrasting *possibly* with *definitely* and *probably* with *definitely*, but only 80% of the questions for stories contrasting *possibly* with *probably*.

According to Hoffner et al. (1990), "apparently, it is easier to understand the distinction between what is certain and what is not certain than it is to understand the distinction between different degrees of probability" (p. 222). They also suggested that "part of the problem may be that adults rarely discuss abstract concepts such as possibility or probability with young children" (p. 230). They called for additional research to determine why children experience difficulty with the terms.

Adverbs of magnitude commonly occur in scientific contexts. For example, a seventh-grade geology teacher, describing the Richter scale, might explain how an earthquake of magnitude 3.5 may cause *slight* damage but one of magnitude 6.0 may cause *severe* damage to populated areas of a country. As students progress through school, they are increasingly able to grasp the subtle differences between adverbs of magnitude. However, it is not until college that they can fully appreciate the distinction between certain semantically adjacent terms such as *considerable* and *severe* that express only slight differences in meaning.

Bashaw and Anderson (1968) examined the development of nine adverbs of magnitude using a paired-comparisons judgment task and a rank-ordering task. Prior research (Cliff, 1959) had indicated that a group of college-educated adults had ranked the adverbs in the following order of increasing magnitude: *slightly, somewhat, rather, pretty, quite, decidedly, unusually, very,* and *extremely.* In the Bashaw and Anderson study, students from Grades 1, 2, 3, 4, 5, 6, 8, 10, and 12 were tested (N = 1365). A control group of college sophomores also participated (N = 163). In constructing the task, each adverb was combined with the adjective *large* (e.g., *slightly large*); each of the resulting combinations was paired with each of the others (e.g., *slightly large–extremely large, slightly large–quite large,* etc.). For each pair, the student was asked to decide which combination expressed a greater degree of largeness. Immediately after the paired-comparisons task, the student was presented with a randomly ordered list of all of the adverb-adjective combinations and was asked to rank the combinations in order from low to high.

Results showed that even the youngest students, the first and second graders, were able to discriminate between some of the adverb combinations, especially when the meanings were semantically further apart (e.g., *slightly large* vs. *extremely large*). As grade level increased, accuracy on both the paired-comparisons and rank-ordering tasks steadily improved, and finer distinctions could be made between semantically adjacent combinations (e.g., *somewhat large* vs. *rather large*). However, even the oldest group, the college students, did not consistently distinguish between all of the adjacent pairs (e.g., *quite large* vs. *decidedly large*) and may have viewed them as synonymous.

Metalinguistic and Metacognitive Verbs

Metalinguistic and metacognitive verbs such as *assert, concede, infer*, and *conclude* are words that are used to talk about language and thought (Olson & Astington, 1986a). Whereas *metalinguistic verbs* refer to acts of speaking, *metacognitive verbs* refer to acts of thinking. Also called *literate verbs*, these words are commonly used in discussions of spoken and written language interpretation, particularly in literature, science, and philosophy classes at the high school and college levels (Astington & Olson, 1987). Literate verbs reportedly were borrowed from Latin during the sixteenth and seventeenth centuries in order to improve the quality of the English language when it became the standard for government, law, science, theology, and philosophy (Olson & Astington, 1986b).

Astington and Olson (1987) examined the understanding of literate verbs in students from Grades 6, 8, 10, and 12 ($N = 99$) and college ($N = 77$). In their study, the literate verbs included a metalinguistic set (*assert, concede, imply, predict, interpret, confirm*) and a metacognitive set (*remember, doubt, infer, hypothesize, conclude, assume*). To assess comprehension of the words, the students were presented with a written multiple-choice task that consisted of 12 short stories, one for each of the 12 different verbs. In each story, the simple verb *say* or *think* was used to mark what a character said or thought. Given the story context, the simple verb could be replaced by a more complex literate verb. Each story was followed by a choice of four sentences, only one of which would best replace the last sentence in the story. The students were instructed to choose the best alternative. Two examples of problems used in the study are presented below, the first for the metalinguistic verb *predict* and the second for the metacognitive verb *remember*:

▶ 1. Susan and Eva are planning to go on a picnic. They want to choose a nice day. One morning they wake up early. Eva says, "Shall we go today?" Susan looks out of the window and *she says, "It will be sunny all day."*
   A. Susan *predicts* that it will be sunny all day.*
   B. Susan *knows* that it will be sunny all day.
   C. Susan *interprets* that it will be sunny all day.
   D. Susan *implies* that it will be sunny all day.

2. Last week in science class, Mr. Jones showed Dave that acid solution turns litmus paper pink. This week there's a test. The first question says, "What color will litmus paper be when you dip it in acid solution?" *Dave thinks that it will be pink.*
   A. Dave *remembers* that it will be pink.*
   B. Dave *hypothesizes* that it will be pink.
   C. Dave *infers* that it will be pink.
   D. Dave *observes* that it will be pink. (Astington & Olson, 1987)

Results showed that comprehension gradually improved with increasing subject age: mean accuracy scores of 45%, 42%, 59%, 71%, and 92%, respectively, were obtained by the students in Grades 6, 8, 10, 12, and college. Although students did not show mastery of the task until college, this was not surprising given the subtle and scholarly nature of the words involved. In fact, it is possible that a large segment of the adult population never masters these and other literate verbs, particularly if their formal education does not continue beyond high school.

Another purpose of the Astington and Olson (1987) study was to examine the relationship between students' comprehension of the literate verbs and their general vocabulary development and critical thinking skills. Accordingly, students in Grades 8 and 12 were also administered the reading vocabulary subtest of the *Canadian Achievement Tests* and the *Cornell Critical Thinking Test* (Ennis & Millman, 1982). Results indicated that performance on the literate verbs task was positively correlated to both of those measures.

Factive and Nonfactive Verbs

Factive verbs (e.g., *know, notice*) are words that presuppose the truth of the complement clause that follows. For example, in the sentence "Bill *knows* that the ball is red," the ball's redness is a certainty. However, with *nonfactive verbs* (e.g., *think, believe*), the truth of the complement clause is uncertain, as in the sentence "Bill *thinks* that the ball is red."

Scoville and Gordon (1980) examined comprehension of factive and nonfactive verbs in students who were ages 5, 8, 11, 14, and 20 years old ($N = 76$). Comprehension of five factive verbs (*know, forget, be sorry, be happy, be surprised*) and five nonfactive verbs (*think, be sure, figure, say, believe*) was assessed using a task where students were asked to judge the truth of the complement clause in a sentence. For each of the 10 verbs, three sentences were presented, with each representing a different combination of positive-negative values. These variations were described as + + (e.g., "Bill knows that the ball is red"), − + (e.g., "Bill does not know that the ball is red"), and + − (e.g., "Bill knows that the ball is not red"). The complement clauses were all of the form " . . . the ball is (red/green/blue/yellow)," with each color term paired randomly with a main verb. The sentences were presented in the context of a television quiz show. Subjects viewed a black-and-white videotape that showed a blindfolded "Dr. Fact," whose job it was to guess the color of a series of Ping-Pong balls drawn randomly from a box by an assistant, "Miss Fancy." On the videotape, all of the balls appeared to be the same shade of gray but it was emphasized to the subject that Miss Fancy always knew the color of the balls. After a ball was drawn, Dr. Fact whispered its color to Miss Fancy, who then produced each stimulus sentence (e.g., "Dr. Fact knows that the ball is yellow"). The subject then repeated the stimulus sentence and was asked by an announcer, "Is the ball (color)?"

The subject answered the question *Yes, No,* or *Don't know* by pushing an appropriate button. For the three sentence variations, $+ +$, $- +$, and $+ -$, the predicted "adult" response pattern for the factive verbs (e.g., *know*) was *Yes–Yes–No,* respectively; for the nonfactive verbs (e.g., *think*), it was *Don't know–Don't know–Don't know,* respectively.

Results showed that the two youngest groups, the 5- and 8-year-olds, showed little understanding of the subtle differences in meaning expressed by the sets of factive and nonfactive verbs. However, knowledge of both types of words gradually improved with each successive age group, and, by early adulthood most of the subjects displayed mastery of the task. In terms of overall accuracy, the 20-year-olds outperformed the 14-year-olds, who outperformed the 11-year-olds and the two youngest subject groups. The results of this study therefore show that knowledge of factive and nonfactive verbs is a protracted and relatively late attainment. The study also suggests that school-age children and adolescents may be confused by these types of verbs, as, for example, when certainty versus uncertainty is expressed in scientific contexts (e.g., "Neuroscientists *know* that the brain stem regulates wakefulness" vs. "Neuroscientists *believe* that the location of memory in the brain is variable").

Summary

Developmental studies have shown that the subtle meanings of literate words are acquired gradually during the school-age and adolescent years. Although preschool children may use many of the words in their spontaneous speech (e.g., *above, below, warm, cold, know, think, believe,* etc.), a full understanding of the words may not be reached until late adolescence or early adulthood and is closely tied to educational experience and performance. For example, studies have shown that literacy as measured by performance on various academic achievement tests is related to students' understanding of polysemous terms, and metalinguistic and metacognitive verbs. Researchers have therefore cautioned that teachers should not assume that school-age children and adolescents have an adequate grasp of these words. Researchers have also recommended that the words be taught directly to students because of their importance to literacy development and academic success.

Future research should examine students' knowledge of additional literate words that might be acquired during the school-age and adolescent years. For example, researchers could track the development of various words that are commonly used in the study of specific domains of philosophy. For example, lectures and writings concerned with the philosophy of religion assume an understanding of *omnipotence, benevolence,* and *omniscience,* just as those concerned with the philosophy of mind assume an understanding of *intention, desire,* and *motivation.* The information obtained from such studies could then be used by teachers and other professionals to facilitate the development of literacy and abstract thought during these important years.

Acknowledgments

Portions of this chapter appeared in the following publications:

Nippold, M. A. (1988). The literate lexicon. In M. A. Nippold (Ed.), *Later language development: Ages nine through nineteen* (pp. 29–47). Austin, TX: PRO-ED.

Nippold, M. A. (1992). The nature of normal and disordered word finding in children and adolescents. *Topics in Language Disorders, 13*(1), 1–14.

Nippold, M. A. (1993). Developmental markers in adolescent language: Syntax, semantics, and pragmatics. *Language, Speech, and Hearing Services in Schools, 24*, 21–28.

Used with permission of PRO-ED, Aspen Publishers, and the American Speech-Language-Hearing Association.

WORD FINDING:
STORAGE AND RETRIEVAL

"Weigh well your words before you give them breath."

—William Shakespeare, *Othello*
(Mieder, Kingsbury, & Harder, 1992, p. 673)

The ability to call up words with speed, clarity, and accuracy is a fundamental aspect of spoken and written communication. Although a seemingly simple phenomenon, word finding depends upon the complex interaction of two key processes, *storage* and *retrieval*. This chapter begins with an explanation of storage and retrieval based on research in cognitive psychology. It then describes the development of word finding during the school-age and adolescent years.

Storage and Retrieval

Storage is the availability of information in memory, and *retrieval* is the accessibility of that information (Kobasigawa, 1977). Bjork and Bjork (1992) described the nature of normal storage and retrieval in human memory. Summarizing a large body of psychological research, they reported that storage and retrieval are distinct but related processes. As they explained, every item in memory (e.g., the name of an exotic tropical fruit) has both a storage strength and a retrieval strength. *Storage strength* is a measure of how well the item has been learned, and *retrieval strength* is a measure of how easily the item can be accessed from memory on a given occasion. Storage and retrieval strength are both increased by opportunities to study an item and to retrieve it from memory. As storage improves, retrieval improves; as retrieval improves, storage improves. Retrieval, however, is the more powerful factor in increasing both storage and retrieval strength.

Bjork and Bjork (1992) explained further that the human capacity for long-term storage is virtually unlimited and that once entrenched in memory, a piece of information remains there indefinitely, even though the individual may have difficulty accessing it. Unlike storage capacity, retrieval capacity is limited and fragile, and it is highly dependent upon four critical factors. These include:

(1) the presence of cues;

(2) the frequency with which an item is retrieved;

(3) competition from other items in memory; and

(4) recency of learning.

First, to retrieve an item from memory (e.g., *mango*), specific cues associated with the item must be present. These cues may be internal or external. Internal cues can include thoughts, feelings, and emotions (e.g., the pleasant memory of eating a mango while on vacation), while external cues can include visual, auditory, tactile, gustatory, or olfactory stimuli (e.g., the smell of ripe mangos at an open air market).

Second, the more frequently an item is accessed (e.g., the individual asks for mangos every day), the easier it becomes to access that item in the future. Conversely, the less frequently the item is accessed (e.g., mangos can no longer be obtained), the less accessible it becomes. In fact, the item may eventually become nonretrievable if it is no longer accessed, despite the fact that it remains in long-term memory and was once accessed frequently. Bjork and Bjork (1992) explained that,

> The act of retrieval is itself a potent learning event. As an overall generalization, the act of retrieving an item of information is considerably more potent in terms of facilitating its subsequent successful recall than is an additional study trial on that item. (p. 37)

Third, given the limited retrieval capacity (and the unlimited storage capacity) of human memory, the probability that an item will be recalled successfully is affected by competition from other items in storage, especially those belonging to the same or a related category (e.g., *persimmon, pomegranate*). According to Bjork and Bjork (1992), "as items are added to memory, or as the retrieval strengths of certain items are increased, other items become less recallable" (p. 43). This was said to result from "the learning or retrieval of other items" (p. 43) and the disuse of older items in the set. To counteract this phenomenon, older items must be retrieved periodically.

Fourth, recency of learning also affects the probability of successful recall. Newly stored words are most accessible soon after they have been learned. If a new word falls into disuse, it soon becomes difficult to recall because of the greater storage strength that characterizes earlier learned items. To retrieve a new word easily, a speaker must continue to use the word, thereby building its storage strength.

It is common for children, adolescents, and adults with language disorders to experience word finding problems, signaled by behaviors such as pauses, hesitations, circumlocutions, and the use of indefinite pronouns (e.g., *something*), empty fillers (e.g., *thing, stuff*), or lexical substitutions (e.g., *dishwasher* for *washing machine*) during spoken communication (e.g., Dennis, 1992; German, 1992; Kail & Leonard, 1986; Rosenbek, LaPointe, & Wertz, 1989; Snyder & Downey, 1991; Wolf & Segal, 1992). It is important to recognize that persons who are free of language disorders also experience word finding problems for a variety of reasons. For example, such difficulties may result from insufficient stimulus cues, incomplete word learning, infrequent or nonrecent word use, or word learning without subsequent use (Bjork & Bjork, 1992; Burke, MacKay, Worthley, & Wade, 1991). However, in these individuals, word finding problems occur with much less frequency, severity, and disruption to communication.

Development of Word Finding

Word finding develops because of changes that occur in storage and retrieval. Storage improves with the expansion of the lexicon. As discussed in Chapters 1 and 2, word knowledge continues to expand throughout childhood, adolescence, and well into adulthood. New words are acquired, old words take on different meanings, and words from semantically related categories become more closely associated, resulting in an organized semantic network. These lexical attainments provide a speaker or writer with a richer and more orderly data base from which to select words for communication. Retrieval improves as accuracy and speed increase and as strategies are used to assist in calling up words. As school-age children and adolescents mature, they can retrieve a greater number and variety of words more efficiently.

Convergent and divergent naming tasks have been used in research to examine the development of word finding. As Guilford (1977) explained, *convergent tasks* require a focused search of the lexicon to produce a specific response (e.g., "Tell me the name of this animal"). *Divergent tasks*, in contrast, require a broad-ranging lexical search and are more flexible in the expected response (e.g., "Tell me all the animals you can think of"). Both types of tasks can reveal changes in the content, speed, and accuracy of naming.

Convergent Naming Tasks

In an early study of the development of naming speed, Milianti and Cullinan (1974) presented a series of 24 pictured objects (e.g., bed, candle, toaster), randomly ordered, to children ages 6 and 9 years ($N = 30$). The names of the objects included both high- and low-frequency words according to published word-frequency estimates (Thorn-dike & Lorge, 1944). As each picture appeared, the child named it as quickly as possible. The results of the study showed that both age groups produced the high-frequency words faster than the low-frequency words, and that 9-year-olds named the pictures faster than 6-year-olds. Mean response latencies obtained by the older and younger groups, respectively, were 911 and 1061 milliseconds.

Developmental improvements in naming speed were also reported by Cirrin (1983) in a similar type of study with children ages 6, 7, and 9 years, and with a con-trol group of adults ($N = 45$). The stimuli consisted of 100 pictured objects, randomly ordered, whose names included high- and low-frequency words, based on published word-frequency estimates (Kolson, 1960; Kucera & Francis, 1967; Rinsland, 1945). The child or adult named each picture as quickly as possible. Response time was found to decrease as subject age increased. Mean response times of the children ages 6, 7, and 9 years and the adults, respectively, were 1037, 1048, 901, and 692 milli-seconds. Moreover, for both children and adults, the high-frequency words were pro-duced faster than the low-frequency words.

Fried-Oken (1984) documented similar developmental changes in naming speed. Additionally, she examined the accuracy of children's naming responses and their error patterns. Children ages 4, 6, and 8 years ($N = 30$) were shown a series of 50 pic-tured items (e.g., animals, foods, musical instruments) in random order. As in previ-ous studies, the names of the pictures included high- and low-frequency words based on published word-frequency estimates (Carroll, Davies, & Richman, 1971). Upon seeing a picture, the child named it as quickly as possible. Fried-Oken's findings showed that naming speed and accuracy steadily increased with subject age, and that high-frequency words were produced more quickly than low-frequency words. When children labeled the pictures incorrectly, the most common error was one in which the substituted word was semantically and perceptually related to the target word (e.g., *broom* for *mop*, *shirt* for *jacket*, etc.). Noninformative responses (e.g., "I don't know") and responses that were semantically but not perceptually related to the tar-get word (e.g., *turtle* for *octopus*) were also common. She suggested that the older chil-dren's superior performance on the task resulted from their more extensive word knowledge and their greater experience with naming tasks.

In addition to the frequency of a word, the category to which it belongs affects the speed and accuracy with which it is named. Denckla and Rudel (1974) examined children's ability to produce the names of different types of words, including single digit numbers, alphabet letters, basic colors, and familiar objects. Children ages 5 through 10 years ($N = 180$) were presented with a series of "naming charts." Each chart contained five different stimuli (e.g., 9, 4, 2, 7, 6) from a certain category (e.g., numbers); the stimuli were repeated in random order 10 times for a total of 50 items per chart. The child named the items on each chart as quickly as possible.

Naming speed for all word types steadily increased as a function of subject age, and naming errors were rare, especially after age 6 years. All age groups named letters and numbers faster than colors and objects. An important finding, this may reflect the fact that letters and numbers are often practiced aloud by children during songs (e.g., "Now I know my ABCs," "One little, two little, three little pumpkins . . ."), games (e.g., counting the number of marbles earned), and repetitive drills (e.g., "One plus one is two, two plus two is four, four plus four is eight . . ."). Indeed, this is consistent with the fact that retrieval is influenced by the frequency with which words are used in spoken communication (Bjork & Bjork, 1992).

The findings of Denckla and Rudel (1974) regarding naming accuracy and speed were largely replicated by Semel and Wiig (1980) during the process of obtaining norms for a standardized test, the *Clinical Evaluation of Language Functions* (CELF). They designed and administered a naming confrontation task to students from kindergarten and Grades 1 through 12 ($N = 159$). This subtest, similar to the naming charts employed by Denckla and Rudel, contained a series of 36 colored shapes arranged in rows of six items each. The student named the color and shape of each item (e.g., "blue circle, red square, black triangle . . ."), moving from left to right, as quickly as possible. Although accuracy reached a maximum by kindergarten (ages 5 and 6 years), with a mean score of 32, naming speed gradually increased through Grade 5 (ages 10 and 11 years) where it stabilized with a mean score of 90 seconds to name the 36 items.

The Role of Stimulus Contexts

Researchers have also examined the effects of different stimulus contexts on children's naming. Rudel, Denckla, Broman, and Hirsch (1980) designed a task in which children ages 5 through 11 years ($N = 202$) produced object names in four different contexts:

(1) *visual naming* (a picture was displayed);

(2) *naming to description* (a question was asked, e.g., "What is the tool for digging a hole in the ground?" p. 113);

(3) *sentence completion* (the child supplied a word at the end of a sentence, e.g., "To find out what to eat in a restaurant, you look at the _____" p. 113); and

(4) *tactual object naming* (the child named objects contained in a bag that were felt but could not be seen).

Forty-eight different nouns were presented, with 12 assigned to each context; words were equated for frequency across contexts.

Accuracy of naming steadily improved as subject age increased. Although the four stimulus contexts were equally easy for the 11-year-olds, certain contexts proved easier than others for the younger children. For the 5- through 10-year-olds combined, accuracy was highest for sentence completion and tactual object naming, lowest for naming to description, and moderate for visual naming. Although the possible reasons for the differences between contexts were not explored, the sentence completion and tactual object contexts may have offered the children a greater number of useful cues than the other contexts.

Wiegel-Crump and Dennis (1986) also examined the effects of stimulus context on naming. Children and adolescents ages 6, 8, 10, 12, and 14 years ($N = 50$) were asked to produce the names of objects and actions under three different conditions:

(1) *semantic,* which was similar to what Rudel et al. (1980) called naming to description (e.g., "I'm thinking of an animal . . . It lives in the jungle . . . It walks on four legs . . . It has a mane . . . and it roars . . . It's a _____?" p. 6);

(2) *rhyming* (e.g., "I'm thinking of an animal . . . It rhymes with dzion . . . It's a _____?" p. 6); and

(3) *visual,* what Rudel et al. called visual naming ("I want you to name the picture for me when I tap with my pencil" p. 6).

The task contained 45 different words, with 9 from each of 5 different semantic categories: animals (e.g., lion, camel), food (e.g., banana, butter), clothing (e.g., hat, glove), household items (e.g., bed, door), and actions (e.g., eat, run). All words were familiar and concrete. For all stimulus contexts, naming speed and accuracy improved as subject age increased. While accuracy plateaued by age 10, speed continued to increase through age 14. In terms of both speed and accuracy, the rhyming context was more difficult than the semantic and visual contexts, and the semantic context was more difficult than the visual, which was inconsistent with Rudel et al. (1980) who found just the opposite effect.

Word Finding and Academic Achievement

Other researchers have also found that as children mature, their performance on naming tasks gradually improves. In a longitudinal study, Wolf and Goodglass (1986) administered the *Boston Naming Test* (BNT) (Kaplan, Goodglass, & Weintraub, 1976) to children ($N = 75$) on three separate occasions. Each child was tested at age 5 years, and again at ages 6 and 7 years. The BNT contained a series of 85 pictured objects that the child named.

Naming accuracy steadily improved as the children got older; mean accuracy scores of 33.6, 41.3, and 43.6 were obtained at ages 5, 6, and 7 years, respectively. It was also found that naming accuracy at age 5 predicted reading ability at age 7, with the more accurate namers showing higher performance on a measure of silent reading comprehension, the *Gates-MacGinitie Reading Test* (Gates & MacGinitie, 1978) and on a measure of connected oral reading accuracy, the *Gray Oral Reading Test* (Gray, 1967). These findings are consistent with a large body of research that has established a close relationship between children's word finding ability and their reading skills (e.g., Badian, 1982; Blachman, 1984; Denckla & Rudel, 1976a, 1976b; Kail & Hall, 1994; Rudel, Denckla, & Broman, 1981; Snyder & Downey, 1991; Wolf, 1984; Wolf, Bally, & Morris, 1986; Wolf & Segal, 1992).

For example, Kail and Hall (1994) recently examined the relationship between naming speed and reading achievement in groups of children who were ages 8, 9, 10, 11, 12, and 13 years old (N = 144). Children were individually administered a task in which they named letters, digits, and colors as rapidly as possible. Fifty stimuli were presented, arranged in rows of five items each. The total length of time required to name all 50 items was recorded. Children were also administered the Reading Recognition and Reading Comprehension subtests of the *Peabody Individual Achievement Test* (PIAT) (Dunn & Markwardt, 1970). The findings showed that the time required to name an item decreased as a function of increasing subject age, and that faster naming was significantly correlated to both measures of reading ability.

Standardized Tests of Convergent Naming

Guilford and Nawojczyk (1988) used standardized tests to examine the development of word finding. They administered the *Boston Naming Test* (BNT) to children at every level from kindergarten through Grade 6 (ages 5 through 12 years) (N = 357). As a comparison measure, they also administered the Noun Picture Naming subtest of the *Test of Word Finding* (TWF) (German, 1986) to every fifth child. The TWF, like the BNT, contains a series of pictured objects that the child names. Although the nouns on both tests are concrete, the BNT contains a greater number of low-frequency words (e.g., *trellis, tongs, abacus, sphinx*) than the TWF.

On both measures, naming accuracy improved as grade level increased, but the TWF proved easier than the BNT, and students reached a ceiling on the TWF by Grade 4. Mean scores for the BNT and the TWF, respectively, ranged from 43% and 55% at kindergarten to 81% and 96% at Grade 6. Performance on the two tests was correlated at kindergarten and at Grades 1 through 4 but not at Grades 5 or 6, perhaps because of the ceiling effects.

Word Finding During Adolescence and Beyond. Older children seem to reach a plateau on naming tasks when simple and common words are to be recalled (Denckla & Rudel, 1974; Garnett & Fleischner, 1983; German, 1986; Guilford & Nawojczyk, 1988; Semel & Wiig, 1980; Wiegel-Crump & Dennis, 1986). However, improvements in naming can be observed throughout adolescence and into adulthood when more difficult words are involved. This was demonstrated by German (1990) who administered the *Test of Adolescent/Adult Word Finding* (TAWF) (German, 1990) to groups of adolescents and adults (N = 1753). The TAWF requires the subject to name a variety of pictured objects, actions, and categories, to complete sentences, and to identify items by description. Many of the items on the TAWF are low-frequency and/or abstract words (e.g., *tambourine, jury, equator, religions*). A total of 107 items are presented.

German's (1990) results showed that groups of subjects ages 13, 18, and 20 through 39 years obtained mean accuracy scores of 88.6, 96.2, and 99.4, respectively. On the Pictured Object subtest of the TAWF, those same groups demonstrated mean item response times of 1.72, 1.47, and 1.39 seconds, respectively. Beyond age 40, however, performance on the TAWF gradually declined in both accuracy and speed. Groups of adults ages 40 through 59 years and 60 through 80 years, respectively, obtained mean accuracy scores of 97.4 and 90.6, and mean item response times of 1.68 and 2.11 seconds.

It would be interesting to know why this age-related decline in naming speed and accuracy occurred in German's (1990) research. The view that word finding gradually deteriorates as part of the normal aging process is controversial. In a recent literature review of picture-naming accuracy in normal older adults, Goulet, Ska, and Kahn (1994) reported that studies were inconsistent in demonstrating a decline in performance associated with increasing age, and they cautioned that there is much variability in naming accuracy among older adults. They suggested that subject factors such as health status, educational background, home environment, and visual perception should be carefully considered when examining naming skills in older adults.

Divergent Naming Tasks

As mentioned previously, divergent naming tasks have also been used to study the development of word finding. Growth in the number of words produced during a divergent naming task was reported by Nelson (1974) in a study with young school-age children. Two groups of children ages 5 and 8 years ($N = 131$) were asked to name as many items as they could think of from nine different semantic categories (animals, colors, furniture, fruit, tools, flowers, vegetables, insects, clothes). Each child was tested individually. The examiner stated a category and encouraged the child to name as many members as possible.

The nine semantic categories differed widely in ease of naming, and both groups of children were able to name more items for animals and colors than for the other seven categories. For the nine categories combined, the mean number of items produced by the 5- and 8-year-olds, respectively, was 4.64 and 8.04. Thus, the older children produced nearly twice as many items as the younger ones. This was accomplished largely by the 8-year-olds producing a greater number of subclass members within categories. For example, when asked to name animals, the older group was more likely to mention different breeds of dogs, types of dinosaurs, or species of birds than the younger group. It was also found that the 8-year-olds produced a greater proportion of appropriate responses than the 5-year-olds. For example, when asked to name vegetables, 8-year-olds were less likely than 5-year-olds to mention items such as pizza, soup, and ice cream that were loosely related to the category but not members of it. Nelson (1974) suggested that the findings reflected the older children's more extensive word knowledge, clearer concept of category boundaries, and greater facility at retrieving words.

In a similar study that included older age groups, Kail and Nippold (1984) asked students ages 8, 12, and 21 years ($N = 39$) to name as many animals and pieces of furniture as they could, allowing 7 minutes per category. The results indicated that the number of appropriate responses gradually increased as a function of age. Combining the two semantic categories, the mean number of words produced by the 8-, 12-, and 21-year-olds, respectively, was 31.6, 33.85, and 47.5. Moreover, each age group tended to name the most typical exemplars of a category (e.g., dog, cat, bird) at the outset, followed by decreasingly typical items (e.g., rat, mongoose, chameleon). Words also tended to be produced in clusters of closely related items. When naming animals, for example, a student might list domestic animals (e.g., cat, dog, hamster), followed by farm animals (e.g., cow, goat, pig), followed by fish (e.g., trout, bass, tuna), and so forth. Although the number of clusters was similar across groups, the number of items within clusters steadily increased as a function of age, reflecting growth in word knowledge.

Developmental data on word finding were obtained during the process of standardizing certain formal tests for children and adolescents. For example, the Divergent Production subtest of the *Fullerton Language Test for Adolescents* (Thorum, 1980) was administered to students ages 11 through 18 years (N = 762). To administer this subtest, five different semantic categories (body parts, modes of transportation, grocery store items, sports, subjects taught in school) were presented, and the student was allowed 20 seconds per category to name as many members as possible. Performance gradually improved over the ages that were tested. Combining the total number of correct responses across the five semantic categories, mean raw scores for students ages 11, 14, and 18 years, respectively, were 57, 61, and 65.

Similarly, the Word Associations subtest of the *Clinical Evaluation of Language Fundamentals–Revised* (CELF–R) (Semel, Wiig, & Secord, 1987) was administered to students ages 5 through 16 years (N = 2426). Each student was asked to name as many members as possible from three different semantic categories (animals, modes of transportation, occupations), allowing 60 seconds per category. Performance gradually improved as a function of age. For all categories combined, mean raw scores for students ages 5, 10, and 16, respectively, were 17, 35, and 45.

Strategies for Word Finding

Developmental studies have also shown that, as children mature, they show greater proficiency in the use of strategies to call up words from memory (e.g., Halperin, 1974; Kail, 1984; Kobasigawa, 1974, 1977; Kobasigawa & Mason, 1982; Paris, 1978). Strategies are goal-oriented behaviors that can facilitate the recall of information (Kail, 1984). Three strategies that can facilitate word recall in either convergent or divergent contexts include *categorical organization*, *categorical cueing*, and *attention to visual cues*.

Categorical Organization

Information is often best retrieved if it can be organized in some manner (Kail, 1984). Children's spontaneous use of categorical organization to call up words from memory was examined by Paris (1978). Groups of 8- and 12-year-olds (N = 40) were read a list of 20 common nouns (e.g., *cow*, *apple*, *boat*) presented in random order. The words included four items from each of five semantic categories (animals, fruit, vehicles, clothes, furniture). Following two successive presentations of the list, the child was asked to recall as many words as possible in any order. After the first recall trial, the child was asked to recall the words two additional times. Three minutes were allowed per trial.

Results showed that the 12-year-olds recalled a greater number of words (mean = 12.4) per trial than the 8-year-olds (mean = 7.8). Both groups tended to recall the words in clusters (e.g., *cow, pig, horse*), which indicated that they had spontaneously organized the words into semantic categories to facilitate recall. However, the 12-year-olds used this strategy more efficiently in that, for each of the three trials, they recalled a larger number of categories and a larger number of words within each category than did the 8-year-olds. The older children also showed greater skill than the younger ones in organizing and recalling the words with each successive trial.

Categorical Cueing

Externally provided categorical cues can also facilitate word recall. Halperin (1974) examined the extent to which children ages 6, 9, and 12 years ($N = 90$) benefited from hearing the names of various categories of words to be recalled. Each child was asked to recall a list of 36 words that the examiner read aloud. The words, which belonged to nine different semantic categories (e.g., zoo animals, tools, buildings), were presented in an organized manner such that all items from one category were listed first, followed by all items from another category, and so on. In addition, the examiner stated the name of each category before reading the words to be recalled (e.g., "Names of zoo animals: lion, elephant, bear . . ."). To recall the words, half the children in each group were cued and half were not. In the cued condition, children were asked to recall the names of all the items that belonged to each category (e.g., "Can you tell me all the zoo animals?"). In the noncued condition, children were asked to recall as many words as possible in any order.

For all three age groups, children in the cued condition recalled a greater number of words than those in the noncued condition, indicating that even the 6-year-olds benefited from hearing the category names before recalling the words associated with them. However, the older children, the 9- and 12-year-olds, recalled a greater number of words than the younger ones in both conditions, indicating that they were more efficient at recalling words with and without the category names made explicit for them.

Attention to Visual Cues

Research has also demonstrated that attention to visual cues can facilitate word recall. Kobasigawa (1974) presented children ages 6, 8, and 11 years ($N = 108$) with a series of 24 pictured objects to be recalled. The pictures included three items (e.g., bear, monkey, camel) from eight different semantic categories (e.g., zoo animals). The examiner displayed each item to be recalled (e.g., bear) along with a related picture cue (e.g., zoo) and explained that the recall item went with the cue (e.g., "In the zoo, you find a bear"). After all items had been presented in this manner, the eight cue cards were given to the child face down and the examiner explained that the child was free to use the cards to help remember the words. The child was then asked to recall as many words as possible in three minutes.

The findings indicated that only 33% of the 6-year-olds used the picture cues to facilitate recall but that 75% of the 8-year-olds and 91% of the 11-year-olds did so. Use of this strategy led to an increase in the total number of items recalled with each successive age group. In addition, the older cue users recalled more items per category than the younger cue users, thereby showing more thorough and efficient use of the strategy.

Summary

Successful word finding results from the operation of two interrelated processes, storage and retrieval. Unlike storage, which is stable and unlimited, retrieval is fragile and highly dependent upon the presence of internal and external cues, the frequency with which a word is accessed, competition from related words in storage, and recency of word learning.

Developmental studies that employed convergent naming tasks have shown that accuracy and speed of naming gradually increase during the school-age and adolescent years and well into adulthood. They have also shown that skill in word finding is closely related to oral and silent reading ability. When simple words are to be recalled, accuracy of naming may reach a plateau as early as kindergarten, although speed of naming continues to increase beyond that point. When more difficult words are to be recalled, improvements in accuracy and speed of naming can be observed to occur well into adulthood. Performance on divergent naming tasks is marked by a gradual increase in the number of appropriate exemplars that can be produced from various semantic categories. This change reflects students' expanding knowledge of words, awareness of subclasses within categories, and their ability to reflect upon the content of the lexicon. Age-related improvements on convergent and divergent tasks also result from increasing competence in the use of organizational strategies that facilitate word recall. As young people mature, they are more likely to spontaneously employ and benefit from a variety of systematic strategies such as categorical organization, categorical cueing, and attention to visual cues to call up words.

Future Research

Although much has been learned about the ability of children and adolescents to call up words during structured naming tasks, little is known about how they accomplish this in less constrained, more naturalistic contexts. Studies are needed to examine developmental changes in the ability to call up words during spontaneous conversational speech in school-age children and adolescents. Research is also needed to examine the development of word finding throughout the life span to determine more precisely the extent to which accuracy and speed of word finding may change as a function of increasing age.

Acknowledgments

Portions of this chapter appeared in the following publication:

Nippold, M. A. (1992). The nature of normal and disordered word finding in children and adolescents. Topics in Language Disorders, 13(1), 1–14.

THE DEFINITION OF WORDS

"The beginning of wisdom is the definition of terms."

—Socrates (469–399 B.C.) (DeVries, 1991, p. 430)

Word definition requires an individual to reflect on the lexicon and to state explicitly what is known implicitly (Watson, 1985). The ability to provide a formal definition of a word is closely related to cognitive and linguistic development, literacy, and academic achievement in school-age children and adolescents (Snow, Cancini, Gonzalez, & Shriberg, 1989; Thorndike, Hagen, & Sattler, 1986; Watson, 1985; Wechsler, 1991).

Long considered to be important, word definition has been examined on formal psychometric batteries since 1905, when Alfred Binet and Theodore Simon published the first modern intelligence test (Binet & Simon, 1905; Thorndike et al., 1986). Currently, many standardized tests of intelligence and language development contain subtests that examine word definition (e.g., Huisingh, Barrett, Zachman, Blagden, & Orman, 1990; Newcomer & Hammill, 1988; Thorndike et al., 1986; Wallace & Hammill, 1994; Wechsler, 1991; Wiig & Secord, 1992; Zachman, Huisingh, Barrett, Orman, & Blagden, 1989).

In addition to its role as an index of human competencies, word definition has practical value in scholarly contexts such as formal debates and scientific reports where individuals must agree on the meanings of certain key terms before purposeful dialogue or information exchange can occur (Freeley, 1993; Makau, 1990). So for example, scientists who debate the ethics of employing nonhuman animals in medical research must define the terms *scientific progress* and *animal welfare* when they are used (Makau, 1990), and a researcher who reports on an innovative treatment for cancer must clarify what is meant by *successful outcome*. Often, the failure to agree on a term prevents a controversy from being resolved as in the case of abortion, where ethicists continue to debate the definition of *life* itself (Freeley, 1993).

Word definition also has practical value in ordinary conversations, as when a parent and teenager discuss the youth's *curfew*. Dissonance may arise within the household if this term is defined in one way by the parent ("Be home by 10 o'clock") and in another way by the teenager ("Start heading home around 10 o'clock"). The failure to explicate the meanings of key terms can result in poor communication, which can negatively impact human relationships in formal and informal contexts.

Types of Definitions

Words can be defined in a variety of ways (Makau, 1990). Perhaps the oldest and most formal type is the Aristotelian, or dictionary, definition. In *Metaphysics* (Book VII), Aristotle (384–322 B.C.) wrote that a definition is a formula containing two essential elements, the genus and the differentiae, which help to distinguish one thing from another; for example, "Man is an animal which is two-footed and featherless" (McKeon, 1941, p. 803). In Aristotle's definition of *man*, *animal* is the genus, and *two-footed* and *featherless* constitute the differentiae. Such definitions can be written symbolically as "X is a Y which Z," where X is the definiendum (i.e., man), Y is its superordinate category (i.e., animal), and Z is one or more characteristics of X (i.e., two-footed, featherless) (Markowitz & Franz, 1988).

Other types of definitions, which are less formal, include *operational*, where a term is defined in relation to a specific situation (e.g., "*Successful outcome* means the patient survives at least 5 years post-treatment"), and those that involve *negation* (e.g., "By *argument*, I don't mean an angry exchange between people"), *comparison* (e.g., "A *marmot* is like a small beaver"), or *example* (e.g., "For example, cricket is a *popular sport* in England") (Makau, 1990). These more naturalistic definitions often are embedded in rich linguistic contexts.

Growth of Word Definition

Word definition is frequently modeled in school (Snow et al., 1989). As early as kindergarten, children are exposed to Aristotelian definitions during classroom discussions with their teachers (Watson, 1985), and beginning at about second grade and continuing throughout their formal educations, children and adolescents are encouraged to use dictionaries to learn the meanings of words (e.g., Coon, Cramer, Fillmer, Lefcourt, Martin, & Thompson, 1980; Eller & Hester, 1980a, 1980b; McDonnell, Nakadate, Pfordresher, & Shoemate, 1979; Smith & Wardhaugh, 1980; Snow et al., 1989).

Growth in the ability to define words is thought to reflect the amount of meaningful exposure one has to formal definitions and the number of opportunities available to practice this literate convention in school (Snow, 1990; Snow et al., 1989; Watson, 1985). Although Piagetian theory has contended that the ability to provide Aristotelian definitions requires class inclusion logic (i.e., understanding how physical objects belong to larger categories), research has not been able to demonstrate such a link (Benelli, Arcuri, & Marchesini, 1988).

The manner in which school-age children, adolescents, and adults define words is discussed in this chapter. The information is derived from two sources: developmental studies and standardized tests that have examined word definition.

Developmental Studies

The development of word definition has been examined by asking individuals of various ages to explain the meanings of words presented out of context (e.g., "What is a *dog*?"). Collectively, those studies have shown that word definition gradually improves during childhood, adolescence, and into adulthood and that quantitative and qualitative changes occur (Al-Issa, 1969; Benelli et al., 1988; Feifel & Lorge, 1950; Johnson & Anglin, 1995; Litowitz, 1977; McGhee-Bidlack, 1991; Shepard, 1970; Snow, 1990; Storck & Looft, 1973; Swartz & Hall, 1972; Watson, 1985, 1995; Wehren, De Lisi, & Arnold, 1981; Wilson, 1975; Wolman & Barker, 1965).

Definitions of young children reflect limitations in semantic content and syntactic form. Litowitz (1977) analyzed the responses of children, ages 4 through 7 years (N = 17), who were asked to define a series of common words (e.g., *bicycle, shoe, hat*). Many of the words were defined in ways that reflected personal or idiosyncratic meanings (e.g., *Bicycle*: "You could use it to ride to Bruce's" p. 296) rather than the socially shared meanings that characterize the definitions of older children, adolescents, and adults (e.g., *Bicycle*: "It's a vehicle that has two wheels").

As children mature, they show a gradual increase in the production of formal, Aristotelian definitions. Al-Issa (1969) examined word definition in children ages 5, 6, 7, 8, 9, and 10 years (N = 201). Each child was asked to define 30 words that were familiar to even the youngest children. Most of the words were nouns that represented common objects (e.g., *dog, chair, window*). Children's responses were classified as functional (e.g., *Dog*: "It barks"), descriptive (e.g., "has a tail"), or categorical (e.g., "It's an animal"). Results showed that at age 5, 72% of the children's responses were functional, 21% were descriptive, and 7% were categorical. By age 10, however, 28% of their responses were functional, 11% were descriptive, and 61% were categorical, indicating a shift toward Aristotelian-like definitions. Other studies using similar procedures (Swartz & Hall, 1972; Wolman & Barker, 1965) have supported these findings.

In Al-Issa's (1969) study, the extent to which the children may have combined response types in their definitions was not examined. Wehren et al. (1981) examined this issue and found that, as children got older, there was a greater tendency for their definitions to include more than one characteristic of the named object. Those researchers asked children ages 5, 7, 9, and 11 years ($N = 80$) and a control group of young adults (mean age = 26 years; $N = 20$) to define 15 nouns, which were the names of common objects (e.g., *hat, book, table*). The extent to which the subjects mentioned both the function and the appearance of an object was of primary interest. Results showed that definitions of the youngest children emphasized functions, but that the tendency to mention both the function and the appearance of an object (e.g., *Hat*: "You wear it on your head to keep warm and it's round") was more common among the older children and the adults. Older children also were more likely to include *general* superordinate category terms in their definitions (e.g., *Clock*: "It's an *object* for telling time"), but Aristotelian definitions that included the *specific* superordinate category term were produced mainly by the adults (e.g., *Clock*: "It's a *timepiece* that hangs on the wall").

Similar findings were made by Benelli et al. (1988) who asked children ages 5, 7, and 10 years ($N = 30$) and a group of adults to explain the meanings of nine familiar nouns from three different categories: *cat, cow, tiger* (*animals*); *sofa, table, wardrobe* (*furniture*); *kite, ball, doll* (*toys*). All words were presented in random order. Performance gradually improved as a function of increasing subject age, particularly in the tendency to produce definitions that contained both functional and perceptual features of the target word (e.g., "A table has legs, is squarish, and is to eat off") and that mentioned the specific superordinate category term (e.g., "It's a piece of *furniture*"). However, unlike Wehren et al. (1981), no differences were found between the oldest children and the adults in defining the words.

Linguistic Versus Metalinguistic Knowledge

It is important to note that optimal performance on word definition tasks involves linguistic and metalinguistic components. Linguistic components include knowledge of the specific superordinate category term and the major characteristics of a word. Metalinguistic components include awareness of what constitutes an appropriate definition (Wehren et al., 1981) and the ability to analyze a word and abstract its category and characteristics. When familiar words are defined, age-related improvements seem to reflect growth in metalinguistic components; when less familiar words are defined, improvements may reflect growth in both linguistic and metalinguistic components. In either case, definition tasks may underestimate a person's knowledge of words (Watson, 1995).

Children often know more about the words they are asked to define than their definitions might indicate. It is clear that preschoolers know that cats and dogs are animals, that apples and cookies are food, and that boys and girls are children. However, when asked to define the words *cat, dog, apple, cookie, boy,* and *girl,* the appropriate category terms (*animal, food, child*) typically are omitted from their responses (Nelson, 1978).

School-age children also show limitations in the extent to which they display their knowledge of word meanings on definition tasks. This was shown by Watson (1985), who asked children ages 5, 7, and 10 years ($N = 107$) to define eight common nouns (e.g., *horse, cat, flower*). After the children had defined the words, they were asked a series of "yes or no" questions that tapped their knowledge of the categories to which the words belonged (e.g., "Is a horse an *animal?*"). Results of the comprehension probe indicated that children of all ages knew the categories of the words. However, the children's definitions of those words often did not mention the categories. Although there was an age-related increase in the frequency of definitions that mentioned the superordinate category term, even the 10-year-olds omitted this term for more than half of their definitions, often substituting a *general* category term (e.g., "A horse is *something* that runs") for the *specific* category term (e.g., "A horse is an *animal* that runs").

Watson (1985) suggested that definitions that contain a general category term may serve as precursors to more complex responses containing the specific category term. She also suggested that an increase in mentioning specific category terms did not result from growth in word knowledge but reflected the gradual adoption of a conventional "literate register" modeled in school through teacher discourse and dictionary usage. Recently, in discussing pragmatic issues that may underlie word definitions, Watson (1995) contended that the use of a specific category term reflects the speaker's desire to provide a maximally informative response in a concise and efficient manner.

Snow (1990), who analyzed children's word definitions using a more fine-grained scoring system than previous researchers, (e.g., Al-Issa, 1969; Watson, 1985; Wehren et al., 1981), also documented gradual improvement during the school-age years. Children from Grades 2, 3, 4, and 5 (ages 7 through 11 years; $N = 137$) defined 10 familiar nouns (e.g., *knife, umbrella, donkey*). Children's responses first were classified as formal or informal. Formal definitions included a specific category term (e.g., *utensil*) or a general one (e.g., *something, thing, a kind of*); informal definitions did not include either type of category term. Formal definitions were then assigned points on several dimensions such as syntactic complexity, quality of the category term (specific or general), and number of characteristics mentioned. Informal definitions were assigned points for the amount of information that was provided about the word. Results showed that 49% of all definitions were formal at second grade but that 76% were formal at fifth grade. Moreover, as grade level increased, formal definitions became more sophisticated whereas informal definitions remained static in quality.

Concrete Versus Abstract Nouns

In an effort to learn about the development of definitions during adolescence, McGhee-Bidlack (1991) asked 10-, 14-, and 18-year-olds ($N = 120$) to define 16 nouns. Half the words were *concrete* and had tangible referents (e.g., *flower, book, car*), while the other half were *abstract* and lacked such referents (e.g., *freedom, courage, wisdom*). All words were familiar to the subjects and were presented in random order. Results indicated that concrete nouns were easier to define than abstract nouns for all three age groups. Concrete nouns were defined mainly in terms of their categories and characteristics (e.g., "A *flower* is a plant that has colorful petals") whereas abstract nouns were defined mainly in terms of their characteristics, with their category terms often omitted (e.g., "*Freedom* means you can do what you want to do"). However, definitions of both types of nouns improved during adolescence, evidenced by a gradual increase in the frequency with which specific category terms and characteristics were mentioned in defining concrete and abstract nouns.

Growth in Categorical Responses

In contrast to the studies discussed so far, Feifel and Lorge (1950) examined the development of word definition without attempting to limit word difficulty. Those researchers asked children ages 6 through 14 years ($N = 900$) to define the 45 words from the vocabulary subtest of the *Stanford-Binet Intelligence Scale* (Thorndike, Hagen, & Sattler, 1986). Nouns, verbs, and adjectives of varying degrees of difficulty (e.g., *orange, eyelash, scorch, roar, priceless, piscatorial*) were presented. To analyze the children's responses, the researchers used the classification system shown in Table 4.1. Quantitatively, they found that the number of correct responses steadily increased as a function of age: mean accuracy scores of 14%, 16%, 18%, 22%, 26%, 31%, 34%, 39%, and 39% were obtained by the groups of 6-, 7-, 8-, 9-, 10-, 11-, 12-, 13-, and 14-year-olds, respectively. Qualitatively, they found that the older children (ages 11 through 14 years) used the Synonym and Explanation response types (see Table 4.1) more often than the younger ones (ages 6 through 10 years), who used the three remaining response types more often than the older ones. Most importantly, as age increased, children's responses reflected a greater tendency to place words into superordinate categories (e.g., to define *orange* as "a fruit which grows in California or Florida," p. 16). Using the same testing procedures and scoring system, those results were later replicated by Wilson (1975) with children of the same age range.

This age-related tendency to produce categorical responses also was observed by Storck and Looft (1973), who not only replicated the Feifel and Lorge (1950) study but extended it to subjects of a very broad age range. Children, adolescents, and adults ($N = 180$) from nine different age groups (6 through 9 years, 10 through 13 years, 14 through 17 years, 18 through 25 years, 26 through 35 years, 36 through 45 years, 46 through 55 years, 56 through 65 years, and 66 plus years) were asked to define the same 45 words that had been presented by Feifel and Lorge. Results showed that the frequency of accurate definitions gradually increased during childhood, adolescence, and into adulthood. The mean number of accurate responses was 10.40 for the 6 through 9 years group, 15.15 for the 10 through 13 years group, 17.85 for the 14 through 17 years group, and 24.50 for the 18 through 25 years group. Of particular importance was the fact that the proportion of accurate definitions that mentioned the specific category term steadily increased during childhood and adolescence but

Table 4.1
Qualitative Classification System Used by Feifel and Lorge

Synonym Category:

Synonym unmodified:	*Orange* = a fruit
Synonym modified by use:	*Straw* = hay that cattle eat
Synonym modified by description:	*Gown* = long dress
Synonym modified by use and description:	*Eyelash* = hair over the eye that protects you
Synonym qualified as to degree:	*Tap* = touch lightly

Explanation Category:

Explanation:	*Priceless* = it's worth a lot of money
	Skill = being able to do something well

Use, Description, and Use and Description Category:

Use:	*Orange* = you eat it
Description:	*Straw* = it's yellow
Use and description:	*Orange* = you eat it and it's round

Demonstration, Repetition, Illustration, and Inferior Explanation Category:

Demonstration:	*Tap* = (performs action)
	Eyelash = (points to eyelash)
Repetition:	*Puddle* = a puddle of water
Illustration:	*Priceless* = a gem
Inferior explanation:	*Scorch* = hot

Error Category:

Incorrect demonstration:	*Eyelash* = (points to eyebrow)
Misinterpretation:	*Regard* = protects something
Wrong definition:	*Orange* = a vegetable
Clang association:	*Roar* = raw
	Skill = skillet
Repetition without explanation:	*Puddle* = puddle
Omits:	When the word is left out

Note. From "Qualitative Differences in the Vocabulary Responses of Children" by H. Feifel and I. Lorge, 1950, *Journal of Educational Psychology*, 41, pp. 4–5.

leveled off during adulthood. Overall performance on the task remained stable between the ages of 25 and 55 years, but gradually declined after that.

Because many of the words contained in the *Stanford-Binet Intelligence Scale* were rather difficult (e.g., *haste, shrewd, priceless, piscatorial*), age-related improvements in word definition reported by Feifel and Lorge (1950), Wilson (1975), and Storck and

Looft (1973) undoubtedly reflected growth in word knowledge as well as growth in metalinguistic components.

Many researchers (e.g., Al-Issa, 1969; Benelli et al., 1988; Snow, 1990; Watson, 1985; Wehren et al., 1981) examined the development of word definition by presenting children with common nouns referring to tangible objects. Other researchers (e.g., Feifel & Lorge, 1950; Storck & Looft, 1973; Wilson, 1975) presented verbs and adjectives in addition to nouns, but the children's performance on the different classes of words was not reported separately. Markowitz and Franz (1988) suggested that nouns may be easier to define than other word classes but had little evidence to support their hypothesis.

Defining Other Types of Words

Recently, Johnson and Anglin (1995) examined the ability of children ages 6, 8, and 10 years (Grades 1, 3, and 5) ($N = 96$) to define words from three different classes—nouns, verbs, and adjectives. Root words (e.g., *home*), compounds (e.g., *homemade*), and words that contained inflectional (*homes*) and derivational (*homeless*) morphemes were included. A master list of 434 words was initially generated through a procedure of systematically sampling an unabridged dictionary. The words in the list ranged from simpler (e.g., *closet, soaking, enjoyable*) to more complex (e.g., *hematology, redefine, spousal*) meanings. Words were selected from this list and presented in order of increasing difficulty. The number of words presented to a child varied, depending on the child's performance. On average, the number of words presented was 10.31 at age 6, 20.50 at age 8, and 42.56 at age 10, reflecting older children's greater knowledge of words.

The results showed that, as subject age increased, children's word definitions reflected growth in semantic content and syntactic form, findings that were consistent with the studies previously discussed. Additionally, Johnson and Anglin (1995) found that these improvements occurred on every class of word (noun, verb, and adjective) and on three of the morphological variants (root, compound, and inflected) they presented. They also found that children provided higher quality definitions for nouns than for verbs and adjectives, and for roots and compounds than for derived and inflected words. Interestingly, problems in defining verbs, adjectives, and derived and inflected words affected the syntactic form more than the semantic content of the response. The researchers suggested that it may be easier for students to provide appropriate syntactic (i.e., *categorical*) definitions of nouns compared to other classes of words because of the way nouns are organized in memory (i.e., *hierarchical*). They also suggested that students may receive more exposure to definitions of nouns than to other types of words during school activities such as dictionary usage.

Naturalistic Research

The studies discussed so far examined the development of definitional skill by presenting words in isolation, divorced from natural conversational contexts. In contrast,

Andersen (1975) employed a more naturalistic approach in an experiment with children ages 3, 6, 9, and 12 years ($N = 23$). The main purpose of her study was to examine children's understanding of the vagueness of boundaries between semantically related categories. Her methods, however, provide interesting insight into children's skill with word definition.

Each child was shown an array of 25 different drinking vessels that varied greatly in shape, size, color, composition, and function (e.g., blue plastic cup, brown ceramic coffee mug, clear wine glass). The prototypicality of the vessels ranged from those that were unequivocally cups (e.g., has handle, made of porcelain) or glasses (e.g., tall, made of clear glass) to those whose category membership was equivocal (e.g., tall, made of red metal). The child was asked first to name each vessel independently and then to sort the vessels into categories—"cup," "glass," or "neither." The child then was asked to define the words *cup* and *glass* as part of a role-playing task. To elicit a definition of *cup*, the examiner said the following:

> Suppose you had a friend from another country and that friend didn't speak English very well. And one day he/she said to you, "My mother told me to go to the store and buy some cups, but I'm not sure what a *cup* is. Can you tell me what it is/what it looks like?" What would you tell him/her? (p. 85)

A definition of *glass* was elicited as follows:

> Now, if that same friend said, "Thank you very much, [child's own name], because with your help I was able to find the cups. But now my mother wants me to buy some glasses. Can you tell me what a glass is/what a glass looks like?" What would you say? (p. 85)

Performance on the activities improved as a function of increasing subject age. In naming the 25 different vessels, the 12-year-olds used a greater number of functional modifiers (e.g., *martini* glass, *beer* mug, *coffee* cup) than the 3-, 6-, or 9-year-olds, reflecting greater knowledge of semantic features. In sorting the vessels, the oldest group assigned more items to the "neither" category than the three younger groups, reflecting greater awareness of the fact that boundaries between objects can be vague. This increased semantic knowledge and awareness of vagueness also was evidenced in the definitions of the 12-year-olds, which contained a greater number of descriptive features (e.g., material, shape, size, etc.) and qualifiers or "hedges" (e.g., "a cup *sometimes* has a handle") than those of the younger groups. The oldest children also produced more Aristotelian definitions (e.g., "a glass is a container for holding something to drink") than the three younger groups.

The Andersen (1975) study is unique in providing insight into the relationship between children's knowledge of words (*linguistic*) and their ability to express that knowledge in their definitions (*metalinguistic*). As children become more aware of the essential elements of a word and the fact that boundaries can be vague, their definitions increasingly reflect that knowledge.

Summary

Developmental studies have shown that word definition gradually improves during childhood and adolescence, and that important changes occur in both semantic content and syntactic form. Quantitatively, the number of words that are accurately defined increases and essential features of the definiendum are mentioned more frequently. Qualitatively, definitions take on a more formal style that includes the specific category term and a phrase that is predicated about the definiendum. Such responses increasingly reflect the socially shared meanings of words. Despite these improvements, definition tasks can be challenging even to adults, particularly when they are asked to define words that are abstract or less familiar.

Standardized Tests

Many standardized tests of language development and intelligence contain subtests that examine word definition in school-age children and/or adolescents. In view of the developmental studies just reviewed, it is interesting to consider the words, scoring procedures, and normative data of some of the tests that were recently published or revised. The following tests are discussed: (1) *Test of Language Development–Second Edition: Primary* (TOLD–2: Primary) (Newcomer & Hammill, 1988); (2) *The Word Test–R: Elementary* (Huisingh et al., 1990); (3) *The Word Test: Adolescent* (Zachman et al., 1989); (4) *Test of Word Knowledge* (TOWK) (Wiig & Secord, 1992); (5) *Comprehensive Receptive and Expressive Vocabulary Test* (CREVT) (Wallace & Hammill, 1994); (6) *Stanford-Binet Intelligence Scale* (Thorndike et al., 1986); and (7) *Wechsler Intelligence Scale for Children–Third Edition* (WISC–III) (Wechsler, 1991).

Descriptive features of the subtests that examine word definition, taken from the test manuals, are contained in Table 4.2. All seven subtests require the child or adolescent to explain the meanings of a series of words presented in isolation (e.g., "Tell me what *house* means").

Words

The words contained in each of the subtests reflect a range of difficulty levels. For example, *The Word Test–R: Elementary* includes the items *house, window, curious,* and *famous*, reflecting both concrete and abstract concepts, and the CREVT (Form A) includes the items *hat, lemon, macaw,* and *teamster*. Although nouns predominate, other word classes (e.g., verbs, adjectives) are included in most of the subtests (see Table 4.2).

The procedure of including words of varying difficulty levels differs from most developmental studies of word definition reported above. With some exceptions (e.g., Johnson & Anglin, 1995), developmental researchers attempted to limit the difficulty of the words so they would be familiar to even the youngest children in their studies, and most researchers used nouns exclusively. The inclusion of more difficult words

Table 4.2

Descriptive Features of Standardized Tests that Examine Word Definition

---

1. *Test of Language Development–Second Edition: Primary* (TOLD–2: Primary) (Newcomer & Hammill, 1988)

Subtest:	Oral Vocabulary
Age range:	4 through 8 years
Words:	30 total: 22 nouns, 1 verb, 6 adjectives, and 1 preposition varying in difficulty; concrete and abstract
Scoring:	1 point per correct response
Criteria:	Must provide a brief explanation, synonym, or two major characteristics (e.g., function, appearance, etc.) of the word, as listed in the manual
Normative data:	Mean raw scores from children (N – 2436) ages 4, 5, 6, 7, and 8 years, respectively, were 4, 9, 11, 16, and 18

2. *The Word Test–R: Elementary* (Huisingh et al., 1990)

Subtest:	Definitions
Age range:	7 through 11 years
Words:	15 total: 8 nouns, 2 verbs, and 5 adjectives varying in difficulty; concrete and abstract
Scoring:	1 point per correct response
Criteria:	Must provide a brief explanation, synonym, or major characteristic (function, appearance, etc.) of the word, as listed in the manual
Normative data:	Mean raw scores from children (N = 1359) at each six-month interval between 7:0 and 11:11. For example, mean = 9.01 at 7:0 through 7:5; mean = 12.21 at 9:0 through 9:5; mean = 13.57 at 11:0 through 11:5

3. *The Word Test: Adolescent* (Zachman et al., 1989)

Subtest:	Definitions
Age range:	12 through 17 years
Words:	15 total: 8 nouns, 3 verbs, and 4 adjectives varying in difficulty; concrete and abstract
Scoring:	1 point per correct response
Criteria:	Must provide a brief explanation, synonym, or major characteristic (function, appearance, etc.) of the word, as listed in the manual
Normative data:	Mean raw scores from adolescents (N = 1042), ages 12:0 through 13:11, 14:0 through 15:11, and 16:0 through 17:11, respectively, were 6.62, 8.19, and 10.32

4. *Test of Word Knowledge* (TOWK) (Wiig & Secord, 1992)

Subtest:	Word Definitions
Age range:	5 through 17 years
Words:	32 nouns varying in difficulty; concrete
Scoring:	1 or 2 points per correct response
Criteria:	1 point for mentioning two correct features of the word; 2 points for mentioning three correct features, as listed in the manual
Normative data:	Mean raw scores for children and adolescents (N = 1570) at each year from ages 5 through 13; data from ages 14 through 17 years were combined. For example, mean raw scores at ages 5, 9, 13, and 14 through 17 years, respectively, were 8.6, 28.5, 41.3, and 47.0

(continues)

Table 4.2. *Continued*

5. *Comprehensive Receptive and Expressive Vocabulary Test* (CREVT) (Wallace & Hammill, 1994)

Subtest:	Expressive Vocabulary
Age range:	5 through 17 years
Words:	25 total: 24 nouns and 1 verb varying in difficulty; concrete
Scoring:	1 point per correct response
Criteria:	Must provide a synonym or brief description (e.g., function, characteristic, etc.) of the word, as listed in the record form; some items require two features
Normative data:	Mean raw scores for children and adolescents (*N* = 1852) ages 5 through 17 years. For example, mean raw scores at ages 5, 9, 13, and 17 years, respectively, were 4, 12, 18, and 19 (Form A)

6. *Stanford-Binet Intelligence Scale* (Thorndike et al., 1986)

Subtest:	Oral Vocabulary
Age range:	7 through 16 years
Words:	32 total: 14 nouns, 8 verbs, and 10 adjectives varying in difficulty; concrete and abstract
Scoring:	1 point per correct response
Criteria:	Must provide synonym or brief description (e.g., function, characteristic, etc.) of the word, as listed in the manual
Normative data:	Mean raw scores for children and adolescents (*N* = 2929) ages 7 through 16. For example, mean raw scores at ages 7, 10, 13, and 16 years, respectively, were 20, 24, 28, and 32 (These means were obtained by combining scores on Oral Vocabulary with scores on a 14-item Picture Vocabulary task.)

7. *Wechsler Intelligence Scale for Children–Third Edition* (WISC–III) (Wechsler, 1991)

Subtest:	Vocabulary
Age range:	6 through 16 years
Words:	30 total: 15 nouns, 7 verbs, and 8 adjectives varying in difficulty; concrete and abstract
Scoring:	1 or 2 points per correct response
Criteria:	Must provide a synonym or brief description of the word, as listed in the manual; to get full credit, response must be specific
Normative data:	Mean raw scores for children and adolescents (*N* = 2200) ages 6 through 16 years. For example, mean raw scores at ages 6, 9, 12, 14, and 16 years, respectively, were 11.5, 22.5, 33.5, 40, and 44

Note: From "School-Age Children and Adolescents: Norms for Word Definition" by M. A. Nippold, 1995, *Language, Speech, and Hearing Services in Schools, 26,* p. 323. Copyright 1995 by American Speech-Language-Hearing Association. Reprinted with permission.

suggests that age-related improvements on standardized tests of word definition reflect growth in word knowledge as well as growth in metalinguistic components.

Scoring Procedures

For each of the subtests, content is emphasized in scoring the responses, and little attention is given to form. For example, on *The Word Test–R: Elementary*, an acceptable response to *window* is, "It's on the wall and you shut it when you're cold" (Huisingh et al., 1990, p. 47). Developmental studies have shown, however, that as children grow older their definitions increasingly approach the Aristotelian style, incorporating changes in both content and form, for example, "A *window* is a piece of glass that you can see through." Although the latter response would also be correct on *The Word Test R: Elementary*, it would not receive a higher score than the simpler response. Similarly, on the TOWK, CREVT, and *Stanford-Binet*, Aristotelian definitions are not necessarily rated higher than less formal types. For example, both of the following definitions of *teacher* would receive full credit on the TOWK, although the first is clearly more sophisticated: (1) "A teacher is a person who helps you learn and corrects your papers"; (2) "She is nice, helps you learn, and reads stories."

Normative Data

Data reported in Table 4.2 indicate that performance on each of the word definition subtests gradually improved over the ages that were included in the normative samples. For example, on the TOLD–2: Primary, 4-year-olds correctly defined 13% of the words, and 8-year-olds correctly defined 60%. Similarly, on the WISC–III, the mean raw was 11.5 at age 6:0 and 44 at age 16:0. With the exception of *The Word Test–R: Elementary*, students did not appear to reach a ceiling in defining the words. For example, on *The Word Test: Adolescent*, which contains more difficult words (e.g., *personnel, chaos, priority*) than those on the TOLD–2: Primary or *The Word Test–R: Elementary*, the oldest group, age 16:0 through 17:11, defined only 69% of the words correctly.

Quantitatively, these results are consistent with developmental studies of word definition in documenting gradual improvement as a function of increasing subject age. Qualitatively, however, it is difficult to discern consistencies between the two developmental data bases because of differences in methodology, particularly in the types of words and the scoring procedures that were employed. For example, as discussed previously, the standardized tests contained more diverse word types and did not separate content and form in scoring responses.

Summary

Standardized tests that examine word definition provide useful information concerning quantitative aspects of development during childhood and adolescence. To discern qualitative aspects of development, however, it is important to analyze both the semantic content and the syntactic form of students' responses. The difficulty of words and the classes to which they belong must also be considered when interpreting the results of standardized tests, because performance may be affected by limitations in word knowledge in addition to or instead of limitations in metalinguistic aspects of development.

Conclusions

When word difficulty is maintained at a low level, performance on definition tasks reflects students' ability to organize their knowledge about the words and to state that knowledge in a succinct, conventional form that is modeled in school. Definition tasks that employ word lists of increasing difficulty also call upon metalinguistic ability, but place additional demands on a student's lexical knowledge base. When asked to define words aloud, young children typically respond by stating a function of the named stimulus (*dog*: "runs") or by producing a personal or idiosyncratic response ("I feed my dog"). With development, the production of categorical or synonymous responses steadily increases well into adulthood and reflects the acquisition of a word's socially shared meaning.

Future Research

Developmental studies and standardized tests of word definition have focused primarily on the ability of children and adolescents to define words presented in isolation. Hence, little is known about the development of word definition in more natural contexts. Word definition is important in facilitating communication in formal and informal situations. Therefore, information is needed concerning the ability of young people to provide appropriate definitions during diverse modes of discourse such as debates, oral reports, and conversations with parents, teachers, and peers. Definitions used in diverse written modes such as term papers, science reports, and informative articles for school newspapers and yearbooks should also be examined.

To analyze the definitions produced in these more natural contexts, innovative approaches will be needed to recognize the diverse types of definitions that can occur. For example, procedures for evaluating the content and form of operational definitions, and definitions by negation, comparison, and example will need to be designed. Many exciting challenges confront researchers of word definition. Those who appreciate the role of words in clarifying thought, as did Aristotle more than 2,300 years ago, will find the effort worthwhile.

Acknowledgments

Portions of this chapter appeared in the following publications:

Nippold, M. A. (1988). The literate lexicon. In M. A. Nippold (Ed.), *Later language development: Ages nine through nineteen* (pp. 29–47). Austin, TX: PRO-ED.

Nippold, M. A. (1995). School-age children and adolescents: Norms for word definition. *Language, Speech, and Hearing Services in Schools, 26,* 320–325.

C H A P T E R

ANALOGIES: INDUCTIVE REASONING

"An insightful detective often draws on his or her experience in order to solve a crime. The detective may bring to mind a previous case in which the clues fit into a similar pattern, and then use this case as a guideline for solving the newly committed crime."

—Davidson (1986, p. 205)

Analogical reasoning occurs when an individual perceives similarities and differences between objects or events and uses that information to solve problems or to learn about the world. A basic human ability (Sternberg, 1982), analogical reasoning is evidenced throughout the life span, beginning in infancy (Wagner, Winner, Cicchetti, & Gardner, 1981) and continuing well into old age (Clark, Gardner, Brown, & Howell, 1990).

The ability of school-age children and adolescents to reason by analogy has been examined most commonly through tasks where incomplete analogies of the form "A is to B as C is to . . . ?" (A : B :: C : D) are presented, and the student must generate the appropriate D item or select it from several alternatives. When verbal (as opposed to perceptual) analogical reasoning is examined in this classic format, the symbols A, B, C, and D are filled by words (e.g., *fish* : *scales* :: *bird* : _?_ beak, molt, *feathers*, wings) or pictured objects to be named.

Collectively, developmental studies have shown that performance on verbal analogy problems gradually improves during the school-age and adolescent years. Growth is characterized by increased speed and accuracy in reaching solutions, greater use of systematic problem-solving strategies, and enhanced comprehension of semantically and structurally complex problems (Achenbach, 1969, 1970; Cashen, 1989;

Feuerstein, 1979; Gallagher & Wright, 1979; Goldman, Pellegrino, Parseghian, & Sallis, 1982; Goldstein, 1962; Goswami & Brown, 1989, 1990; Levinson & Carpenter, 1974; Nippold, 1994; Nippold & Sullivan, 1987; Piaget, Montangero, & Billeter, 1977; Sternberg & Downing, 1982; Sternberg & Nigro, 1980). Growth also occurs metalinguistically in that students become more adept at explaining and defending their solutions to analogy problems (Gallagher & Wright, 1979; Goldman et al., 1982; Goswami & Brown, 1990; Levinson & Carpenter, 1974; Piaget et al., 1977).

A variety of internal and external factors are related to the development of verbal analogical reasoning. Internal factors include the chronological age, cognitive level, academic achievement, and problem-solving style of the child or adolescent, whereas external factors include the semantic and structural complexity of the problems themselves.

Internal Factors

Piaget et al. (1977) examined verbal analogical reasoning in children ages 5 through 12 years. Each child was given a stack of pictures (e.g., ship, bicycle, cork, helm, bottle, lid, handlebars, saucepan) and was asked to sort them into pairs that went together well (e.g., ship–helm, bottle–cork, bicycle–handlebars, saucepan–lid). Next, the child was encouraged to place the pairs into 2 × 2 matrices so that all four pictures went together well (e.g., ship–helm placed above bicycle–handlebars; bottle–cork placed above saucepan–lid). After completing a matrix, the child was asked to explain the arrangement to the examiner and was offered a related alternative for the picture in the lower right corner (e.g., a bell to replace the handlebars, a stove to replace the lid). This counter-suggestion served to examine the stability of the child's understanding of the solution to the analogy problem.

Piaget et al. (1977) reported that children passed through three distinct stages in performing this task, stages that corresponded to the cognitive levels of preoperational, concrete operational, and formal operational thought. During the preoperational stage, 5- and 6-year-old children successfully formed pairs but usually could not coordinate the pairs to complete the analogies. Even when they occasionally did complete an analogy, they could not explain why it was correct, and they were easily swayed by related alternatives. During the concrete operational stage, which included 7- through 10-year-olds, more analogies were completed and better explanations were provided, but related alternatives were still accepted, particularly by the 7- and 8-year-olds. Moreover, when analogies were completed successfully, this was usually accomplished through much trial-and-error behavior. Finally, during the formal operational stage, the 11- and 12-year-olds successfully completed most of the analogies and did so without using a trial-and-error strategy. Additionally, their explanations were superior to those of the younger children, and they were better able to resist counter-suggestions, thereby showing greater stability in their solutions to the analogy problems.

The relationship of chronological age and cognitive level to verbal analogical reasoning was also investigated by Feuerstein (1979). The participants in his research included students with normal cognitive development, ages 8 through 14 years ($N = 253$). A group of adolescents with mild mental retardation ($N = 551$), ages 13 through 17 years (mean age = 15:3), also participated. A written multiple-choice task that included 20 problems was presented. Each problem consisted of a 2×2 matrix in which the two boxes at the top each contained a printed word (e.g., *house* and *door*). Together, these two words implied a certain relationship (e.g., "One enters a house through a door"). For the lower half of the matrix, the box on the left also contained a printed word (e.g., *garden*), and the box on the right was empty. The student's task was to select a word from a set of choices (e.g., gate, plot, fence, apartment, flowers) that best completed the matrix (i.e., *gate*). All analogies were composed of high-frequency words selected from children's books.

For the students with normal cognitive development, mean scores of 23%, 60%, 72%, 75%, 87%, 89%, and 91%, respectively, were obtained by groups of 8-, 9-, 10-, 11-, 12-, 13-, and 14-year-olds, indicating that accuracy improved as a function of increasing age. By age 12, however, performance appeared to reach a plateau, most likely because the analogies were comprised of simple words. Had analogies with more complex words been presented (e.g., *frugal : parsimonious :: generous : ?* miserly, *philanthropic*, stubborn, cooperative, compassionate), the task undoubtedly would have been more challenging to the older students (see discussion on the role of semantics later in this chapter). For the adolescents with mental retardation, a mean score of 57% was obtained. This contrasted markedly to a mean of 89% obtained by combining the results of the three oldest groups of normal learners, ages 12 to 14 years ($N = 112$), whose mean age was 13:0.

Armour-Thomas and Allen (1990) examined the relationship between verbal analogical reasoning and academic achievement in a group of ninth-grade students (ages 14 and 15 years) ($N = 54$). Half the students were high achievers and half were low achievers as determined by their classroom performance (i.e., grades). All students were administered three sets of problems, each of which contained 16 test items, for a total of 48 items. The first two sets were designed to examine their ability to handle the various components of an analogy problem. For the first set, students were asked to state how the A and B terms of an analogy (e.g., *toe* and *foot*) were related to one another. For the second set, they were asked to state how the A and B terms (e.g., *small : big*) were related to the C and D terms (e.g., *happy : sad*) of an analogy. The third set was a measure of their ability to solve analogy problems of the form A : B :: C : D (e.g., *tree : branch :: clock : ?* time, hand, second, watch). None of the problems contained words that exceeded a third-grade reading level. The Reading Vocabulary and Reading Comprehension subtests of the *Metropolitan Achievement Tests* (Durost, 1959) were also administered as a measure of academic ability.

As expected, the high achievers outperformed the low achievers on all three sets of problems. For the 16 verbal analogies, mean accuracy scores of 84% and 63% were obtained by the high and low groups, respectively. It was also found that, for all students combined, the ability to solve each of the three sets of problems was correlated to both subtests of the *Metropolitan Achievement Test*.

In an earlier study, Achenbach (1970) examined age-related improvements in analogical reasoning, strategies that students use to solve analogy problems, and the relationship of these factors to measures of cognitive level and academic achievement. He developed the *Children's Associative Responding Test* (CART) (Achenbach, 1969), a measure designed specifically to distinguish children who solve analogies through word association from those who use their analogical reasoning skills. This is a written, multiple-choice task consisting of 68 analogies of the form A : B :: C : D. Of these, the first three terms, called the stem of the analogy, are presented, and the fourth is left to be inferred. Each stem is followed by five single-word answer choices. For half of the test items, the correct choice is a distant associate of the C term, but one of the other choices, a plausible foil, is a close semantic associate of C. For example, for the item *bear : cave :: boy* is to ____?____, the correct answer, *house*, is pitted against the foil, *girl*. For the other half of the test items, none of the choices is a particularly close associate of C (e.g., *piano : fingers :: whistle : _?_* throat, loud, face, *lips*, song). Associative responding is measured by subtracting the number of nonfoil errors from the number of foil errors to obtain a difference (D) score. Thus, the higher the D score, the greater the tendency to respond associatively.

Achenbach (1970) administered the CART to students ages 11, 12, 13, and 14 years old ($N = 1085$). Mean accuracy scores of 71%, 81%, 85%, and 89% were obtained by the four age groups, respectively, indicating that the CART was sensitive to age-related growth in analogical reasoning. Achenbach also examined the relationship between performance on the CART and the students' grade point averages, and their scores on standardized tests of intelligence and academic achievement. He found that for all four age groups, the low D scorers (i.e., $D \leq 1$) surpassed the high D scorers (i.e., $D \geq 4$) on all three variables. It was interesting, however, that although the high D scorers made more errors on the test items for which associative responding was possible, the two groups performed equally well on the items for which this was not possible. This showed that the associative responders had the capacity to solve the problems through analogical reasoning, but did not consistently do so.

A difference in problem-solving style between associative and non-associative responders was also explored by Achenbach (1969) using the *Matching Familiar Figures Test* (MFFT) (Kagan, Rosman, Day, Albert, & Phillips, 1964). This is a timed task that requires careful and systematic analysis. In it, a pictured object (e.g., a teddy bear) is displayed, and a child must pick out the identical object from a set of six choices, five of which represent slight variations of the target picture (e.g., the shape of the mouth or feet vary, the angle of the head or bow tie vary, etc.). Children with an impulsive problem-solving style tend to perform the task quickly and inaccurately, while those with a reflective style perform more slowly and accurately. In Achenbach's study, a short version of the CART was administered to 191 11-year-olds.

The 20 students with the highest D scores (associative responders) and the 20 with the lowest D scores (non-associative responders) were then given the MFFT. As predicted, the high D scorers showed an impulsive problem-solving style on the MFFT, while the low D scorers were more reflective.

Research has also shown that the associative response strategy diminishes during the school-age years and that by early adolescence, if not before, analogies of the form $A : B :: C : D$ (called second-order analogies) are solved through appropriate reasoning processes (Gallagher & Wright, 1979; Goldman et al., 1982; Sternberg & Nigro, 1980). This change in strategy represents a qualitative improvement in verbal analogical reasoning. However, Sternberg and Downing (1982) hypothesized that young adolescents would revert to the old associative response strategy when confronted with more complex third-order analogies of the form $[(A : B :: C : D) :: (A : B :: C : D)]$. As with second-order analogies, these "analogies between analogies" can vary in their "goodness" depending on the relationships expressed by the terms. For each of the component analogies, the C and D terms must be related to one another in the same way as the A and B terms (Criterion 1); moreover, the component analogies must be related to one another analogously (Criterion 2). The following third-order analogy meets these two criteria:

$$[(sand : beach :: star : galaxy) :: \\ (water : ocean :: air : sky)]$$

In contrast, the next example satisfies the first criterion but fails to satisfy the second because the two component analogies are associatively related to one another:

$$[(bench : judge :: pulpit : minister) :: \\ (chair : courtroom :: pew : church)]$$

To test the *associative reversion* hypothesis, Sternberg and Downing (1982) constructed a task that consisted of 60 third-order analogies. All of the problems satisfied the first criterion for goodness but varied in the extent to which the second criterion was satisfied, with many of the component analogies associatively related. Adolescents who were ages 13, 16, and 18 years ($N = 60$) were asked to judge the relatedness of the component analogies in each problem using a scale of 1 ("extremely poorly related") to 9 ("extremely well related"). According to the investigators, high scores assigned to the associatively related problems constituted an associative response strategy in dealing with third-order analogies. Results indicated that ratings of the associative problems were highest among the youngest adolescents and declined with each successive age group. This lead the investigators to conclude that the associative response strategy observed among younger students in relation to second-order analogies resurfaces among adolescents in relation to third-order analogies, but shows the same diminishing pattern as a function of increasing chronological age.

External Factors

Semantics

To study the role of semantics in the understanding of analogies, Goldstein (1962) constructed a task to determine whether problems that expressed different types of meanings would present variations in difficulty. He developed a written, multiple-choice task similar to Achenbach's (1970) CART, which consisted of 120 analogies of the form A : B :: C : D, with the D term omitted. Each stem was accompanied by five answer choices. The task consisted of 15 analogies of 8 different types as shown in Table 5.1.

In contrast to Achenbach (1969, 1970), Goldstein (1962) attempted to exclude problems that could be solved by simple word association and hence did not require analogical reasoning. For example, an analogy such as *glove : hand :: shoe : ?* would not be included because the correct answer, *foot*, is a close associate of the third term, *shoe*. However, an item such as *garden : gate :: room : ?* was acceptable because the correct answer, *door*, is not a particularly close associate of *room*. The degree of association between words had been determined through prior screening procedures. Goldstein's task was administered to students who were ages 8 through 13 years ($N = 120$). To ensure that the students' performance was not hampered by reading difficulties, the vocabulary of the analogies did not exceed a third-grade level.

Results indicated that the synonymous, antonymous, and characteristic property analogies were easiest to solve, followed by superordinate and part-whole analogies. Causal, functional, and sequential analogies were the most difficult. Task performance was found to improve with age, and mean scores of 40%, 39%, 44%, 56%, 59%, and 64%, respectively, were obtained by the six age groups. With the exception of the 8-year-olds, those percentages are markedly lower than those obtained by Feuerstein

Table 5.1
Types of Analogies Used by Goldstein

1. *Antonymous* (e.g., *clear* is to *cloudy* as *shallow* is to: _?_ narrow, pool, muddy, swift, *deep*)
2. *Synonymous* (e.g., *weep* is to *cry* as *smile* is to: _?_ joke, *grin*, play, sorry, mouth)
3. *Characteristic Property* (e.g., *wheel* is to *round* as *arrow* is to: _?_ bow, strong, wood, shoot, *straight*)
4. *Part-Whole* (e.g., *leg* is to *knee* as *arm* is to: _?_ hand, wrist, *elbow*, sleeve, head)
5. *Superordinate-Subordinate* (e.g., *shirt* is to *clothing* as *hammer* is to: _?_ nails, hit, claw, *tools*, screw-driver)
6. *Functional* (e.g., *time* is to *clock* as *weight* is to: _?_ pound, size, hour, watch, *scale*)
7. *Sequential* (e.g., *Tuesday* is to *Sunday* as *Friday* is to: _?_ Monday, *Wednesday*, Sunday, Thursday, week)
8. *Causal* (e.g., *fire* is to *smoke* as *water* is to: _?_ liquid, wet, ice, *steam*, drink)

Note. Adapted from *Developmental Studies in Analogical Reasoning* (pp. 186–195) by G. Goldstein, 1962, Lawrence, KS: University of Kansas, unpublished doctoral dissertation.

(1979). Reasons for this discrepancy are unknown, as both investigators carefully controlled the vocabulary level of their analogies, presented similar types of analogies (e.g., synonymous, functional, part-whole, etc.), used a written, multiple-choice task, and took steps to ensure that the children understood the task prior to testing.

Sternberg and Nigro (1980) also examined the influence of semantic factors in a developmental study of verbal analogical reasoning, but they tested students of a wider age range: 9-, 12-, 15-, and 18-year-olds ($N = 80$). Sixty analogies of the form used by Goldstein (1962) were presented in a written, multiple-choice task, with 12 items representing each of five semantic types: synonymous, antonymous, functional, linear ordering (i.e., sequential), and categorical (i.e., superordinate-subordinate). Unlike in Goldstein's study, Sternberg and Nigro did not attempt to exclude (or include) items that could be solved by word association. As with Goldstein's study, the vocabulary of the analogies did not exceed a third-grade level.

Results indicated that functional and antonymous analogies were considerably easier than problems that expressed synonymous, sequential, and categorical relationships. Their findings were only partially consistent with Goldstein (1962) who found that functional analogies were difficult and that synonymous analogies were easy to solve. This discrepancy suggests that it is important to consider variations in difficulty within any particular type of analogy. For example, it is possible that the underlying meanings of Goldstein's functional analogies (e.g., *compass : direction :: tape measure : distance*) were conceptually more challenging than those used by Sternberg and Nigro (1980) (e.g., *horn : play :: horse : ride*). Nevertheless, the results of Sternberg and Nigro's study were consistent with Goldstein's results in that overall performance steadily improved as subject age increased. However, accuracy for the 9-, 12-, 15-, and 18-year-olds, respectively, was 72%, 78%, 83%, and 92%, means that were much higher than those obtained by Goldstein for the two overlapping age groups, the 9- and 12-year-olds. This inconsistency may be due in part to the presence of analogies in Sternberg and Nigro's study that could be solved by simple word association. In fact, Sternberg and Nigro noted that the two youngest age groups did show greater accuracy on analogies of this type compared with those that actually required analogical reasoning, a discrepancy that was not seen in the older students. This suggested to Sternberg and Nigro that younger children use different strategies to solve analogies than older children, who are more likely to use their analogical reasoning skills.

Gallagher and Wright (1979) also considered the possibility that different types of meanings would affect the difficulty level of analogies, but they focused on a different aspect of semantics than Goldstein (1962) and Sternberg and Nigro (1980). In Gallagher and Wright's study, a written, multiple-choice task consisting of 20 analogies was designed. Ten of the test items were "concrete" analogies in which the relationship shared by the two pairs of terms was easily observable (e.g., *picture : frame :: yard : fence*); the other 10 analogies were "abstract" in that the common relationship was less observable (e.g., *engine : car :: man : bicycle*). The response choices always included at least one plausible foil, which was a term that was related to the analogy but not in the appropriate manner (e.g., *tree* was a foil in the "picture" analogy). Following each response, children were asked to explain their answers in writing.

Children who were ages 9, 10, 11, and 12 years ($N = 260$) participated in the study. Results indicated that the abstract analogies were more difficult to solve than the concrete. Performance on the multiple-choice task steadily improved with increasing subject age, and the younger children were more easily swayed by plausible foils, thus showing a greater tendency to respond associatively. Developmental change in the written explanations of answers was characterized by an improved ability to capture the shared relationship between the two pairs of terms. For example, the 9-year-olds tended to think of the pairs as independent units (e.g., "A car needs an engine, a bicycle needs a person"), whereas the 12-year-olds were better able to integrate the two (e.g., "Because engine and man power the car and the bicycle").

The studies discussed so far have focused on semantics by comparing the difficulty of analogies expressing different types of relationships (e.g., functional versus sequential) or levels of abstractness. However, it is important to note that the difficulty of analogies can also be increased simply by raising the vocabulary level of the words contained in the problems (Sternberg, 1982). For example, the following analogies both express antonymous meanings that are easily observed, but the second example is more complex because of the words employed:

top : bottom :: front : back
apex : base :: anterior : posterior

Research has shown that students continue to be challenged well into adolescence by classic four-part analogies when the problems contain more difficult words. Cashen (1989) (cited by Nelson & Gillespie, 1991) designed a task that contained 10 problems for each of three difficulty levels: low (*happy : glad :: angry : _?_ mad*, excited, silly); moderate (*silly : foolish :: thoughtful : _?_ wise*, stupid, rich); and high (*belligerent : warlike :: mollifying : _?_ peacemaking*, arguing, ridiculous). Difficult analogies contained words that were less common and expressed more subtle meanings.

Students in Grades 5, 8, and 11 ($N = 201$) read the problems and selected the best answer for each. Results showed that overall performance on the task steadily improved with each successive grade level, and that for each group of students, the three types of problems were differentially challenging. For the sets of low, moderate, and high level problems, respectively, mean accuracy scores for each group were: Grade 5 = 90%, 73%, 42%; Grade 8 = 95%, 85%, 59%; Grade 11 = 95%, 93%, 66%. Thus, even the oldest students were challenged by analogy problems that contained less common words expressing more subtle meanings.

This raises an interesting point concerning the contribution of word knowledge versus logical thought to the development of verbal analogical reasoning. When investigators control the vocabulary level of their analogy problems, age-related improvements do occur (Feuerstein, 1979; Goldstein, 1962; Sternberg & Nigro, 1980) and therefore seem attributable to growth in logic apart from word knowledge. However, the common practice of choosing words from elementary reading lists as a way of con-trolling vocabulary level does not fully consider the child's understanding of those words, which may be only partially developed (see Chapter 2). Thus, when age-related improvements are reported in studies of verbal analogical reasoning, it is likely that the superior performance of older students is also the result of a more refined and extensive knowledge of the words contained in the analogies. It is important to remember that verbal analogical reasoning is a mental construct where language and cognition converge, and that competence in both areas is essential to solving such problems. It should also be mentioned that *world* knowledge, which is often closely related to word knowledge (Crais, 1990), can also be expected to influence students' ability to understand verbal analogies. For example, to solve the following problem, some knowledge of American and British politics is necessary:

Republican : Democrat :: Tory : _?_
(Monarch, Socialist, Conservative, *Whig*, Loyalist)

Structure

Several investigators have examined structural factors that affect verbal analogical rea-soning. For example, Goldman et al. (1982) examined 8- and 10-year-olds ($N = 47$) under two different conditions, a generative task and a multiple-choice task. In the generative task, 50 analogy stems were presented (e.g., *cat : tiger :: dog : _?_*), and the child was asked to supply the missing term (i.e., *wolf*). Two weeks later, each child received a multiple-choice task in which the same 50 stems were presented but each was followed by five alternative answers, some of which were close associates of the third term of the analogy. After children selected an answer, they were asked to explain that choice to the examiner.

Results showed that the generative task was more difficult than the multiple-choice task, and that the 10-year-olds as a group outperformed the 8-year-olds on both tasks. In agreement with the findings of Gallagher and Wright (1979) and Sternberg and Nigro (1980), the younger children in this study showed a greater ten-dency to respond associatively on the multiple-choice task. However, much variabil-ity within age groups was found, with some 8-year-olds outperforming the less skilled 10-year-olds. Goldman et al. also found that less skilled children in both age groups had greater difficulty defending their correct responses on the multiple-choice task and tended to provide irrelevant (e.g., "Dogs and wolves bark") or personalized (e.g., "I like wolves") explanations compared with those of more skilled children, whose answers often reflected proportional thinking (e.g., "Cats and tigers are in the same family and dogs and wolves are too").

Levinson and Carpenter (1974) also addressed the issue of structural factors in analogical reasoning. Those investigators used a generative task in which students who were ages 9, 12, and 15 years ($N = 42$) were asked to solve a set of 16 analogies written in two different forms, true and quasi. A *true analogy* is written in the form of a proportion (e.g., *bird* is to *air* as *fish* is to *water*), whereas a *quasi analogy* is written in sentence form and contains verbs that specify the relationship between the terms (e.g., a *bird* flies in the *air*; a *fish* swims in the *water*). In this study, each age group received a different set of analogies (with missing fourth terms) so that the vocabulary level could be controlled for each group. In addition, care was taken to ensure that none of the correct answers to the analogies was a close associate of the third term. Half of the students in each group received the analogies in the true form first, followed one week later by the quasi analogies; the other half in each group received the two forms in the reverse order. Four students, randomly selected from each group, were also asked to explain their solutions orally for both the true and the quasi analogies so that proportional thinking could be examined.

The results of the study revealed that quasi analogies were significantly easier than true analogies for the 9-year-olds, with mean scores of 64% versus 50% obtained by this age group for the two forms, respectively. However, the quasi analogies offered no advantage to the 12- or 15-year-olds, who outperformed the younger students on both types of analogies. In the oral explanations of solutions, evidence of proportional thinking in relation to the true analogies steadily increased as a function of subject age, a result that supplements the research of Piaget et al. (1977), Gallagher and Wright (1979), and Goldman et al. (1982), who found that children who were better at solving analogies were also better at defending them. However, the explanations for the quasi analogies showed no age-related improvements. Perhaps this lack of change resulted from the fact that the key relationship was already provided for the children in the verbs of the quasi analogies, thus reducing the advantage to the older children, who could already identify those relationships for themselves.

Given that second-order analogies comprised of simple vocabulary are easily solved by young school-age children, Nippold (1994) was interested in determining if older children and adolescents would be challenged by third-order analogies, also comprised of simple vocabulary. Students who were ages 10, 12, 14, and 16 years ($N = 180$) were presented with a task that contained 35 third-order analogy problems, expressing five different semantic relationships: functional, categorical, antonymous, synonymous, and sequential. There were seven problems representing each type, presented in random order. The vocabulary level of the task did not exceed a fourth-grade reading level. An example of a problem that expressed a categorical relationship was as follows:

> [(bee : insect :: rose : flower) :: (?)]
> A. baboon : gibbon :: tiger : lion
> B. zoo : cage :: farm : barn
> C. python : snake :: fir : tree*
> D. butterfly : wings :: ant : legs

For each problem, the student was asked to select the second-order analogy that best completed the third-order analogy.

Mean accuracy scores of 59%, 73%, 88%, and 86% were obtained by the groups of 10-, 12-, 14-, and 16-year-olds, respectively, indicating that performance steadily improved through age 14. For the students as a whole, the analogies varied in difficulty according to the semantic relationships they expressed. Listed in order of increasing difficulty, they were: functional, categorical, antonymous, synonymous, and sequential. This pattern was similar to that which was reported by Sternberg and Nigro (1980) in relation to second-order analogies. Although the students appeared to reach a plateau on this particular task by age 14, it is likely that older adolescents and young adults would be challenged by tasks of third-order verbal analogical reasoning comprised of more abstract and less common words. Research should be conducted to examine this possibility.

Analogical Reasoning in Younger Children

Most developmental studies of verbal analogical reasoning have focused on children ages 8 years and older, reflecting an assumption that younger children have little or no ability to reason by analogy. However, this assumption has been disproved (Goswami & Brown, 1989, 1990; Nippold & Sullivan, 1987). It is important to note that most of the analogy tasks employed in the studies discussed so far have required complex linguistic and metalinguistic skills. Many of them have also required sophisticated world knowledge (for further discussion, see Goswami, 1991, 1992; Goswami & Brown, 1989, 1990) or an understanding of complex concepts such as sequential relationships (Sternberg & Nigro, 1980). Some of the tasks have required children to read the problems (Achenbach, 1969, 1970; Feuerstein, 1979) or to justify their solutions to problems orally or in writing (Gallagher & Wright, 1979; Piaget et al., 1977). However, when investigators began to design and administer tasks to younger children that were free of these additional linguistic, metalinguistic, and conceptual demands, it became apparent that a basic ability to reason by analogy is present very early in life (for a discussion of analogical reasoning in infants, see Wagner et al., 1981).

For example, Gentner (1977) employed a more naturalistic method to study analogical reasoning in young children. The participants were 10 preschoolers (ages 4 and 5), 10 first graders (ages 6 and 7), and 10 college sophomores (ages 19 and 20). Gentner designed two simple tasks in which various parts of the human body were compared to certain features on pictured objects. In the first task, the participants were shown pictures of trees that were turned upside down, right-side up, or sideways. They were then asked to point to the location where various body parts would be, as in, "If this tree had a knee, where would it be?" Six different parts of the human body were used—knees, feet, arms, stomach, head, and shoulders. In the second task, participants were shown pictures of mountains and were asked to point to the locations where the eyes and a mouth would be. Drawn into each mountain was a different set of crags that could be facial features, some of which were irrelevant and distracting.

To receive credit, an individual had to place the eyes above the mouth, regardless of the details of the picture.

All groups were equally successful with the first task. On the second task, the preschoolers and first graders performed equally well and slightly better than the adults, who seemed to be distracted by the irrelevant details of the pictures. Gentner (1977) suggested that when analogical reasoning is assessed using simple directions, familiar materials, and a nonspoken response mode, even preschoolers demonstrate a basic ability in this area.

In view of Gentner's findings, Nippold and Sullivan (1987) were encouraged to explore the possibility that if certain adjustments were made in the more traditional methods of assessing analogical reasoning, children under 8 years of age might perform successfully. Children ages 5, 6, and 7 ($N = 90$) participated in their study. A multiple-choice task for nonreaders was designed, using pictures and simple vocabulary and syntax. The task consisted of sixteen 2 x 2 matrices representing the classic form, "A is to B as C is to D." Cells A, B, and C contained pictured objects, and the D cell was empty (e.g., *sandwich–sack* placed above *hammer–?*). Three alternative pictures were shown below each matrix, consisting of one correct answer (e.g., *toolbox*) and two foils (*nail, saw*). The foils were always associates of C but did not bear the same relationship to it that B bore to A. However, the correct alternative always related to C in the same way that B related to A. All analogies used in the study expressed simple functional relationships and had passed a series of screening measures to ensure that their meanings were unambiguous and that the words contained in them were familiar to children as young as 5 years of age. The examiner presented each test item aloud, using a moderate speaking rate, and pointed to each picture as it was named. In lieu of the obscure "is to . . . as" syntactic phrasing, the examiner substituted the phrase "goes with," (e.g., "*sandwich* goes with *sack* and *hammer* goes with . . . . Is it *nail, saw*, or *toolbox?*"). Children responded by pointing to or naming the picture of their choice.

As predicted, even the 5-year-olds performed well above the level of chance on this modified, yet traditional, type of verbal analogical reasoning task. Mean scores of 50%, 62%, and 67% were obtained by the 5-, 6-, and 7-year-olds, respectively, indicating that the years between 5 and 7 are marked by steady and rapid growth in this area of development. In agreement with Goldman et al. (1982), much variability in task performance was seen within each of the three age groups. For example, although the 7-year-olds as a group outperformed the 5-year-olds, there were 5-year-olds in the study who performed as well as the average 7-year-old, and 7-year-olds who performed much like the average 5-year-old.

Using very similar procedures, Goswami and Brown (1989) examined verbal analogical reasoning in children who were even younger than those who participated in the Nippold and Sullivan (1987) study. In their investigation, children ages 3-, 4-, and 6-years-old ($N = 80$) were asked to solve a set of eight analogy problems, all of which involved common objects and events. The key to solving each problem was to understand how certain objects had been transformed (e.g., a dog and a pair of shorts had become dirty; a chocolate bar and a snowman had melted; an egg and a lamp had broken). For each problem, the examiner first displayed a sequence of three picture cards that represented the stem of the analogy (e.g., *dog* : *dirty dog* :: *shorts* : _?_). The examiner then displayed five additional cards in random order (e.g., *muddy shorts*, *muddy boots*, *wet dog*, *push-toy dog*, *pig*) that represented the answer choices. The child named each picture as it was displayed and then was asked to select the card that best completed the pattern.

Mean accuracy scores of 37%, 63%, and 91% were obtained by the 3-, 4-, and 6-year-olds, respectively. Although performance on the task improved with each successive age group, even the 3-year-olds performed above the level of chance. Goswami and Brown (1989) concluded that children can reason by analogy at a very young age, and they attributed the age-related improvement to growth in children's understanding of the underlying relationships.

Using the same procedures but a different set of analogy problems, Goswami and Brown (1990) replicated their previous findings (1989) with children who were ages 4, 5, and 9 years old (*N* = 60). In this study, the pictured analogies expressed relationships such as function (e.g., *train* : *track* :: *boat* : *water*) and location (e.g., *bird* : *nest* :: *dog* : *kennel*). After the children had selected the picture that best completed a pattern, they were asked to explain their choice. Mean accuracy scores of 59%, 66%, and 94% were obtained by the 4-, 5-, and 9-year-olds, respectively, showing steady improvement throughout this age range. Children's explanations for their correct picture choices also improved as a function of increasing age, with the 9-year-olds demonstrating the clearest explanations.

Summary

During the school-age and adolescent years, students show an increasing ability to solve verbal analogy problems and to provide appropriate explanations for those solutions. Improvement also occurs in the strategies used to solve analogy problems. For example, by late childhood the associative response strategy observed earlier in relation to second-order analogies is replaced by true analogical reasoning. Although the associative response strategy resurfaces during early adolescence in relation to third-order analogies, it diminishes soon thereafter, as it did at an earlier age.

Aside from these age-related findings, research has demonstrated that children within any particular age group show a wide range of competence in solving verbal analogy problems, with the more successful problem solvers also showing higher cognitive levels, greater academic achievement, and a more reflective problem-solving style. Explanations of analogy solutions provided by these children also tend to be superior, indicating that their verbal skills in general are above average.

The ability to solve analogies is greatly affected by semantic factors. For example, concrete analogies are easier than abstract, and analogies that express antonymous relationships are easier than those that express sequential relationships. Moreover, analogies comprised of difficult words may challenge individuals throughout adolescence and well into adulthood. Structural factors also affect performance, with quasi analogies easier than true analogies for younger school-age children, and multiple-choice response modes easier than generative modes. Another structural factor concerns the juxtaposition of second-order analogies to create third-order analogies. Students generally find these "analogies between analogies" more difficult to solve than second-order problems.

Acknowledgments

Portions of this chapter appeared in the following publications:

Nippold, M. A. (1986). Verbal analogical reasoning in children and adolescents. *Topics in Language Disorders*, 6(4), 51–63.

Nippold, M. A. (1988). Verbal reasoning. In M. A. Nippold (Ed.), *Later language development: Ages nine through nineteen* (pp. 159–177). Austin, TX: PRO-ED.

Used with permission of Aspen Publishers and PRO-ED.

C H A P T E R

SYLLOGISMS: DEDUCTIVE REASONING

"The study of logic provides a means of facilitating the attempt to develop well-argued positions and to evaluate critically the positions espoused by others."

—Gorovitz and Williams (1969, p. 3)

Since the days of Aristotle (384–322 B.C.), syllogisms have been used in spoken and written communication to establish truths or to express points of view in an orderly and reasoned manner. A *syllogism* is a form of argument that contains two premises and a conclusion that follows logically from those premises. Major types of syllogisms include *conditional, categorical, disjunctive* (Freeley, 1993), and *conjunctive* (Sternberg, 1979). A *conditional syllogism* may be written symbolically as follows:

▶ If P then Q. (major premise)
   P. (minor premise)
   Therefore, Q. (conclusion)

This example is a common type of conditional syllogism, also called an *if–then* argument. Other types of conditional syllogisms include *only–if* (P only if Q) and *biconditional* (P if and only if Q) arguments. Regarding the if–then argument, there are two valid forms, *modus ponens* and *modus tollens* (Markovits, 1995). With *modus ponens*, the minor premise *affirms the antecedent* of the major premise, as in the following example:

▶ If a glass is dropped on concrete, it will break.
   A glass was dropped on concrete.
   Therefore, the glass broke.

73

With *modus tollens*, the minor premise *denies the consequent* of the major premise, as in this example:

> ▶ If a glass is dropped on concrete, it will break.
> The glass did not break.
> Therefore, the glass was not dropped on concrete.

Invalid forms of *modus ponens* occur when the minor premise *affirms the consequent*:

> ▶ If a glass is dropped on concrete, it will break.
> The glass broke.
> Therefore . . .

Nothing can be concluded logically from the premises of this argument because not enough information was provided. For example, it is unknown whether or not the glass broke for some reason other than being dropped on concrete (e.g., it was stepped on, a car rolled over it, etc.).

Invalid forms of *modus tollens* occur when the minor premise *denies the antecedent*:

> ▶ If a glass is dropped on concrete, it will break.
> The glass was not dropped on concrete.
> Therefore . . .

Similarly, nothing can be concluded logically. Without further information about the glass and what might have happened to it, its status (intact, broken, scratched, etc.) remains unknown. A *categorical syllogism* may be written symbolically as follows:

> ▶ All Ps are Qs. (major premise)
> R is a P. (minor premise)
> Therefore, R is a Q. (conclusion)

With a valid categorical syllogism, the major premise makes a general statement, beginning with an inclusive term such as "all," "every," or "any." The minor premise makes a statement about a specific instance of P, and the conclusion follows logically from the two premises (Freeley, 1993), for example:

> ▶ All one-celled animals are protozoa.
> Sarcodines are one-celled animals.
> Therefore, sarcodines are protozoa.

Moreover, each term (P, Q, R) in the categorical syllogism may occur only once in any premise but must be used twice throughout the argument. Violations of these rules prevent logical connections between premises, resulting in invalid categorical arguments, for example:

▶ All cats are felines.
  Trixie is a dog.
  Therefore . . .

A *disjunctive syllogism* presents two alternatives in the major premise, separated by the word *or*. The minor premise makes a statement about one of the alternatives, and the conclusion follows logically, for example:

▶ We'll either go to the beach or to the park.
  We'll go to the beach.
  Therefore, we won't go to the park.

Disjunctive syllogisms may be *exclusive* or *inclusive*. An exclusive argument takes the form "P or Q but not both," allowing only one of the alternatives to stand (e.g., "I'll take pie or cake but not both"). In contrast, an inclusive argument takes the form "P or Q or both," allowing both alternatives to stand (e.g., "I'll take pie or cake or both").

A *conjunctive syllogism* simply states that two conditions co-occur and may be expressed as follows:

▶ P and Q. (major premise)
  P. (minor premise)
  Therefore, Q. (conclusion)

Such an argument might be used to explain the rules of a game, for example:

▶ White beads move diagonally and red beads move horizontally.
  White beads move diagonally.
  Therefore, red beads move horizontally.

Syllogistic reasoning is called upon in a variety of academic, professional, and personal endeavors. It is important for individuals to be able to produce valid arguments and to detect invalid ones when they occur. For example, in studying geometry, high school students are required to write proofs and to provide reasons for their statements such as the following:

▶ A point is the midpoint of a line segment iff [if and only if] it is between its endpoints and divides it into two equal segments. (Jacobs, 1987, p. 133)

Moreover, in a court of law, a defense attorney must be able to show how an argument, such as the following, is illogical and therefore should be disregarded:

▶ If a man robs a bank (P), he will have a large sum of money in his possession (Q).
  Jim had a large sum of money in the trunk of his car (Q). Therefore, Jim robbed the bank (P).

Note that this argument is an invalid form of *modus ponens*.

On a personal level, negative and inaccurate assumptions about others may be drawn when invalid syllogistic arguments are left unquestioned. For example, a teenager was informed by his car insurance company that if he received a speeding ticket (P), his rates would increase (Q). When his rates increased the following year (Q), his mother erroneously assumed that the youth had been caught speeding (P). This also is an invalid form of *modus ponens*.

Considerable attention has been focused on the manner in which children and adolescents come to understand valid and invalid forms of syllogisms. As with analogical reasoning (Chapter 5), developmental studies have shown that syllogistic reasoning begins in early childhood (Dias & Harris, 1988, 1990; English, 1993; Hawkins, Pea, Glick, & Scribner, 1984) and steadily improves throughout the school-age and adolescent years (Keating & Caramazza, 1975; Kodroff & Roberge, 1975; Markovits, 1995; Markovits, Schleifer, & Fortier, 1989; O'Brien & Shapiro, 1968; Roberge & Flexer, 1980; Roberge & Paulus, 1971; Shapiro & O'Brien, 1970; Sternberg, 1979, 1980; Taplin, Staudenmayer, & Taddonio, 1974). It has also been shown that syllogistic reasoning is related to internal factors such as cognitive and linguistic development (Keating & Caramazza, 1975; Sternberg, 1979) and to external factors such as the type of argument (e.g., categorical versus conditional), the content dimensions of an argument (e.g., common objects versus abstract symbols; objects present versus objects absent), and the presentation mode (e.g., written versus conversational style) (Kodroff & Roberge, 1975; Kuhn, 1977; Roberge & Flexer, 1979; Roberge & Paulus, 1971; Sternberg, 1979; Taplin et al., 1974).

Internal Factors

In a developmental study that examined factors of age, intelligence, and language ability, Keating and Caramazza (1975) presented 64 if–then conditional syllogisms in a written, multiple-choice format to groups of 11- and 13-year-old boys (N = 109). Each age group was composed of two subgroups, one with high intelligence and one with average intelligence. Students with high intelligence had all scored at the 98th or 99th percentile on the composite arithmetic scale of the *Iowa Tests of Basic Skills* (Lindquist & Hieronymous, 1956); those with average intelligence had all scored between the 45th and 55th percentiles on the *Iowa*.

Results showed that the 13-year-olds performed the syllogism task significantly better than the 11-year-olds, with mean accuracy scores of 81% and 76% obtained by the two age groups, respectively. Moreover, for both age groups, students with high intelligence performed the task significantly better than those with average intelligence. To examine the relationship between syllogistic reasoning and other abilities, all students in both age groups were also administered a vocabulary test and a nonverbal reasoning test, the *Standard Progressive Matrices* (Raven, 1960). Significant correlations were obtained between the syllogism task and each of those measures, indicating that the ability to solve syllogisms involves both cognitive and linguistic processes.

Sternberg (1980) examined changes in speed and accuracy in syllogistic reasoning during the school-age and adolescent years. Students who were ages 8, 10, 13, 15, and 16 years ($N = 124$) were tested using a written, multiple-choice task that contained 32 if–then conditional syllogisms. The responses of each student were timed automatically using a tachistoscopic device with an attached centisecond clock. The student read each problem silently and pushed a button to indicate an answer choice. Results showed that accuracy improved significantly as a function of increasing subject age. Mean scores of 60%, 75%, 77%, 82%, and 84% were obtained by the groups of 8-, 10-, 13-, 15- and 16-year-olds, respectively. Response latency steadily declined with each successive age group, a finding that was consistent with research in analogical reasoning (Sternberg & Nigro, 1980).

Roberge and Flexer (1980) also demonstrated age-related improvements in syllogistic reasoning in a study of young adolescents, ages 12 and 14 years old ($N = 80$). The task consisted of 16 syllogisms of a variety of types, including biconditional (e.g., "A bug is big if and only if it is red. This bug is red. Therefore, _?_") and if–then conditional (e.g., "If a bug is big, then it is red. This bug is not big. Therefore, _?_"). Students selected a conclusion that followed logically from the two premises. Results showed that the 14-year-olds, whose mean accuracy score was 70%, outperformed the 12-year-olds, whose mean accuracy score was 64%. Students were also administered the Word Knowledge subtest of the *Metropolitan Achievement Tests* (Durost, 1959) to determine if syllogistic reasoning was related to vocabulary level. However, the correlation coefficient between the two tasks was not significant, a result that was inconsistent with other studies that supported an association between language development and syllogistic reasoning (Keating & Caramazza, 1975; Sternberg, 1979). Perhaps this was due to the fact that words contained in the syllogisms presented by Roberge and Flexer were simple and therefore did not prove sufficiently challenging.

External Factors

Valid Versus Invalid Arguments

Investigations have been conducted in which children and adolescents were presented with valid versus invalid syllogisms (e.g., English, 1993; Markovits, 1995; Markovits et al., 1989; Shapiro & O'Brien, 1970; Taplin et al., 1974). Collectively, those reports have indicated that students experience greater difficulty understanding invalid arguments.

For example, Markovits, Schleifer, and Fortier (1989) administered a task of syllogistic reasoning to children ages 6, 8, and 11 years old ($N = 85$). Six of the problems were *valid* categorical syllogisms, for example:

▶ Every Zobole is yellow.
  All yellow things have a nose.
  Do Zoboles have a nose? (p. 793)

Six additional problems were *invalid* categorical syllogisms, lacking logical connections between premises, for example:

▶ Every Zobole is yellow.
All red things have a nose.
Do Zoboles have a nose? (p. 793)

The examiner read each problem aloud. Children responded "Yes," "No," "Don't know," or "There's no answer," and then were asked to explain their answers (e.g., "How do you know that?" p. 788). For the valid syllogisms, children performed very well, and mean accuracy scores of 76%, 80%, and 89% were obtained by the groups of 6-, 8-, and 11-year-olds, respectively. However, for the invalid syllogisms, mean accuracy scores were only 1%, 4%, and 20% for the three groups, respectively, indicating that even the 11-year-olds had difficulty recognizing illogical arguments. Regarding the children's explanations for their answers, age-related improvements occurred in relation to the valid problems in that older children showed a greater tendency than younger ones to refer to information stated in the premises. However, little improvement occurred in explaining the invalid problems.

Similar findings have been made with respect to conditional syllogisms. For example, Shapiro and O'Brien (1970) administered two versions of a task of syllogistic reasoning to students in every grade from first through eighth (ages 6 through 13 years) ($N = 384$). Both versions of the task contained 100 problems, all of which were if–then conditional syllogisms. For version A, the correct answer to each problem was either "Yes" or "No," and there were no problems that represented invalid arguments. An example of a version A problem was as follows:

▶ If this is Room 9, then it is fourth grade.
This is Room 9.
Is it fourth grade?
Yes/No (p. 824)

For version B, the correct answer was "Yes," "No," or "Not enough clues." One-third of the problems, randomly distributed, represented invalid arguments, lacking sufficient information to reach a definite conclusion. For example, the problem below was an invalid form of *modus tollens*:

▶ If this is Room 9, then it is fourth grade.
This is not Room 9.
Is it fourth grade?
Yes/No/Not enough clues (p. 824)

Half the students in each grade level were administered version A and half were administered version B. Results showed that version B was substantially more difficult

Table 6.1
Types of If–Then Conditional Syllogisms Used by Taplin, Staudenmayer, and Taddonio

Type of Syllogism	1st Premise	2nd Premise	Conclusion
1. Affirming the antecedent	if p then q	+p	+q
2. Affirming the antecedent	if p then q	+p	−q
3. Denying the antecedent	if p then q	−p	+q
4. Denying the antecedent	if p then q	−p	−q
5. Affirming the consequent	if p then q	+q	+p
6. Affirming the consequent	if p then q	+q	−p
7. Denying the consequent	if p then q	−q	+p
8. Denying the consequent	if p then q	−q	−p

Answers: 1 = always; 2 = never; 3 = sometimes; 4 = sometimes; 5 = sometimes; 6 = sometimes; 7 = never; 8 = always

Note. Adapted from "Developmental Changes in Conditional Reasoning: Linguistic or Logical?" by J. E. Taplin, H. Staudenmayer, and J. L. Taddonio, 1974, *Journal of Experimental Child Psychology, 17*, 360–373.

The student indicated if the conclusion was "Always correct," "Sometimes correct," or "Never correct."

than version A, owing to the greater difficulty of version B problems that were invalid arguments. On version A, performance reached a ceiling by third grade, where a mean accuracy score of 83% was obtained. In contrast, the mean accuracy score on version B was only 55% by third grade. However, performance continued to improve beyond that point, reaching a high of 73% accuracy by eighth grade.

A study by Taplin, Staudenmayer, and Taddonio (1974) indicated that even by late adolescence, valid and invalid syllogisms are difficult to understand. The students in their investigation were ages 9, 11, 13, 15, and 17 years old (N = 296). The task contained 96 conditional problems, with 12 representing each of the eight types shown in Table 6.1. Each problem consisted of two premises that were always true, and a conclusion that varied in its truthfulness. Capital letters were used in all problems, as shown in the following example, which affirmed the antecedent and had an affirmative conclusion:

▶ If there is a Z, then there is an H.
  There is a Z.
  There is an H.

In responding to an argument, a student evaluated the truthfulness of the conclusion by circling the best choice—"Always correct," "Sometimes correct," or "Never correct." For all students combined, the most difficult types of syllogisms were both forms of denying the antecedent (Table 6.1, Items 3 and 4) and both forms of affirming the consequent (Items 5 and 6). Note that each of these types is an *invalid* argument. In contrast, the syllogisms for both forms of affirming the antecedent (Items 1 and 2) and denying the consequent (Items 7 and 8) were substantially easier, types that are *valid* arguments. As expected, performance on the task improved as a function of increasing subject age. Combining all types of syllogisms, mean accuracy scores for the 9-, 11-, 13-, 15-, and 17-year-olds, respectively, were 39%, 44%, 45%, 54%, and 63%, indicating that syllogisms continue to be challenging throughout adolescence.

Tasks with Concrete Objects

Research has also shown that syllogisms are easier to solve when they are accompanied by concrete objects. Kodroff and Roberge (1975) presented children from Grades 1, 2, and 3 (ages 7 through 9 years) ($N = 36$) with an if–then conditional reasoning task that contained 12 problems: half of the problems were *modus ponens* ("If there is a knife, then there is a fork. There is a knife. Is there a fork?" p. 23), and half were *modus tollens* ("If there is a knife, then there is a fork. There is not a fork. Is there a knife?" p. 23). The task was presented to each child on two separate occasions. During one presentation, concrete objects were displayed as the examiner read the problems aloud. During the other presentation, the problems were presented orally without the accompanying objects. After responding, children were always asked to explain their answers.

Performance on the task improved with increasing grade level, and overall mean accuracy scores of 64%, 74%, and 84% were obtained by the first-, second-, and third-grade students, respectively. *Modus ponens* problems were easier than *modus tollens*, but accuracy on both types of problems was higher when they were accompanied by concrete objects. However, students of all grades had difficulty explaining their correct answers to the questions and frequently offered explanations based on their own world experience rather than on facts stated in the syllogisms (e.g., "Because if there's a kitten, there has to be a mother to take care of the kitten" p. 23).

This pattern, in which children's ability to explain syllogisms lags behind their more passive understanding of those problems, is consistent with many other aspects of later language development. For example, understanding has been shown to precede explanation in the development of the lexicon (Chapters 2–4) and figurative meanings including ambiguity (Chapters 7–10).

Different Types of Syllogisms

Roberge and Paulus (1971) compared the difficulty of categorical versus if–then conditional syllogisms for groups of students enrolled in Grades 4, 6, 8, and 10 (ages 9, 11,

13, and 15 years, respectively) ($N = 200$). The researchers were also interested in determining if content dimensions affected the difficulty of the problems. Content dimensions included *concrete–familiar*, where common objects were used in the problems in unimaginative ways, *suggestive*, where common objects were used in imaginative ways, and *abstract*, where letters, symbols, or nonsense words were used. Examples of categorical and conditional syllogisms expressing the three different content dimensions are contained in Table 6.2. For both categorical and conditional syllogisms, 12 problems were presented for each of the three content dimensions. Students were asked to respond "Yes," "No," or "Maybe" to the last statement in each problem.

For the students as a whole, categorical syllogisms were easier to solve than conditional syllogisms. Significant differences also were obtained as a function of content dimension: when grade level and syllogism type were combined, concrete–familiar problems were easiest, suggestive were intermediate, and abstract were most difficult. Consistent with the studies reported earlier (e.g., Markovits et al., 1989; Taplin et al., 1974), accuracy in responding to categorical and conditional syllogisms improved as a function of increasing subject age. Across the three content dimensions, mean accuracy scores for the 9-, 11-, 13-, and 15-year-olds, respectively, were 43%, 45%, 54%, and 63% for categorical syllogisms, and 42%, 41%, 56%, and 59% for conditional.

Other investigators have also documented the greater difficulty of if–then conditional syllogisms in comparison to other types. For example, Roberge and Flexer (1979) administered a syllogistic reasoning task to groups of 13-year-olds and adults ($N = 144$). The task contained 16 syllogisms, with four representing each of the four types shown in Table 6.3: biconditional, if–then conditional, exclusive disjunctive, and inclusive disjunctive. For each problem, students were asked to write a conclusion that followed logically from the two premises.

Surprisingly, the adolescents and adults did not differ in their performance on the task. For the subjects as a whole, exclusive disjunctive problems were easiest to solve, if–then conditional were most difficult, and inclusive disjunctive and biconditional problems were moderate in difficulty. Mean accuracy scores for those four types, respectively, were 85%, 63%, 71%, and 70%.

Similar results were obtained by Sternberg (1979), who conducted a larger developmental study of syllogistic reasoning. Participants in his investigation were ages 7, 9, 11, 13, 17, and 19 years old ($N = 224$). The task involved a cardboard box, a towel to cover the box, and two objects such as a cardboard circle and a cardboard square. A game was played where the examiner secretly placed one, both, or neither of the two objects into the box. The subject's goal was to figure out what the examiner had done. To "assist" the subject, the examiner always gave two hints, which were actually the first two premises of a syllogism. The subject was then asked to respond "True," "False," or "Maybe" to the conclusion of the syllogism. The premises and conclusion were always presented in both spoken and written form. The task consisted of 80 syllogisms, with 16 representing each of five different types—conjunctive, disjunctive (both inclusive and exclusive), if–then conditional, only–if conditional, and

Table 6.2
Types of Syllogisms Used by Roberge and Paulus

Concrete–Familiar:

Categorical:

All of the green coats in the closet belong to Sarah.
The coat in the closet is green.
Therefore, the coat in the closet does not belong to Sarah. (no)

If–Then Conditional:

If the hat on the table is blue, then it belongs to Sally.
The hat on the table is blue.
Therefore, the hat on the table does not belong to Sally. (no)

Suggestive:

Categorical:

All ants that can fly are bigger than zebras.
This ant can fly.
Therefore, this ant is bigger than a zebra. (yes)

If–Then Conditional:

If mice can fly, then they are bigger than horses.
Mice are bigger than horses.
Therefore, mice can fly. (maybe)

Abstract:

Categorical:

All pittles are cloots.
This is a pittle.
Therefore, this is a cloot. (yes)

If–Then Conditional:

If there is a nupittle, then there is a coolt.
There is not a coolt.
Therefore, there is a nupittle. (no)

Note: Adapted from "Developmental Patterns for Children's Class and Conditional Reasoning Abilities" by J. J. Roberge and D. H. Paulus, 1971, *Developmental Psychology, 4*, 191–200.

Students were asked to provide a "Yes," "No," or "Maybe" response to the last statement in each problem.

Table 6.3
Types of Syllogisms Used by Roberge and Flexer

Biconditional:

There is a P if and only if there is a Q.
There is a P.
Therefore, (there is a Q).

If–Then Conditional:

If there is a P, then there is a Q.
There is a Q.
Therefore, (none).

Exclusive Disjunctive:

Either there is a P or there is a Q (but not both).
There is not a P.
Therefore, (there is a Q).

Inclusive Disjunctive:

Either there is a P or there is a Q (or both).
There is not a Q.
Therefore, (there is a P).

Note. Adapted from "Further Examination of Formal Operational Reasoning Abilities" by J. J. Roberge and B. B. Flexer, 1979, *Child Development, 50,* 478–484.

Students were asked to write a conclusion that followed logically from the two premises or to write "None" if nothing followed.

biconditional. Examples of each type are contained in Table 6.4. Sternberg called this the "combination task" because the subject had to mentally combine the first two premises in order to evaluate the validity of the conclusion. To accomplish this, the subject had to comprehend each of the three sentences (*linguistic encoding*) and then reason deductively (*logical combination*).

For the subjects as a whole, mean accuracy scores indicated that the conjunctive syllogisms (69%) were easiest, followed by the exclusive disjunctive syllogisms (35%). Only–if conditional (21%) and biconditional (20%) were intermediate in difficulty, and inclusive disjunctive (6%) and if–then conditional (6%) were most difficult. Results also showed that performance steadily improved with age. Mean accuracy scores obtained by the groups of 7-, 9-, 11-, 13-, 17-, and 19-year-olds, respectively, were 8%, 17%, 24%, 31%, 44%, and 57%. Thus, even the oldest subjects, who were college students, did not approach mastery of the task.

Table 6.4
Types of Syllogisms Used by Sternberg

Conjunctive:

There is a circle in the box *and* there is a square in the box.
There is a circle in the box.
There is a not square in the box. (false)

Disjunctive:

Inclusive (P or Q or both):

There is a circle in the box *or* there is a square in the box.
There is a circle in the box.
There is a square in the box. (maybe)

Exclusive (P or Q, but not both):

There is a circle in the box *or* there is a square in the box.
There is a square in the box.
There is not a circle in the box. (true)

If–Then Conditional:

If there is a circle in the box *then* there is a square in the box.
There is a square in the box.
There is a circle in the box. (maybe)

Only–If Conditional:

There is a circle in the box *only if* there is a square in the box.
There is not a circle in the box.
There is not a square in the box. (maybe)

Biconditional:

There is a circle in the box *if and only if* there is a square in the box.
There is not a square in the box.
There is not a circle in the box. (true)

Note. Adapted from "Developmental Patterns in the Encoding and Combination of Logical Connectives" by R. J. Sternberg, 1979, *Journal of Experimental Child Psychology, 28,* 469–498.

Students were asked to respond "True," "False," or "Maybe" to the conclusion of the syllogism.

Another purpose of Sternberg's study was to compare the contribution of linguistic versus logical factors to the development of syllogistic reasoning. To accomplish this, another task called *encoding* was presented to the same groups of students. The encoding task employed the same problems and procedures as the combination task, except that the second premise of each problem was omitted (e.g., "There is a circle in the box and there is a square in the box. There is not a circle in the box—True, False, Maybe"). By omitting the second premise, the need for deductive reasoning dissolves and the task simply assesses the subject's linguistic encoding of the sentences. By comparing the difficulty of the encoding and combination tasks, one can infer the contribution of linguistic versus logical factors to performance on the combination task. For example, if few errors occur on the encoding task but many occur on the combination task (which requires sentence comprehension as well as deductive reasoning), this would indicate that logical factors play a greater role than linguistic factors in solving syllogisms. Alternatively, if the encoding task is equal to or only slightly easier than the combination task, this would indicate that linguistic factors play a major role in solving syllogisms. Sternberg (1979) found that the encoding task was only slightly easier than the combination task for each of the six age groups, leading to the conclusion that linguistic factors (e.g., sentence comprehension) account for a large portion of students' success in solving syllogisms.

Syllogistic Reasoning in Younger Children

Many of the tasks employed in the studies discussed above have been rather formal. Kuhn (1977), in contrast, suggested that formal written tasks might underestimate children's ability to reason syllogistically. Therefore, she developed a more naturalistic task where pictures were presented and described in a conversational manner, and the child was asked questions that required categorical or conditional reasoning. For example, in one task, the child was shown a large color photograph of a "far-away city" called Tundor and additional pictures of people who lived there. The examiner made statements about the pictures (e.g., "All of the people in Tundor are happy. Here is a picture of Jean. Jean lives in Tundor") and then asked questions requiring a "Yes," "No," or "Maybe" response (e.g., "Is Jean happy?"). Children ages 6, 7, 8, and 9 years old (Grades 1, 2, 3, and 4) participated ($N = 60$).

Interestingly, no developmental differences were found as a function of increasing subject age. Regarding the oldest children, the 9-year-olds, mean accuracy scores of 77% and 67% were obtained for the questions requiring categorical and conditional reasoning, respectively. Importantly, the results were markedly higher than those that had been obtained by the 9-year-olds in the Roberge and Paulus (1971) study (43% and 42% for categorical and conditional items, respectively), or by the 9-year-olds in the Taplin et al. (1974) study who were presented with conditional items only (39%). These comparisons across studies suggest that problems of syllogistic reasoning are easier for children to solve when concrete, conversational tasks are employed as opposed to more abstract, written tasks.

Since the publication of Kuhn's (1977) study, other investigators have examined syllogistic reasoning in even younger children and have obtained positive results. Hawkins, Pea, Glick, and Scribner (1984) presented 4- and 5-year-old children

($N = 40$) with a task in which some of the problems involved fantasy characters, as in the following example:

▶ Pogs wear blue boots.
  Tom is a pog.
  Does Tom wear blue boots? (p. 587)

The examiner read each problem aloud and asked the child to respond "Yes" or "No" to each question. Following their responses, children were asked to explain their answers.

For problems involving fantasy characters, the children achieved a mean accuracy score of 73%, a level well above chance performance. Moreover, the explanations for their correct responses often referred back to information that had been stated in the premises ("Yes, because he's a pog" p. 588), providing further evidence that they had reasoned deductively. The investigators speculated that the use of fantasy characters in the problems helped the children achieve an "abstract attitude" that allowed them to think hypothetically without interference from practical world knowledge. Other investigators (Dias & Harris, 1988, 1990; English, 1993) have supported this view, reporting that even preschool children can reason deductively when the task involves fantasy conditions and the children are encouraged to imagine hypothetical situations.

Summary

Developmental studies have shown that syllogistic reasoning is present in early childhood and gradually improves during the school-age and adolescent years. Growth occurs primarily in the speed and accuracy with which problems are solved and in students' ability to provide cogent explanations of arguments. Performance continues to improve into adulthood, and even college students may be challenged by certain types of syllogisms. Students of all ages are better able to detect and explain valid arguments than invalid ones that are marked by insufficient information or illogical connections between premises.

Studies have also shown that syllogisms that express conjunction, exclusive disjunction, and categorical relationships are generally easier than those that express inclusive disjunction and if–then conditional arguments. Biconditional and only–if conditional syllogisms appear to be of intermediate difficulty. Factors responsible for these differences among types of syllogisms are unknown, although frequency of exposure through ordinary conversation may be a relevant factor. For example, speakers use the exclusive *or* (e.g., "I'll take cake or pie") more often than the inclusive variety (e.g., "I'll take cake or pie or both") (Sternberg, 1979). It is also noteworthy that syllogisms within a particular type can vary greatly in difficulty according to content factors. For example, syllogisms that contain abstract terms (e.g., capital letters) are more difficult than those that contain concrete terms (e.g., the names of common objects). Mode of presentation has also been found to affect performance in that formal written syllogisms are more difficult than those that occur in conversational contexts.

Acknowledgments

Portions of this chapter appeared in the following publication:

Nippold, M. A. (1988). Verbal reasoning. In M A Nippold (Ed.), *Later language development: Ages nine through nineteen* (pp. 159–177). Austin, TX: PRO-ED.

C H A P T E R

METAPHORS AND SIMILES

"Just as the repeated use of a hammer may strengthen the arm, the repeated use of metaphors may strengthen the powers of analysis and synthesis."

—Sticht (1979, p. 485)

Metaphors and similes are figurative expressions that draw comparisons between items that are normally viewed as distinct. A *metaphor* contains a term, called "the topic," which is likened to another term, called "the vehicle," on the basis of one or more shared features, called "the ground" (Gardner, Winner, Bechhofer, & Wolf, 1978). For example, in the metaphor "The giraffe was a flagpole living at the zoo," *giraffe* is the topic, *flagpole* the vehicle, and *tallness* the ground.

Two main types of metaphors are the *predicative* (also known as *similarity*) and the *proportional* (Billow, 1977; Miller, 1979). In a *predicative metaphor*, such as the "giraffe–flagpole" example, there is one topic and one vehicle (Ortony, 1979; Winner, Engel, & Gardner, 1980a). *Proportional metaphors*, however, contain two topics and two vehicles that express an analogical relationship at an underlying level; at the surface level, one topic is unstated (Gardner et al., 1978; Miller, 1979; Ortony, 1979). For example, the proportional metaphor, "The artist was an apple tree with no fruit" contains the analogy, "Apple tree is to fruit as artist is to _____," leaving the topic, artwork, to be inferred.

A *simile* is a variation of a predicative metaphor that makes the comparison between the topic and vehicle more explicit by inserting the word *like* (e.g., "The giraffe was *like* a flagpole living at the zoo") or the phrase *as (adjective) as* (e.g., "The giraffe was *as tall as* a flagpole living at the zoo"). Note that in the latter type of simile, the comparison is so explicit that the ground is actually stated and does not need to be inferred.

When used skillfully, metaphors and similes can capture peoples' attention, stimulate their imaginations, and communicate complex ideas in a clear and convincing manner. For example, in her book *The Sense of Wonder*, Rachel Carson (1965) used metaphors masterfully to convey to parents the importance of teaching children about nature by keeping alive the child's "inborn sense of wonder" through joyful outdoor experiences. She wrote:

> I sincerely believe that for the child, and for the parent seeking to guide him, it is not half so important to *know* as to *feel*. If facts are the seeds that later produce knowledge and wisdom, then the emotions and the impressions of the senses are the fertile soil in which the seeds must grow. The years of early childhood are the time to prepare the soil . . . (p. 45)

Moreover, *Silent Spring*, Carson's (1962) most famous book, was so beautifully written, with metaphoric language woven into scientific text, that readers were captivated by it, and the world was awakened to the life-threatening dangers of pesticides (Brooks, 1972; McCay, 1993).

Metaphor and Simile Comprehension

Children's comprehension of metaphors and similes has been studied for many years. Collectively, studies have shown that metaphors and similes are first understood during the preschool years (Boynton & Kossan, 1981; Dent, 1984; Gardner, 1974; Gentner, 1977; Nippold & Sullivan, 1987; Pearson, 1990; Vosniadou & Ortony, 1983; Vosniadou, Ortony, Reynolds, & Wilson, 1984), and that comprehension steadily improves throughout childhood, adolescence, and into adulthood (Boswell, 1979; Evans & Gamble, 1988; Karadsheh, 1991; Keil, 1986; Kogan & Chadrow, 1986; Kubicka, 1992; Nippold, Leonard, & Kail, 1984; Nippold & Sullivan, 1987; Siltanen, 1981, 1989; Vosniadou et al., 1984; Waggoner, Messe, & Palermo, 1985; Waggoner & Palermo, 1989).

The Role of Cognition

An early school of thought emphasized the difficulty of metaphors and similes, and the need for certain cognitive prerequisites to be present before a child could comprehend such expressions. For example, Billow (1975) examined metaphor comprehension in relation to Piagetian cognitive level. Children ages 9, 11, and 13 years old ($N = 30$) were asked to explain the meanings of 12 predicative (similarity) metaphors (e.g., "Hair is spaghetti") and 12 proportional metaphors (e.g., "My head is an apple without any core"). Billow had hypothesized that concrete–operational thinking was required before a child could comprehend predicative metaphors, and that formal operational thinking was required before proportional metaphors could be understood. Each child was also administered a class-inclusion task as a measure of concrete operational thought, and a combinatorial reasoning task as a measure of formal operational thought.

Results showed that for both types of metaphors, explanations steadily improved as subject age increased. For the predicative metaphors, mean accuracy scores obtained by the 9-, 11-, and 13-year-olds, respectively, were 60%, 85%, and 90%. For the proportional metaphors, those means were 47%, 65%, and 75%, respectively. In addition, significant correlations were obtained between class inclusion and predicative metaphor comprehension, and between combinatorial reasoning and proportional metaphor comprehension. However, the cognitive-prerequisite hypothesis was not supported for either type of metaphor. Children who performed poorly on the class-inclusion task sometimes understood the predicative metaphors, and those who performed poorly on the combinatorial reasoning task sometimes understood the proportional metaphors.

Siltanen (1981) studied metaphor comprehension by grouping children and adolescents ages 9 through 18 years ($N = 126$) into Piagetian cognitive stages: concrete–operational (ages 9 through 11), late concrete–early formal operational (ages 12 through 14), and formal operational (ages 15 through 18). The experimental task consisted of 16 metaphors that had been classified as "easy" (e.g., "Butterflies are rainbows"), "moderate" (e.g., "Jealousy is a green-eyed monster"), or "difficult" (e.g., "Genius is perseverance in action"). Each metaphor was presented within a contextually supportive paragraph. Students read the paragraphs and wrote down the meanings of the metaphors.

Explanations of the metaphors were analyzed in terms of accuracy and completeness. As expected, the formal operational group outperformed the transitional group, which outperformed the concrete–operational group. However, even the formal operational group had not completely mastered the task and found the difficult metaphors especially challenging. Although the author implied that performance on the task was determined by Piagetian cognitive level, no evidence was presented that would establish a cause-and-effect relationship between cognitive level and metaphor understanding. However, verbal ability scores from subtests of the *Iowa Tests of Basic Skills* (Lindquist & Hieronymus, 1956) were available for some of the students. Significant correlation coefficients were obtained between metaphor understanding and the subtests Language Use, Language Total, Reading Comprehension, and Total Listening, indicating that linguistic competence is related to figurative understanding.

Other investigators such as Arlin (1978), Cometa and Eson (1978), and Smith (1976) also tried to demonstrate that certain Piagetian cognitive stages were prerequisites to metaphor comprehension, but none were successful. Vosniadou (1987) provided an insightful discussion of this issue and outlined the methodological problems affecting the research in this area.

The relationship between cognition and metaphor comprehension has also been examined from a non-Piagetian perspective, but the results have been inconsistent.

For example, Kogan, Connor, Gross, and Fava (1980) examined the relationship between performance on a metaphoric-triads task (MTT) and performance on various standardized tests such as the *Otis–Lennon Mental Ability Test* (Otis & Lennon, 1967) and the *Iowa Tests of Basic Skills* (Lindquist & Hieronymus, 1956). The MTT is a measure of metaphor comprehension where three pictures are displayed in a row in front of the subject. Two pictures express a metaphoric relationship (e.g., a coiled snake and a winding river) whereas the third picture (e.g., a fish) is related to the other two in a literal manner. Each subject was asked to select and explain all possible pairs. A response was credited if the metaphoric relationship was appropriately identified. Kogan et al. found that the MTT was sensitive to age-related improvements in metaphor comprehension: mean accuracy scores for groups of 9-, 10-, 12-, 18-, and 19-year-olds ($N = 448$) were 29%, 28%, 41%, 61%, and 60%, respectively. Scores on the *Iowa* and *Otis–Lennon* tests were available for some of the 9-year-olds and for all of the 12-year-olds, but no correlations between these measures and the MTT reached significance. However, some of the 9-year-olds were also administered the *Children's Associative Responding Test* (CART, Achenbach, 1969), a measure of analogical reasoning (see Chapter 5), and it was found that better performance on the MTT was associated with better performance on the CART.

Malgady (1977) also employed a non-Piagetian approach to the study of metaphoric language. In his investigation, 11 different similes (e.g., "The hair is like spaghetti," "The clouds are like ice cream") were presented to children from three different age groups: 5 through 6 years, 8 through 9 years, and 11 through 12 years ($N = 60$). The sentences were presented in spoken form to the youngest group, and in written form to the two oldest groups. Children explained or wrote down the meanings of each. Results showed that the percentage of valid interpretations increased with each successive age group; means of 67%, 71%, and 83% were obtained by the younger to older groups, respectively. It was also found that for the oldest group, performance on the simile task was significantly correlated to verbal intelligence as measured by the *Lorge–Thorndike Intelligence Test* (Lorge & Thorndike, 1957), and to reading comprehension as measured by the *Metropolitan Achievement Tests* (Durost, 1959).

Summary

Studies that have focused on cognitive factors have shown that comprehension of metaphors and similes steadily improves during the school-age and adolescent years. However, no investigators were able to identify any specific cognitive prerequisites for the understanding of metaphors or similes. Children's performance on tasks of figurative understanding is definitely related to their performance on measures of cognition, language, and academic achievement. However, the cognitive prerequisite hypothesis is no longer widely accepted. The fact that even preschool children can comprehend metaphors and similes when age-appropriate materials and testing procedures are employed casts doubt upon the need for certain Piagetian stages to be present prior to the attainment of figurative understanding.

The Role of Linguistic, Metalinguistic, and Nonlinguistic Factors

In addition to cognitive factors, research has demonstrated that a variety of linguistic, metalinguistic, and nonlinguistic factors are related to children's comprehension of metaphors and similes.

Semantic Features

Children's knowledge and awareness of the relevant semantic features of the topic and the vehicle of a metaphor or simile has been shown to play a key role in their understanding of such expressions. Evidence for this position was provided by Evans and Gamble (1988) who examined metaphor interpretation in children who were ages 8, 10, and 12 years old ($N = 72$). A list of predicative metaphors was initially generated. All contained words that were familiar to even the youngest children in the study (e.g., "Camels are the trucks of the desert," "Flowers are the calendars of the garden," "Roosters are the alarm clocks of the farm," etc.) (p. 448). Each child participated in two tasks. For the first task, the topic and the vehicle of each metaphor (e.g., *camel, truck, flower, calendar, rooster, alarm clock*) had been incorporated into a list of randomly ordered terms. The child was asked to tell what the important or special features of each term were. The purpose of this task was to determine what attributes of each term were most salient for the child. Six weeks later, the child was asked to explain what each of the metaphors meant (e.g., "What does it mean to say, Camels are the trucks of the desert?").

As expected, metaphor interpretations steadily improved with each successive age group. For the 8-, 10-, and 12-year-olds, respectively, 62%, 75%, and 83% of the metaphors were explained correctly. It was also found that when children misinterpreted metaphors, they frequently did so when they had listed incorrect or irrelevant features for the topic or vehicle of that expression during the initial feature-listing task. These results indicate that an understanding of metaphors requires a child to have more than a general familiarity with the words contained in the expressions. For example, even though a child may know what camels and trucks look like, the metaphor "Camels are the trucks of the desert" will not be well-understood without knowledge of the fact that camels, like trucks, are used in some countries to transport goods over long distances. Importantly, this view of metaphor understanding, which can be called the *semantic feature hypothesis*, is consistent with the information discussed in Chapter 2 concerning the gradual manner in which words are acquired during the school-age and adolescent years and the notion of partial lexical knowledge.

Additional support for the semantic feature hypothesis was provided by Baldwin, Luce, and Readence (1982). Fifth-grade students ($N = 39$) were presented with metaphors and similes (e.g., "The pieces of ice hanging from the roof were carrots," "The man's feet were like blocks of ice," "The clouds that hung in the sky were like cotton candy") and were asked to explain the meaning of each sentence in writing. Immediately following this explanation task, the students were given a list of the vehicles from each of the sentences (e.g., carrots, blocks of ice, cotton candy), randomly ordered, and were asked to write down the important features of each term.

The results indicated that the students correctly interpreted 57% of the figurative sentences and misinterpreted 43%. Moreover, their performance in interpreting the sentences was closely related to their performance on the feature-listing task. When students interpreted the sentences correctly, they were more likely to have listed the appropriate semantic features of the vehicle than when they misinterpreted the sentences. It was also found that students could improve their ability to interpret metaphors and similes when they were later "coached" by an experimenter to attend to the relevant semantic features of the vehicle. The authors concluded that the important role of word knowledge in the understanding and teaching of metaphors and similes to children should not be underestimated.

Concrete Versus Abstract Nouns

The concreteness of the nouns contained in a metaphor also affects its ease of understanding. This was demonstrated by Siltanen (1981) who examined the development of metaphor understanding in children from three age groups: 6 through 8 years, 9 through 11 years, and 12 years ($N = 256$). Children were asked to interpret three types of metaphors: *concrete*, in which both the topic and the vehicle were concrete nouns (e.g., "The *moon* is the Earth's *kite*"); *mixed*, which contained one concrete noun and one abstract noun (e.g., "A circus *clown* is *loneliness* all dressed up"); and *abstract*, in which both the topic and the vehicle were abstract nouns (e.g., "*Genius* is *perseverance* in action"). Metaphors were presented either without context, with a short context (8 to 10 words preceding the metaphor), or with a long context (60 to 100 words forming a short story). Overall performance on the task steadily improved with each successive age group, and, as predicted, the concrete metaphors were easier than the abstract, and the mixed were intermediate in difficulty. It was also found that children's performance was enhanced when metaphors were presented with short or long contexts. Other reports have also indicated that story contexts facilitate children's understanding of metaphors and similes (e.g., Ortony, Schallert, Reynolds, & Antos, 1978; Reynolds & Ortony, 1980; Vosniadou et al., 1984; Waggoner et al., 1985).

Conceptual Domain

In order to understand an abstract metaphor such as "Genius is perseverance in action," a child must appreciate the subtle meanings of words. Keil (1986) argued that the amount and quality of knowledge that a child possesses concerning the topic and vehicle of a metaphor plays a particularly important role in the child's comprehension of the expressions. He was interested in children's knowledge of conceptual domains, and its relationship to their understanding of metaphors. In his investigation, children ages 5, 7, and 9 years old ($N = 48$) were asked to explain the meanings of metaphors that represented a variety of conceptual domains. For all groups, metaphors that described human personalities (e.g., "She was a stormy person") were more difficult than those that expressed simpler concepts (e.g., "The car was thirsty," "The wind howled").

Other researchers have also examined the issue of conceptual domain in relation to children's comprehension of metaphors. For example, Winner, Rosenstiel, and Gardner (1976) compared children's understanding of "psychological-physical" metaphors to their understanding of "cross-sensory" metaphors. Psychological-physical metaphors were said to express "a psychological experience by appealing to an event in the physical domain" (p. 290) (e.g., "After many years of working at the jail, the prison guard had become a hard rock that could not be moved" [p. 293]); cross-sensory were said to express "an experience in one sensory modality by referring synesthetically to another sensory modality" (p. 290) (e.g., "The smell of my mother's perfume was bright sunshine" [p. 293]).

Children who participated in the Winner et al. (1976) study were drawn from six different age groups: 6, 7, 8, 10, 12, and 14 years ($N = 180$). An examiner read 16 metaphoric sentences to the child—eight psychological-physical and eight cross-sensory. Comprehension of each sentence was assessed under two different conditions—explanation and multiple choice. To accomplish this, the examiner asked half the children in each age group to explain the meanings of the sentences, and the other half to select from four alternative interpretations that the examiner read to them. For each sentence, the four choices always included one appropriate metaphoric interpretation and three foils that expressed various literal interpretations.

The results for both response conditions indicated that comprehension steadily improved through age 14, and that the cross-sensory metaphors were easier to understand than the psychological-physical, particularly for the younger children. It was also found that for both conditions, literal interpretations decreased and figurative interpretations increased as age increased. The multiple-choice condition revealed a higher level of performance than the explanation condition, indicating that adequate figurative explanations for the metaphors were infrequent before age 10. However, this was not surprising, given the greater metalinguistic demands of the explanation task in requiring a child to talk about language.

Although metaphors that describe personality traits, emotions, and other psychological phenomena may be more difficult to understand than those that express more tangible concepts, it would be incorrect to assume that psychological metaphors are completely beyond the competence of young children. Waggoner and Palermo (1989) constructed a task where metaphors expressing psychological concepts such as happiness (e.g., "Betty was a bouncing bubble"), fear (e.g., "Rosemary was a shaking mouse"), and anger (e.g., "Betty was a bucking horse") were presented within contextually supportive stories. Children ages 5, 7, and 9 years ($N = 32$) listened to the stories and were asked to choose which of two emotions (e.g., happiness, sadness) was being expressed by the metaphor. After the children had selected an emotion, they were asked to explain that choice. On the forced choice task, overall accuracy scores of 69%, 71%, and 86%, respectively, were obtained by the 5-, 7-, and 9-year-olds, indicating that performance improved with increasing subject age but that even the youngest children responded above the level of chance performance. In contrast, on the explanation task, children from all age groups had difficulty, indicating that explanation tasks may underestimate a child's understanding of psychological metaphors.

Surface Structure

In addition to a child's knowledge and awareness of relevant semantic features and familiarity with conceptual domains, factors such as the surface structure of an expression may contribute to the ease or difficulty with which it is understood. This was demonstrated by Winner et al. (1980a), who examined metaphor comprehension in children ages 6, 7, and 9 years ($N = 120$). In their investigation, 15 predicative metaphors were written such as, "The skywriting was a scar marking the sky." Then, for each predicative metaphor, four syntactically different but semantically equivalent variations were written. These were in the form of topicless metaphors (e.g., "The scar marked the sky"), similes (e.g., "The skywriting was like a scar marking the sky"), quasi analogies (e.g., "A scar marks someone's skin and something marks the sky"), and riddles (e.g., "What is like a scar but marks the sky?"). Thus, there were five syntactic variations for each metaphor: predicative, topicless, simile, quasi analogy, and riddle. Each variation was assigned to one of five forms of the task, so that each form contained 15 different metaphors. There were three instances of each syntactic variation on each form. Children were randomly assigned to receive one of the five forms. The examiner read the 15 metaphors to each child. As in the earlier study (Winner et al., 1976), half the children in each age group responded through a multiple-choice condition, and half were asked to explain the meanings of the metaphors. In the multiple-choice condition, the examiner read four alternative answers and asked the child to choose the best one.

The results of the study indicated that for both response modes and for all syntactic variations, performance improved as children got older, but even the youngest children understood many of the metaphors. Consistent with the findings of the earlier study (Winner et al., 1976), the multiple-choice condition yielded greater accuracy than the explanation condition for all five syntactic variations. For both response modes, topicless metaphors were easier to understand than predicative, and riddles were easier to understand than topicless metaphors. However, similes and predicative metaphors were equal in difficulty. Whereas quasi analogies were easier to understand than topicless metaphors in the multiple-choice condition, they were equal in difficulty for children in the explanation condition.

Although Winner et al. (1980a) had predicted that similes would be easier for children to comprehend than predicative metaphors, suggesting that the additional word *like* might help a child realize that the metaphorical statement was not intended literally, their results did not support that prediction. Reynolds and Ortony (1980), however, made that same prediction and did find that similes were easier to comprehend than predicative metaphors, at least for younger children.

Reynolds and Ortony (1980) developed a more naturalistic task involving contextual support. Children who were ages 7, 8, 9, 10, and 11 years old ($N = 171$) read short stories and selected the most appropriate continuation sentence for each from among four alternatives. The continuation sentences were expressed either as predicative metaphors or as semantically matched similes. For example, one story was about a boy who wanted to hide his new baseball mitt from his friends. Expressed as a metaphor, the appropriate continuation sentence was "Johnny was a dog burying a bone in the backyard" (p. 1116), and as a simile it was "Johnny was like a dog burying a bone in the backyard" (p. 1116).

For metaphors and similes combined, accuracy in selecting the appropriate continuation sentence steadily improved as subject age increased: mean scores of 50%, 53%, 67%, 72%, and 80%, respectively, were obtained by the 7-, 8-, 9-, 10-, and 11-year-olds. It was also found that similes were easier to understand than metaphors for the two youngest groups but offered no advantage to any of the three oldest groups.

Nippold et al. (1984) also examined the influence of syntactic form and conceptual domain on children's metaphor comprehension. They constructed a multiple-choice listening task in which 7- and 9-year-olds ($N = 60$) were presented with nine instances of four different types of metaphoric sentences: (1) perceptual-predicative (e.g., "The bird was a rainbow flying in the sky"); (2) psychological-predicative (e.g., "Tommy was a vacuum cleaner listening to the story"); (3) perceptual-proportional (e.g., "The bird's nest was a piggy bank that had no coins"); and (4) psychological-proportional (e.g., "The artist was an apple tree that had no fruit"). Perceptual metaphors expressed a visual resemblance between different items, and psychological metaphors expressed an emotion, mental state, or personality characteristic.

In constructing the task, Nippold et al. (1984) ensured that the sentences were approximately the same length, that the vocabulary was familiar to 7- and 9-year-olds, and that the metaphors were novel so that children would actively think about their meanings. In presenting the task, the examiner read each sentence aloud, asked the child to repeat it, and read two alternative interpretations from which to choose. One alternative represented an appropriate figurative interpretation, and the other expressed an inappropriate nonliteral interpretation. For example, in presenting the alternatives for the "bird-rainbow" metaphor, the examiner said, "That means the bird: (1) was very colorful; (2) was making a nest" (p. 200).

The results indicated that the 9-year-olds outperformed the 7-year-olds, although even the younger children responded well above the level of chance performance. It was also found that both age groups had more difficulty with proportional metaphors than with predicative metaphors. However, psychological metaphors did not differ from perceptual metaphors in ease of understanding, perhaps because the children were already familiar with all of the words in the two types of sentences.

In a subsequent study, Nippold and Sullivan (1987) examined the ability of even younger children to comprehend proportional metaphors. A similar type of multiple-choice listening task was administered to children ages 5, 6, and 7 years ($N = 90$). Twelve proportional metaphors (e.g., "The house was a box with no lid") were presented, each followed by a choice of three alternative interpretations (i.e., "That means the house: had no furniture, had no people, had no roof"). Performance on the task improved with each successive age group, and mean accuracy scores of 43%, 58%, and 73% were obtained by the 5-, 6-, and 7-year-olds, respectively. Thus, even the 5-year-olds performed above the level of chance (33%). It was also found that children's ability to interpret the proportional metaphors was correlated to their receptive vocabulary scores as measured by their performance on the *Peabody Picture Vocabulary Test-Revised* (Dunn & Dunn, 1981).

Nonlinguistic Factors

Dent (1984) developed an unusual perceptual task for assessing metaphor comprehension in the visual modality. In her investigation, children ages 5, 7, and 10 years ($N = 48$) and a group of adults ($N = 32$) were shown triads of filmed scenes (e.g., a ballerina leaping, a ballerina spinning, a top spinning) and were told to pick two that went together. In each triad, there were three possible pairings: (1) literal, in which the same type of object was shown in two different ways (e.g., ballerina leaping, ballerina spinning); (2) metaphoric, in which one particular property characterized two different types of items (e.g., ballerina spinning, top spinning); and (3) control, in which there was little similarity between two scenes (e.g., top spinning, ballerina leaping).

Ten triads were presented to each subject, half consisting of moving or event scenes (e.g., ballerina leaping, ballerina spinning, top spinning), and half consisting of stationary or object scenes (e.g., wrinkled face, smooth face, and wrinkled apple). After a metaphoric pairing was made, the subject was asked to think about the two scenes at the same time and to describe what came to mind. The purpose of the description task was to determine to what extent the subject could articulate the overlapping properties (i.e., the ground) between the topic and vehicle of a visual metaphor when specifically asked to do so.

The results showed that control pairings occurred infrequently but that literal pairings were frequent at all ages. Metaphoric pairings steadily increased until the adult level, but even the 5-year-olds had some success with these pairings. Regarding the two metaphor types, subjects had greater success detecting the moving metaphors than the stationary metaphors. Dent (1984) suggested that the greater "attention-capturing" properties of moving metaphors may have accounted for this difference. She also reported that the ability to explain a metaphor lagged behind metaphoric detection but improved with age. However, the 10-year-olds did not differ from the adults in explaining the metaphoric pairings, a finding that contrasted with many other studies indicating that metaphoric explanations continue to improve during the school-age and adolescent years (Billow, 1975; Gardner, 1974; Kogan et al., 1980;

Malgady, 1977; Pollio & Pickens, 1980; Silberstein, Gardner, Phelps, & Winner, 1982; Siltanen, 1981; Winner et al., 1976).

Gardner (1974) also developed a metaphor comprehension task that involved nonlinguistic components. In his investigation, children were asked to match familiar polar adjectives, such as *happy-sad* and *loud-quiet*, to stimuli in various sensory modalities, such as colors, facial expressions, and auditory tones. Materials had been collected to represent the literal and metaphoric interpretations of the adjective pairs in the various modalities. For example, the literal interpretation of the pair *happy-sad* was represented by pictures of happy and sad faces; the metaphoric interpretations of this pair were represented by yellow-orange and violet-blue color swatches and by musical tones played in a major key and in a minor key. Gardner had ensured that the metaphoric matches were legitimate by presenting them to adult judges in a prior experiment.

Gardner's (1974) subjects were ages 3, 7, 11, and 19 years old (N = 101). Each subject was first presented with materials representing the literal interpretations of an adjective pair, such as a happy face and a sad face, and was told to decide, for example, which was happy and which was sad. After establishing that the literal meanings of the pairs were understood, the examiner presented the subject with pairs of stimuli representing metaphoric interpretations from the various modalities. The subject then was told that he or she would see two colors (or hear two tones, etc.) and was to decide which was happy and which was sad. The subject was then asked to explain each match.

Accuracy in assigning the metaphoric interpretations to the sensory stimuli improved as a function of age, but even the youngest subjects performed well on this task. However, the 3-year-olds usually were unable to explain their matches, and the 7-year-olds typically gave literal explanations (e.g., "An easel is *loud* because you hear the brush"). The 11-year-olds, however, frequently gave appropriate explanations (e.g., "An angry face is *cold* because it makes you feel cold"); the 19-year-olds gave an even greater variety of appropriate explanations and showed greater awareness of the multiple meanings of words.

Thus, a discrepancy was found between the younger children's detection of metaphoric matches and their ability to verbalize that knowledge. Gardner (1974) concluded that, although metaphoric understanding steadily improves with age, a basic ability to deal with metaphors is present in very young children.

Novel and Frozen Metaphors

A developmental study conducted by Pollio and Pollio (1979) indicated that the novelty of a metaphoric expression affects its understandability. They presented a comprehension task involving 17 frozen and 17 novel metaphors to children ages 9 through 14 years old (N = 149). A *frozen metaphor* was defined as one that frequently occurred in the language, whereas a *novel metaphor* rarely occurred. Each metaphor used in the study had been classified as frozen or novel by a panel of adult judges. To assess comprehension, each metaphor was presented within the context of a short paragraph or sentence that was followed by four randomly ordered answer choices. One choice expressed the correct nonliteral meaning of the metaphor, and the others were foils. Children read the test items and circled the best answer choice for each. As predicted, frozen metaphors were easier to comprehend than novel metaphors for all five grade levels. The results also showed a pattern of steady improvement as grade level increased: in fourth grade, accuracy in comprehending the novel and frozen metaphors was 45% and 58%, respectively, but increased to 60% and 80%, respectively, by eighth grade.

Pollio and Pickens (1980) later presented that same comprehension task to additional groups of subjects representing a broader age range. Children ages 8 through 17 years, from Grades 3, 5, 6, 7, 9, and 11 ($N = 180$), participated in the second study. Consistent with the first study (Pollio & Pollio, 1979), frozen metaphors were easier to comprehend than novel, and comprehension of both types of metaphors steadily improved as children got older. Although the two oldest groups approached a ceiling on the task, accuracy in comprehending the novel and frozen metaphors was 88% and 95%, respectively, by Grade 11.

Summary

Studies have shown that students' performance on tasks of metaphor and simile comprehension is related to a number of factors. These include knowledge of semantic features and conceptual domains, the ability to manage syntactic complexities, the presence of linguistic contextual support, the type of response mode employed, novelty versus frozenness of the expressions, and moving versus static visual presentations.

Metaphoric Productions

A number of questions might be asked concerning the production of metaphoric language during the school-age and adolescent years. For example, how often are such expressions produced and under what conditions? Does the frequency of metaphoric productions increase or decrease as children grow older? What types of metaphors are produced during this age range and to what extent are they novel versus frozen?

Formal Tasks

Most research focusing on metaphoric productions in school-age children and adolescents has been conducted using formal elicitation tasks. Pollio and Pollio (1974) studied the development of metaphoric productions in children from Grades 3, 4, and 5, who were ages 8 through 11 years ($N = 174$). In a compositions task, students wrote stories about imaginative topics (e.g., a talking goldfish, adventures in space), and the frequency of novel and frozen metaphors occurring in their stories was analyzed. The results showed that the production of both types of metaphors steadily decreased as grade level increased, and that all three grade levels produced a greater proportion of frozen than of novel metaphors. Pollio and Pollio suggested that during formal writing assignments, elementary school students are increasingly concerned about achieving good grades, and so they are less likely to "rock the boat" by using words in unconventional or nonliteral ways.

However, when Pollio and Pollio (1974) presented a different task to the same students in that study, the results suggested that the capacity for metaphor productions actually increased during the 8-through-11-year age range. The second task required students to make comparisons between different items. Pairs of unrelated words (e.g., *boy—clock*) were presented, and the students were asked to describe how the two items were similar. As before, students' responses were analyzed for the frequency of frozen and novel metaphors. In contrast to the compositions task, the comparisons task showed that for all three grade levels, a greater proportion of novel than frozen metaphors occurred in the responses. The results also showed that the production of both types of metaphors increased with grade level. To study the development of metaphoric productions over a wider age range, Pollio and Pickens (1980) administered a compositions task similar to the one used by Pollio and Pollio (1974) to groups of students ages 8 through 17 years, who were enrolled in Grades 3, 5, 6, 7, 9, and 11 ($N = 180$). Consistent with the previous study (Pollio & Pollio, 1974), a greater proportion of frozen than novel metaphors were produced at each grade level, and both types of metaphors steadily decreased in frequency from third through sixth grades. This reflected the "don't rock the boat" strategy seen earlier with the compositions task. Whereas novel metaphors continued to decrease through eleventh grade, interestingly, the frequency of frozen metaphors sharply increased from seventh to eleventh grades. Pollio and Pickens (1980) suggested that these results were consistent with the view that formal writing tasks tend to discourage unusual uses of words, and that adolescents are even more sensitive to this issue than younger students. The fact that frozen metaphors actually increased during adolescence was simply interpreted to mean that as students got older, they no longer considered the frozen metaphors to be unusual.

Polanski (1989) found that the particular mode of formal writing plays a role in students' spontaneous production of metaphors. In her investigation, students from Grades 4, 8, and 12, and a group of college juniors wrote compositions in three different modes: expressive (descriptive), explanatory (expository), and persuasive. All writing was carried out in natural classroom settings, and students were unaware that their compositions would be analyzed for instances of figurative language. Results indicated that metaphoric productions increased as a function of grade level in all three modes of writing, but that they occurred most often in the expressive mode and least often in the persuasive mode. For example, at Grade 4, 25% of the students produced one or more metaphors in their expressive writing, but only 15% did so in their persuasive writing. By college, 78% did so in their expressive writing, and 52% did so in their persuasive writing. These results indicate that it is important to examine students' production of figurative language in a variety of written modes.

Gardner, Kircher, Winner, and Perkins (1975) employed a sentence-completion task to study spoken metaphoric productions developmentally. Children and adolescents ages 7, 11, 14, and 19 years old (N = 84) were presented with a set of short stories and asked to complete the last sentence in each, as in the following example:

▶ Things don't have to be huge in size to look that way. Look at that boy standing over there. He looks as gigantic as . . . (p. 128)

The responses subsequently were scored as literal, conventional (i.e., frozen), appropriate (i.e., novel), or inappropriate. Results showed that frozen metaphoric productions were the most frequent response at all ages but did not show any developmental changes. Although literal, inappropriate, and novel productions were low at all ages, novel productions did show a slight increase in frequency as subject age increased.

Gardner et al.'s (1975) finding that frozen metaphors were produced more frequently than novel metaphors during a spoken sentence-completion task was consistent with the findings of Pollio and Pollio (1974) and Pollio and Pickens (1980), where students wrote compositions. However, the results of Gardner et al. were inconsistent with those two studies in terms of the developmental patterns for the two types of metaphors. Thus, it is difficult to draw firm conclusions concerning the development of metaphoric productions. More research should be conducted in this area, particularly when students can be observed in both formal and informal situations using spoken and written language.

Informal Tasks

Spontaneous metaphors spoken by preschool children in natural settings were recorded and analyzed in several investigations (e.g., Billow, 1981; Chukovsky, 1968; Winner, 1979; Winner, McCarthy, & Gardner, 1980b; Winner, McCarthy, Kleinman, & Gardner, 1979), and a relatively high frequency of such language was reported. No known investigator has conducted this type of systematic study with school-age children and adolescents. However, Ortony, Turner, and Larson-Shapiro (1985) questioned African-American children from Grades 4, 5, and 6 (N = 319) living in Harlem, New York, about their participation in "sounding," a verbally aggressive street game where insults are exchanged that often contain metaphors and other types of figurative language. Ortony et al. provided the following example of sounding:

LARRY: "Man, you so poor your roaches and rats eat lunch out!"

REGGIE: "Well, you so poor the rats and roaches take you out to lunch!" (p. 26)

Many of the children in the study reported that they often used sounding, which, when executed skillfully, was a mark of status among their peers. The investigators were also interested in the relationship between sounding and the comprehension of figurative language. Therefore, all children were also administered the Reynolds and Ortony (1980) metaphor-simile comprehension task previously described. It was found that those who used sounding more frequently also understood figurative language better than those who used it less often. Consistent with Reynolds and Ortony, performance on the figurative comprehension task improved as children got older, but the frequency of sounding for each grade level was not reported. Thus, it is unknown to what extent developmental changes may occur in children's sounding behavior.

Summary

Research indicates that the capacity to produce metaphors and similes increases during the school-age and adolescent years, but that the actual use of such language is affected by situational factors. Certain formal writing assignments may discourage spontaneous metaphoric productions, especially in younger students, but other types of writing may encourage its use. For example, the frequency of metaphoric productions increases as a function of age when students write in a formal expressive mode. Divergent production tasks (e.g., comparing dissimilar objects) also seems to encourage the use of metaphors as students grow older. Informal encounters with peers tend to encourage spontaneous spoken metaphoric productions in the form of sounding. It would be interesting to examine the extent to which children's capacity for metaphoric productions is related to factors such as leadership, conversational dominance, verbal competence, and other social, cognitive, and linguistic factors.

Acknowledgments

Portions of this chapter appeared in the following publications:

Nippold, M. A. (1985). Comprehension of figurative language in youth. *Topics in Language Disorders, 5*(3), 1–20.
Nippold, M. A. (1988). Figurative language. In M. A. Nippold (Ed.), *Later language development: Ages nine through nineteen* (pp. 179–210). Austin, TX: PRO-ED.

C H A P T E R

IDIOMS AND SLANG TERMS

"Two butterflies are on a daisy in a polo field with poloists bearing down upon a ball at rest beneath them. The caption, a speech of one of the butterflies, connects the language of teenagers incongruously with the situation of pastoral: 'The first one to fly off is chicken.'"

—Redfern (1984, p. 23)

This chapter covers the development of idioms and slang terms during the school-age and adolescent years. *Idioms* are expressions such as "skating on thin ice," "paper over the cracks," and "read between the lines" that can have both a literal and a figurative interpretation, depending on the linguistic context. For example, the literal meaning of "paper over the cracks" comes to mind upon reading, "The interior decorator, in restoring the old house, decided to paper over the cracks," but the figurative meaning is sparked by the sentence, "The mechanic, urged by the dealer to repair the car quickly, decided to paper over the cracks." *Slang* terms such as "five-finger discount" (stolen goods) and "grandma lane" (slow line of traffic) are an informal type of figurative expression used by particular subcultures. Adolescents are especially adept at generating and promoting the use of slang (Chapman, 1988), and each generation seems to have its own unique set of terms. For example, teenagers living in Oregon in the 1990s are fond of the terms "chillin'" (relaxing), "scamming" (observing members of the opposite sex), and "numnuts" (stupid) (Romero, 1994). In contrast, during the 1960s, teenagers in Southern California favored such terms as "bitchin'" (outstanding), "wipe out" (when a person gets knocked off a surfboard or otherwise suffers defeat), and "boss" (excellent, wonderful) (Chapman, 1988) that are now out-of-date.

Whereas idioms commonly occur in both spoken and written forms of language, slang terms are used mainly in spoken contexts and frequently have an off-color status. Idioms have fixed and conventionalized meanings that result from years of repeated use (Ackerman, 1982). Although some slang terms eventually become conventionalized if adopted by the mainstream culture, others drop out of the language or are used mainly by persons of a particular subculture or generation as when baby-boomers continue to say "groovy" and "right-on" (Romero, 1994).

Idioms

Idioms as giant lexical units are an important part of semantic development. Such expressions often occur in the speech of classroom teachers directed toward their students and in textbooks for school-age children and adolescents (Arter, 1976; Hollingsed, 1958; Lazar, Warr-Leeper, Nicholson, & Johnson, 1989; Nippold, 1990). However, research has shown that students' reading comprehension is sometimes hindered by the presence of idioms in written passages (Edwards, 1975; May, 1979). Thus, an understanding of idioms is important for attaining literacy. A growing number of studies have formally examined the development of idiom understanding in school-age children and adolescents. In some of those studies, adults also participated. Collectively, their findings show that idiom understanding begins in early childhood and gradually improves throughout the school-age and adolescent years, and well into adulthood (Ackerman, 1982b; Brasseur & Jimenez, 1989; Brinton, Fujiki, & Mackey, 1985; Cacciari & Levorato, 1989; Douglas & Peel, 1979; Gibbs, 1987, 1991; Levorato & Cacciari, 1992; Lodge & Leach, 1975; Lutzer, 1991; Nippold & Martin, 1989; Nippold & Rudzinski, 1993; Nippold & Taylor, 1995; Nippold, Taylor, & Baker, 1996c; Prinz, 1983; Strand & Fraser, 1979; Thorum, 1980).

In an early investigation, Lodge and Leach (1975) examined the understanding of idioms in students who were ages 6, 9, 12, and 21 (N = 80). The task consisted of 10 idiomatic sentences (e.g., "He kicked the bucket," "He spilled the beans"), each accompanied by four pictures. Two pictures were accurate illustrations—one of the literal meaning and one of the figurative—and two were foils. After each sentence was read aloud by the examiner, the student was asked to point to the pictures that best expressed the two meanings. All groups understood the literal meanings, but the 6- and 9-year-olds had considerable difficulty with the figurative meanings. Although the 12-year-olds understood some of the figurative meanings, only the 21-year-olds had mastered them. Lodge and Leach suggested that younger children lacked a capacity for "semantic duality" and tended to "literalize nearly all inputs" (p. 529).

However, the findings of Lodge and Leach (1975) were questioned by Strand and Fraser (1979), who suggested that the simultaneous presentation of literal and figurative pictures in the earlier study may have been confusing. Therefore, Strand and Fraser designed a task in which comprehension of the literal meanings of idiomatic sentences was assessed separately from comprehension of the figurative meanings. In Strand and Fraser's study, children ages 5, 7, 9, and 11 ($N = 40$) listened to 20 idiomatic sentences, each of which was accompanied by two sets of four pictures—one set for the literal meanings and one set for the figurative meanings. Each set contained one correct illustration and three foils. The literal and figurative comprehension tasks were both administered during one session, with the literal task always following the figurative. For both tasks, the examiner read a sentence and asked the child to choose the one picture that best expressed its meaning. For the figurative task, the child also was asked to explain the meaning of the sentence.

In agreement with Lodge and Leach (1975), Strand and Fraser (1979) found that all groups comprehended the literal meanings of the idioms better than the figurative meanings. However, for the figurative meanings, the results differed markedly in that Strand and Fraser found that even the youngest children in their study understood some of the figurative meanings and that the oldest children understood most of them.

However, it is possible that factors other than presentation style may have contributed to the discrepancy between the findings of these two studies. For example, Strand and Fraser (1979) presented twice as many idioms to the children in their study, and only five of those idioms had also been used by Lodge and Leach (1975). They were "hit the sack," "spill the beans," "face the music," "kick the bucket," and "break the ice." It is noteworthy that those particular idioms were frequently misunderstood at a figurative level by the youngest children in Strand and Fraser's study. In contrast, two idioms that proved easiest for the children had not been used by Lodge and Leach. They were "feeling blue" and "get ripped off." To explain the difficulty of the idioms, Strand and Fraser compared the syntactic structure of the "difficult" and "easy" idioms but found no differences. Therefore, they suggested that ease of understanding may be a function of the extent to which children are exposed to various idioms and find them relevant to their own experiences.

Additional support for the view that individual idioms can vary widely in difficulty was provided by Brinton, Fujiki, and Mackey (1985). In their study, children who were ages 5, 7, 9, and 11 ($N = 20$) were individually administered a task designed to examine their understanding of six different idioms that occurred on Saturday morning cartoons: "hit the ceiling," "got carried away," "now you're cooking," "let the cat out of the bag," "all tied up," and "lend me a hand." Each child was tested individually. For each idiom, the examiner read a short story, accompanied by some pictures. For "got carried away," the story was as follows:

> Mom and Nancy went to the store. Mom said, "Nancy, you may have one candy bar." Nancy got excited and grabbed ten candy bars. "Nancy, that's too many," Mom said. (p. 249)

Following the story, the child was asked to select from among four pictures the one that best illustrated the idiom (e.g., "Show me: Nancy got carried away") (p. 249).

The choices always included one correct figurative interpretation, one literal interpretation, and two additional nonliteral foils.

Results showed that performance steadily improved as subject age increased. For the groups of children ages 5, 7, 9, and 11, respectively, mean accuracy scores of 22%, 44%, 56%, and 62% were obtained. It was also found that idioms varied widely in difficulty. For example, "let the cat out of the bag" and "hit the ceiling" were especially difficult, while "now you're cooking" and "got carried away" were generally quite easy for children.

As with metaphors and similes, research has demonstrated that comprehension of idioms is influenced by the manner in which it is assessed. For example, Prinz (1983) compared the difficulty of idiom comprehension under two conditions—multiple-choice versus explanation. Students who were ages 7, 9, 12, and 15, and a group of adults ($N = 60$) were tested. The same procedures and idiomatic sentences that had been used by Lodge and Leach (1975) served as the multiple-choice task in this investigation. For the explanation task, each subject was simply asked to explain the meanings of the idiomatic sentences. Performance on both tasks steadily improved as subject age increased, but multiple-choice was easier than explanation. For multiple-choice, mean accuracy scores for the 7-, 9-, 12-, 15-year-olds, and adults, respectively, were 10%, 50%, 80%, 90%, and 100%; for explanation, those means were 2%, 20%, 35%, 50%, and 95%, respectively. Thus, the active interpretation of idioms lagged behind their passive understanding for all subject groups except the adults, for whom the tasks were equally easy.

Many questions remain unanswered concerning students' understanding of idioms. For example, in the four studies just described (Brinton et al., 1985; Lodge & Leach, 1975; Prinz, 1983; Strand & Fraser, 1979), idioms were presented with picture cues. However, it is unknown to what extent pictures may enhance students' comprehension of figurative meanings. It is also possible that students respond differently to idioms in contrived testing situations compared to natural settings.

Douglas and Peel (1979) developed a more naturalistic procedure for examining idiom understanding. In their study, children ages 7, 9, 11, and 13 (Grades 1, 3, 5, and 7) ($N = 120$) listened to six different idioms, each presented in a spoken story context (e.g., "Billy was racing his model car. Waiting at the starting line, he was so excited that he 'jumped the gun,'" p. 117). The student was then asked to explain the idiom (e.g., "What does the phrase 'jumped the gun' mean?"). Responses were evaluated for the degree to which literal interpretations (e.g., "Billy stepped over the gun") versus figurative interpretations (e.g., "Billy started too soon") were provided.

Consistent with other studies (Brinton et al., 1985; Lodge & Leach, 1975; Prinz, 1983; Strand & Fraser, 1979), Douglas and Peel (1979) found that idiom understanding steadily improved as subject age increased. Although a full understanding of the idioms was not attained until age 13, even the youngest students, the 7-year-olds, sometimes gave figurative interpretations.

Ackerman (1982b) provided direct support for the importance of context in interpreting idioms, especially for younger children. In Ackerman's study, children ages 6, 8, and 10 years and a group of college students ($N = 96$) listened to a series of simple stories, each of which ended in an idiomatic sentence. Each story had three versions that were biased toward different interpretations of the final sentence—idiomatic, literal, and neutral. The question of interest was the extent to which a student could interpret the figurative meaning of the final sentence in the presence of varying linguistic contexts. For example, one story with its three versions was as follows:

▶ **Idiomatic Context:**

Karen was up in her room doing her homework when she heard her brother Larry talking to their mother. Larry was blaming Karen for something *he* had broken. Karen said, "I'll *fix his wagon*." (p. 444)

▶ **Literal Context:**

Karen was always helping her little brother Larry. This time Larry was crying to their mother over something that had broken. Karen said, "I'll *fix his wagon*." (p. 445)

▶ **Neutral Context:**

Karen was up in her room doing her homework when she heard her brother Larry talking to their mother. Larry was upset over something that was broken. Karen said, "I'll *fix his wagon*." (pp. 444–445)

Following each story, the subject was asked to explain the final sentence (e.g., "What was Karen going to do?"). Results showed that the 6-year-olds had difficulty interpreting the sentences, but that the 8-year-olds could interpret them in the presence of idiomatic contexts. In contrast, both the 10-year-olds and the adults could interpret the sentences not only in the presence of idiomatic contexts but also in the presence of neutral and literal contexts. These findings suggested to Ackerman (1982b) that younger children rely on linguistically biasing contexts to a greater extent than older children when interpreting idioms, and that for older children and adults, "idiom interpretations are relatively fixed and not strongly dependent on contextual support" (p. 450). However, it is important to note that the idioms presented in Ackerman's study were considered to be "common." It is possible that if less common idioms had been presented, the older subjects might have relied on context to a greater extent than they did.

Nippold and Martin (1989) examined idiom interpretation in adolescents. They predicted that idioms presented in context would be easier for adolescents to interpret than idioms presented in isolation. Students who were ages 14, 15, 16, and 17 ($N = 475$) participated. The task consisted of a modified version of the Idioms subtest from the *Fullerton Language Test for Adolescents* (Thorum, 1980). Normally, the Idioms subtest is administered individually and a student is asked to explain to the examiner the meanings of 20 different idioms that are presented out of context (e.g., "take a back seat," "talk shop," "have a chip on one's shoulder"). However, in the Nippold and Martin study, the 20 idioms were presented in written form, and the students were asked to write down an interpretation of each expression. The task was modified in this manner so that a large number of students could be tested quickly. The task was also modified so that half the idioms were presented in isolation (e.g., "What does it mean to 'take a back seat?'"), and half were presented within two-sentence story contexts where the idiom was the last phrase in the second sentence (e.g., "Billy often gets into fights with other kids at school. His mother says he 'has a chip on his shoulder.' What does it mean to 'have a chip on one's shoulder'?"). Care was taken to ensure that the idioms assigned to the two conditions, isolation and context, were balanced for difficulty. In writing the stories, familiar situations were depicted, and simple vocabulary and syntax were used so that idiom understanding would not be hampered by reading complexities.

Results showed that idioms in context were easier for adolescents to interpret than idioms in isolation. For all students combined, the mean accuracy score was 60% for idioms in isolation and 69% for idioms in context. Although the context effect was small, greater benefits might have accrued had the idioms been presented within larger contextual units (e.g., paragraphs). The study also showed that performance under both presentation modes improved as subject age increased. Mean accuracy scores obtained by the 14-, 15-, 16-, and 17-year-olds, respectively, were 54%, 57%, 63%, and 67% for idioms in isolation, and 65%, 68%, 72%, and 72% for idioms in context. Thus, although accuracy of idiom interpretation slowly improved as subject age increased, even the oldest students had not completely mastered the task in either presentation mode. These results were consistent with Prinz (1983) in showing quantitative improvement but non-mastery of idiom interpretation during adolescence. However, they were inconsistent with Douglas and Peel (1979) who reported mastery by the age of 13. This discrepancy may be due, in part, to the fact that different sets of idioms were employed in the different studies.

Also in the Nippold and Martin (1989) study, results of the *National Educational Development Tests* (1984) were available for 89% of the 16-year-olds. This is a group-administered, standardized test of academic achievement that contains three subtests that measure literacy: English Usage, Natural Sciences Reading, and Social Studies Reading. Significant correlations were obtained between the idiom interpretation task and each of the subtests. Similar findings have been made by other researchers. For example, Edwards (1975) reported that eighth-grade students (ages 13 through 14), who had obtained high intelligence test scores, showed better comprehension of written passages of text containing idioms than their classmates who had obtained lower intelligence scores.

To examine growth in idiom explanation during adulthood, Brasseur and Jimenez

(1989) presented the Idioms subtest from the *Fullerton Language Test for Adolescents* (Thorum, 1980) to college students from three different age groups: 18 through 21, 22 through 29, and 30 through 43 years ($N = 71$). Each of the 20 idioms was presented in isolation, in keeping with the standardized testing procedures. However, as in the Nippold and Martin (1989) study, students wrote down their explanations of the idioms, rather than explaining them orally. Responses were scored as correct or incorrect using guidelines provided in the test manual.

Performance improved as subject age increased, and mean accuracy scores of 60%, 73%, and 83% were obtained by the three groups, respectively. In considering these results in relation to those of Nippold and Martin (1989), it becomes apparent that idiom explanation continues to improve throughout adolescence and well into adulthood. It is interesting, however, that the two oldest groups of adolescents (ages 16 and 17) in the Nippold and Martin study obtained slightly higher accuracy scores on idioms in isolation than did the youngest group of adults (ages 18-21) in the Brasseur and Jimenez (1989) study. Given the similarities in testing procedures employed in the two studies, differences in the subjects who participated in the two studies might help to explain this discrepancy. For example, frequency of exposure to idioms is an important factor related to their understanding (Nippold & Rudzinski, 1993; Nippold & Taylor, 1995; Nippold, et al., 1996c). Perhaps the young adults in the Brasseur and Jimenez study were less familiar with the idioms than the adolescents in the Nippold and Martin study.

It is often assumed that there is little relationship between the literal and the figurative meanings of an idiom, and that knowing the literal meaning is not very helpful in learning the figurative meaning (Ortony, Schallert, Reynolds, & Antos, 1978). This view has led several investigators to hypothesize that people learn idioms as giant lexical units rather than by analyzing their constituents (e.g., Ackerman, 1982b; Hoffman & Honeck, 1980; Strand & Fraser, 1979). However, Gibbs (1987, 1991) distinguished two types of idioms: *opaque* and *transparent*. With the opaque type (e.g., "beat around the bush," "shoot the breeze," "spill the beans"), there is little relationship between the literal and the figurative meanings. However, with the transparent type (e.g., "hold your tongues," "skating on thin ice," "keep a straight face"), the figurative meaning is actually an extension of the literal meaning. For example, "skating on thin ice" implies a precarious situation literally and figuratively. Gibbs therefore hypothesized that transparent idioms would be easier for children to analyze and interpret than opaque idioms.

In a developmental study of children ages 5, 6, 8, and 9 ($N = 80$), Gibbs (1987) examined the effects of context on the interpretation of idioms while comparing the difficulty of opaque and transparent idioms. He also compared the difficulty of two response modes, explanation and multiple-choice. Ten opaque and 10 transparent idioms were presented. Half the children in each age group received the idioms in context, while the other half received them in isolation. In the context condition, each idiom served as the final sentence of an idiomatically biasing story. The examiner read each story aloud, and then asked the child to explain the final sentence. Following the explanation, the child was asked to choose the best interpretation of the idiom from two alternatives. Examples of test items used in the study are as follows:

▶ **Opaque Idiom:**

When Betty got home from school early for disrupting the class, she knew that her mother would be angry. When her mother asked her why she was home so early, Betty started to ask her mother what was for dinner that night. Finally her mother said, "Stop beating around the bush." (p. 585)

Explanation Question:

What did Betty's mother mean when she said, "Stop beating around the bush"? (p. 586)

Forced-Choice Questions:

1. Did she want Betty to stop avoiding the question? (yes)
2. Did she want Betty to stop hurting the plants? (no) (p. 586)

▶ **Transparent Idiom:**

Jim and Tina got into a big argument out on the playground over whose turn it was to get on the swing. When the teacher came over to see what the problem was, Jim and Tina shouted their complaints at her at the same time. The teacher said, "Hold your tongues." (p. 585)

Explanation Question:

What did the teacher mean when she said, "Hold your tongues"? (p. 585)

Forced-Choice Questions:

1. Did she want them to grab their tongues? (no)
2. Did she want them to be quiet? (yes) (p. 585)

In the isolation condition, the child was asked to explain each idiomatic sentence without hearing the story and then to choose the best interpretation of the sentence from two alternatives.

Results showed that idioms in context were easier to understand than idioms in isolation; that transparent idioms were easier than opaque, particularly during the explanation task when context was present; and that the multiple-choice task was easier than the explanation task. It was also found that performance on both the explanation and multiple-choice tasks steadily improved as subject age increased but that not even the oldest children knew all of the idioms. The results were consistent with other studies of figurative language development (e.g., Nippold, Martin, & Erskine, 1988; Prinz, 1983; Winner, Engel, & Gardner, 1980; Winner, Rosenstiel, & Gardner, 1976) in showing that multiple-choice tasks are easier than explanation tasks, and that contextually supportive information facilitates children's understanding of figurative expressions. The finding that transparent idioms were easier to explain than opaque added an exciting dimension to the literature on children's understanding of idioms. Prior to Gibbs' (1987) study, the common assumption that there is little relationship between the literal and the figurative meanings of idioms had not been questioned.

Given that the oldest children in Gibbs' (1987) study were only 9 years old, it was unknown if transparency would affect idiom understanding in older children and adolescents. The extent to which the familiarity of an idiom might affect its ease of understanding was also unknown. To examine the role of transparency and familiarity on idiom understanding in youth, Nippold and Rudzinski (1993) designed a task that contained 24 different idioms representing three levels of familiarity—high, moderate, and low—with eight expressions for each level. Each idiom also had a transparency rating that ranged from high to low.

The familiarity and transparency ratings of the idioms had been determined during a separate experiment in which adolescents ($N = 20$) and adults ($N = 20$) were presented with a list of 100 idioms in random order. First, they performed a familiarity rating task where they were asked to use a 5-point Likert scale to indicate how often they had heard or read each idiom before (1 = many times; 5 = never). Next, they performed a transparency rating task where they were asked to indicate how closely the literal and nonliteral meanings of each idiom compared using a 3-point Likert scale (1 = closely related; 3 = not related). For the transparency rating task, each expression was accompanied by a brief explanation of its literal and nonliteral meanings. This was to ensure that all students interpreted the idioms similarly. The results showed that the adolescents rated the expressions as less familiar but more transparent than did the adults. Given these differences between groups, only the ratings of the adolescents were used in selecting idioms for the main experiment in the Nippold and Rudzinski (1993) study. The entire set of ratings for all 100 idioms from both groups is reported in Appendix 8.1. These ratings may be useful to other researchers in figurative language.

After the 24 idioms had been selected based on their familiarity and transparency ratings, an idiom explanation task was written. This task was presented to additional groups of students who were ages 11, 14, and 17 ($N = 150$). Each idiom occurred in a brief, written story. Students read the stories silently and provided written explanations of the idioms. An example of a problem on the task was as follows:

▶ Rick was working on his chemistry report one evening. The next day, the teacher asked for the report. Rick told the teacher that his little brother had thrown it into the fireplace.

The teacher said, "That 'has a hollow ring.'"

What does it mean to 'have a hollow ring'? (p. 737)

The results showed that performance on the task steadily improved with each successive age group. For the 11-, 14-, and 17-year-olds, respectively, overall mean accuracy scores of 50%, 68%, and 75% were obtained. It was also found that idiom familiarity and transparency affected students' performance: idioms that were higher in familiarity and transparency were generally easier to understand than those that were lower in those two factors. The results concerning familiarity were consistent with the *language experience hypothesis*, the view that the development of figurative language depends to a large extent upon the amount of meaningful exposure one has to such expressions (Ortony, Turner, & Larson-Shapiro, 1985). Moreover, the results concerning transparency were consistent with the *metasemantic hypothesis*, the view that in addition to exposure, figurative understanding develops as the learner applies a metalinguistic strategy of attempting to infer the nonliteral meaning of an expression from the literal meaning of the words comprising it. This view contrasts with the hypothesis that idioms are learned as giant lexical units (Ackerman, 1982b; Hoffman & Honeck, 1980; Strand & Fraser, 1979). Nippold and Rudzinski (1993) concluded that "although opaque idioms may be learned in this more holistic manner, transparent idioms seem to be learned through a more dissecting strategy" (p. 736). Thus it appears that young people may employ different strategies as they attempt to learn the meanings of different idioms.

In a subsequent study, Nippold and Taylor (1995) presented the same set of 24 idioms and story contexts that had been used in the Nippold and Rudzinski (1993) study to additional groups of students who were ages 11, 14, and 17 ($N = 150$). This time, however, students responded through a multiple-choice mode rather than an explanation mode. As in the previous study, performance on the task increased with each successive age group, and the factors of familiarity and transparency played a key role in the students' ability to understand the expressions. In comparing the performance of the students in the two studies, it was found that the multiple-choice response mode was easier than the explanation mode at each of the three age levels. This result was consistent with other studies of idiom understanding (e.g., Ackerman, 1982b; Gibbs, 1987, 1991; Prinz, 1983).

Although the factors of familiarity and transparency both play a critical role in the development of idiom understanding, it is important to note that both factors are inherently relative and, like many aspects of the lexicon (Crystal, 1988), are constantly undergoing change. This is reflected in the fact that adults, having lived longer and having had more life experiences, generally show greater familiarity with idioms than do adolescents (Nippold & Rudzinski, 1993). Moreover, certain idioms that may be highly transparent to adults may be uninterpretable to young people because of different life experiences. For example, children born during the 1980s and 1990s, raised in the era of CDs, Walkmen, and working mothers, may be baffled by sentences such as "Jim's a 'broken record,'" or "Mrs. Jones 'wears the pants' in that family."

Summary

Developmental studies have shown that the understanding of idioms gradually improves during the school-age and adolescent years, but even in adulthood certain idioms may cause confusion. It is clear that individual idioms vary greatly in their ease of understanding. For example, low-frequency idioms whose literal and nonliteral meanings have little overlap can be expected to cause difficulty for children, adolescents, and adults. In contrast, idioms that are common and transparent may be well understood even by very young children.

As with metaphors and similes, the understanding of idioms is also influenced by certain task factors. For example, idioms presented in isolation are more difficult than those presented in supportive linguistic contexts, and tasks requiring students to explain the figurative meanings of idioms are more difficult than multiple-choice tasks where students can choose an appropriate interpretation or simply point to a picture that best illustrates the meaning. Explanation tasks therefore tend to underestimate a child's passive understanding of idioms. However, they do provide insight into qualitative changes that occur as children grow older, and indicate, for example, that concrete and literal interpretations decline as abstract interpretations increase. It has also been shown that students with higher literacy skills and cognitive levels demonstrate greater understanding of idioms than their peers with average or below-average abilities.

Future Research

Much remains to be learned concerning children's competence with idioms. For example, it is unknown to what extent the understanding of idioms that occur in natural settings (e.g., listening to parents talk about sports or politics) differs from that which occurs in contrived testing situations. In addition, little is known about the development of children's ability to spontaneously produce appropriate idioms in natural settings. Another topic for future research suggested by Gibbs (1987) is the comprehension of "ambiguous idioms," expressions such as "give a hand" that have two distinct figurative meanings (i.e., to applaud or to assist another person). It would be interesting to compare children's understanding of ambiguous idioms with other types of ambiguities such as jokes and riddles (see Chapter 10).

Slang Terms

The use of slang terms unique to the peer group is an important aspect of later language development, particularly during adolescence (Donahue & Bryan, 1984; Hyde,

1982; Leona, 1978; Lewis, 1963; Nelsen & Rosenbaum, 1972; Schwartz & Merten, 1967). People use slang terms for a variety of reasons. These include the desire to promote social interaction, to show that one belongs to a group, to exclude others from the group, to be playful, and to reduce the seriousness of a situation (Crystal, 1987).

Slang terms used by adolescents often occur in the form of metaphors. Leona (1978) studied adolescents at a high school near Boston, Massachusetts, and reported that the general student population had special names for members of various cliques. These cliques included "jocks," who were actively involved in sports; "motorheads," who spent most of their time driving or repairing their cars; and "fleabags," who used drugs and had a countercultural lifestyle. In addition, each clique had its own slang terms that served to distinguish it from outsiders. For examples, jocks had special names for other athletes (e.g., "The Jumping Machine," "Speedy," "East to West"), motorheads had names for particular cars (e.g., "Bondo," "Six-Pack," "Goat"), and fleabags had names for drugs (e.g., "joints," "bones," "j's"). Although slang terms are frequently associated with illiterate and, in some cases, illegal activities, the ability to create and to use such terms appropriately in varied situations requires a high level of verbal sophistication.

Little is known about developmental changes that may occur in the spontaneous use of slang terms by older children and adolescents. However, Nelsen and Rosenbaum (1972) indirectly examined this issue in a study where boys and girls ($N = 1916$) from Grades 7 through 12 (ages 12 through 18) were compared in their ability to generate lists of slang terms used by their peers when talking about various topics. Nine different topics were presented, one at a time, which included money, cigarettes and smoking, autos and motorbikes, alcohol and drinking, clothing and appearance, boys, girls, popular people, and unpopular people. Students worked in groups of four persons of the same gender and grade level. Each group was allowed five minutes per topic to generate as many slang terms as possible.

Results showed that boys generated more slang terms than girls for the topics of money, and autos and motorbikes, but that girls outperformed boys on the topics of clothing and appearance, boys, popular people, and unpopular people. The results also showed that the mean number of slang terms steadily increased as a function of grade level, and that larger increases were seen for some topics than for others. For example, seventh-grade boys generated a mean of 10.4 terms for the topic of girls, whereas twelfth-grade boys generated a mean of 24.4 terms for that same topic. Other topics showing large increases for boys included autos and motorbikes, and alcohol and drinking. Topics showing large increases for girls included unpopular people, alcohol and drinking, and girls.

Future Research

Although Nelsen and Rosenbaum (1972) showed that older adolescents knew more slang terms than younger ones, this did not prove that the older adolescents actually used more slang terms than the younger ones. Thus, it would be interesting to examine the frequency with which slang terms are actually used by adolescents of different ages. To accomplish this, instead of asking adolescents to generate lists of slang terms, an indirect approach might be employed where adolescents in small groups are asked to discuss among themselves various topics of interest (e.g., "What do clothes tell you about another person?," "What makes a boy or a girl popular? Unpopular? Why?"). As the students are talking, tape recordings could be made so that the spontaneous usage of slang terms could later be analyzed. Adolescents of different ages (e.g., 13, 15, 17, and 19 years old) should be studied in this manner in order to observe developmental changes. It would also be important to study adolescents' use of slang terms in many different settings and with persons of different ages, genders, and levels of status.

Another interesting aspect of slang is that such terms can have multiple non-literal meanings, often signaled by subtle variations in vocal stress, pitch, and intonation, and by nonlinguistic contextual factors. For example, the ever-popular term "awesome" can serve as a sincere comment about the excellence of persons or events (e.g., "We have an 'awesome' basketball team," spoken after winning the state championship). However, it can also be used sarcastically to deflate another's ego (e.g., "Jim's an 'awesome' athlete," in reference to the weakest player on a team) (see Chapter 10). Little is known about the ability of older children and adolescents to use and understand the multiple nonliteral meanings of slang terms. Hence, this would also be an interesting and worthwhile topic for future research.

Appendix 8.1
Mean Familiarity and Transparency
Ratings for 100 Idioms*

	Familiarity		Transparency	
	Adolescents	Adults	Adolescents	Adults
1. Beat around the bush	1.30	1.15	2.40	2.85
2. Bet one's bottom dollar	1.90	1.90	1.50	2.30
3. Blow off some steam	1.30	1.40	1.85	1.55
4. Blow one's own horn	2.00	1.55	2.25	2.85
5. Blow the cobwebs away	2.80	3.15	2.15	2.55
6. Blow the lid off	2.35	2.10	2.25	2.60
7. Breathe down one's neck	1.50	1.55	1.95	2.05
8. Bring home the bacon	1.35	1.30	2.10	2.20
9. Bring the house down	2.05	1.70	2.30	2.85
10. Cast the first stone	2.65	1.55	1.55	1.70
11. Comes home to roost	2.70	2.85	2.60	2.80
12. Cross swords with someone	3.10	3.35	1.85	2.20
13. Cut down to size	1.90	1.80	2.25	2.60
14. Draw a long breath	2.90	3.55	1.45	1.05
15. Get away with murder	1.60	1.05	1.55	1.50
16. Get off the ground	2.50	2.00	2.20	2.20
17. Get off the hook	2.00	2.05	1.70	1.85
18. Get the ball rolling	1.95	1.80	1.75	2.15
19. Get the lead out	1.85	1.80	2.75	2.90
20. Gets in one's hair	2.10	1.75	2.05	2.65
21. Gets under one's skin	1.70	1.55	2.15	2.05
22. Give someone enough rope	3.25	2.95	1.85	2.25
23. Give up the ship	3.20	3.30	1.95	1.95
24. Go against the grain	2.60	1.50	2.50	2.65
25. Go around in circles	1.45	1.35	2.05	2.15
26. Go by the board	3.75	4.10	2.70	3.00
27. Go by the book	1.60	1.30	1.15	1.15
28. Go into one's shell	3.05	2.45	1.70	1.70
29. Go through the mill	3.60	3.10	2.60	2.55
30. Go through the motions	2.35	1.70	1.90	1.65
31. Go through the roof	1.75	2.30	2.15	2.70
32. Go to the dogs	2.75	2.55	2.55	3.00
33. Hang by a thread	1.60	1.70	1.60	2.05
34. Hang on one's coat-tails	3.45	2.80	2.35	2.50
35. Haul over the coals	3.45	3.00	2.20	2.35
36. Have a hollow ring	4.00	3.55	2.40	2.60
37. Have a soft spot	1.95	1.25	2.05	2.65

(continues)

Appendix 8.1. *Continued*

	Familiarity		Transparency	
	Adolescents	Adults	Adolescents	Adults
38. Hit below the belt	1.70	1.45	2.05	2.40
39. Hoe one's own row	4.35	3.55	2.65	2.45
40. Hold one's head up	1.95	1.45	1.80	1.85
41. Jump through a hoop	3.30	2.05	2.30	2.65
42. Keep one's chin up	1.45	1.30	1.75	2.05
43. Keep one's nose clean	1.70	1.90	2.30	2.90
44. Keep one's shirt on	1.60	1.65	2.35	2.80
45. Keep the pot boiling	3.40	3.75	2.00	2.20
46. Keep under one's hat	2.35	2.10	1.60	1.80
47. Keep up one's end	2.75	2.20	1.85	1.60
48. Kick up one's heels	1.95	1.55	2.20	2.20
49. Lay at one's door	3.75	3.80	2.35	2.65
50. Lead with one's chin	4.15	3.75	2.65	2.95
51. Leave the door open	2.25	2.30	2.35	2.40
52. Let one's hair down	1.80	1.20	2.00	2.45
53. Make one's hair curl	2.60	2.10	2.45	2.90
54. Make the fur fly	3.60	3.30	2.35	2.45
55. Paddle one's own canoe	3.45	3.35	1.65	1.75
56. Paint the town red	2.00	1.50	2.50	3.00
57. Paper over the cracks	4.25	4.30	2.00	1.80
58. Pick up the threads	3.70	3.40	2.60	2.80
59. Play one's cards well	2.20	1.85	1.90	2.00
60. Pull in one's belt	3.55	3.60	2.15	2.75
61. Pull up one's socks	3.95	4.20	2.80	2.95
62. Put one's foot down	1.20	1.10	2.10	2.75
63. Put their heads together	1.45	1.35	2.05	2.10
64. Put up the shutters	3.60	4.35	2.50	2.30
65. Read between the lines	1.15	1.35	2.20	2.40
66. Remain in the saddle	3.40	3.45	1.95	2.15
67. Rise to the bait	4.05	3.55	2.30	2.35
68. Roll up one's sleeves	2.55	2.00	1.84	2.25
69. Run circles around someone	1.65	1.80	2.55	2.85
70. Run out of steam	2.05	1.35	1.35	1.40
71. Sail against the wind	2.40	2.70	1.95	1.80
72. See beyond one's nose	3.30	2.95	1.90	2.00
73. Shake in one's shoes	1.75	1.70	1.90	2.00
74. Shoot from the hip	2.45	2.20	2.00	2.35
75. Sing a different tune	2.35	1.75	1.95	1.85
76. Sing for one's supper	3.75	2.45	2.10	2.25
77. Sit on one's hands	3.35	2.90	2.40	2.50
78. Skating on thin ice	1.30	1.30	1.35	1.55

(continues)

Appendix 8.1. *Continued*

	Familiarity		Transparency	
	Adolescents	Adults	Adolescents	Adults
79. Slip through one's fingers	1.85	1.80	2.05	2.45
80. Spread it on thick	1.75	1.85	2.25	2.65
81. Step into one's shoes	2.15	2.10	1.95	2.45
82. Strike the right note	2.95	2.25	1.95	1.90
83. Swear black is white	3.95	3.75	1.45	1.50
84. Swim against the tide	2.40	2.05	1.70	1.90
85. Take a back seat	2.50	1.95	2.40	2.75
86. Take a long view	3.30	3.45	1.85	1.90
87. Take down a peg	4.30	3.30	2.60	2.70
88. Take for a ride	2.30	1.90	2.65	2.90
89. Take under one's wing	2.20	1.55	1.55	1.70
90. Talk the same language	2.20	2.20	1.85	1.80
91. Talk through one's hat	4.70	3.70	2.70	2.80
92. Throw out of gear	3.20	3.65	2.25	2.50
93. Throw to the wolves	2.65	2.15	1.50	1.75
94. Turn back the clock	1.75	1.50	1.75	1.85
95. Turn the other cheek	1.35	1.20	1.95	1.90
96. Vote with one's feet	4.55	4.35	2.65	2.80
97. Walk the chalk line	3.30	4.35	2.20	2.60
98. Wave a white flag	2.50	2.35	2.20	2.20
99. Whistle in the dark	3.70	3.65	2.30	2.75
100. Wither on the vine	3.65	3.20	2.15	2.05
Mean (M)	2.60	2.38	2.09	2.29
Standard Deviation (SD)	.91	.94	.36	.46
Range	1.15–4.70	1.05–4.35	1.15–2.80	1.05–3.00

Note. Some of the data are from "Familiarity and Transparency in Idiom Explanation: A Developmental Study of Children and Adolescents," by Marilyn A. Nippold and Mishelle Rudzinski, 1993, *Journal of Speech and Hearing Research, 36*, p. 733. Copyright 1993 by the American Speech-Language-Hearing Association. Adapted with permission.

Familiarity is a measure of how often one has heard or read the idiom before:
1 = many times; 2 = several times; 3 = a few times; 4 = once; 5 = never.

Transparency is a measure of how closely the literal and nonliteral meanings of the idiom compare:
1 = closely related; 2 = somewhat related; 3 = not related.

Acknowledgments

Portions of this chapter appeared in the following publications:

Nippold, M. A. (1985). Comprehension of figurative language in youth. *Topics in Language Disorders, 5*(3), 1–20.

Nippold, M. A. (1988). Figurative language. In M. A. Nippold (Ed.), *Later language development: Ages nine through nineteen* (pp. 179–210). Austin, TX: PRO-ED.

Nippold, M. (1993). Developmental markers in adolescent language: Syntax, semantics, and pragmatics. *Language, Speech, and Hearing Services in Schools, 24*, 21–28.

Nippold, M. A. & Rudzinski, M. (1993). Familiarity and transparency in idiom explanation: A developmental study of children and adolescents. *Journal of Speech and Hearing Research, 36*, 728–737.

Used with permission of Aspen Publishers, PRO-ED, and the American Speech-Language-Hearing Association.

C H A P T E R

PROVERBS AND FABLES

"Hold fast to the words of your ancestors."

—Anonymous

Proverbs are statements that express the collective values, beliefs, and wisdom of a society (Hirsch, Kett, & Trefil, 1988; Mieder, 1993; Ridout & Witting, 1967). As such, they serve a variety of communicative functions. For example, proverbs are used to offer encouragement ("Every cloud has a silver lining") or advice ("Don't count your chickens before they're hatched"), warn a person of danger ("When a wolf shows his teeth, he isn't laughing"), or comment on events ("When the cat's away, the mice will play"). Some proverbs may offer contradictory messages, as in the case of "Too many cooks spoil the broth" compared with "Many hands make light work" (Hirsch et al., 1988, p. 46). However, this confusion is easily resolved upon realizing the important role that context plays in the interpretation of proverbs. In different situations, each proverb may be perfectly appropriate. When proverbs are used apart from communicative contexts, their meanings may be unclear or only partially understood.

Exposure to proverbs is an important part of cultural literacy (Hirsch et al., 1988). Proverbs often occur in the context of fables such as those of Aesop (620–560 B.C.), the Greek storyteller. *Fables* are short and imaginative stories that conclude with a proverbial statement or moral. Animals that talk and otherwise act like people are usually the main characters, but the intent of the story is to provide insight into human behavior and to offer an important lesson about life (Welch & Bennett, 1981). Children often encounter proverbs as preschoolers when their parents read fables to them, and later when they can read themselves. Beginning in elementary school,

A hare jeered at a tortoise for the slowness of his pace. But the tortoise laughed and said that he would run against her and beat her any day she should name. "Come on," said the hare, "you shall soon see what my feet are made of." So it was agreed that they should start at once. The tortoise went off jogging along, without a moment's stopping, at his usual steady pace. The hare, treating the whole matter very lightly, said she would first take a little nap, and that she should soon overtake the tortoise. Meanwhile, the tortoise plodded on, and the hare oversleeping herself, arrived at the goal, only to see that the tortoise had got in before her. *Slow and steady wins the race.*

Figure 9.1. Aesop's fable, "The Hare and the Tortoise."

children read fables and are encouraged to abstract the meaning of the proverb by attending to the story. For example, in an elementary literature textbook (Welch & Bennett, 1981), students were assigned to read Aesop's fable, "The Hare and the Tortoise" (see Figure 9.1), and then they were asked to explain the meaning of the concluding proverb, "Slow and steady wins the race." They were also asked to explain how the lesson taught by the fable could be useful today. This assignment illustrates how a child's skill at comprehending a story plays a major role in determining how well a proverb will be interpreted and applied to daily situations.

Are Proverbs Difficult to Understand?

Although children are exposed to proverbs at a young age, some reports have indicated that these expressions may be more difficult for them to understand than other types of figurative expressions such as metaphors, similes, and idioms (Billow, 1975; Douglas & Peel, 1979). In fact, some researchers have argued that children have little or no understanding of proverbs before adolescence (Billow, 1975; Douglas & Peel, 1979; Gorham, 1956; Holden, 1978; Lutzer, 1988; Piaget, 1926; Richardson & Church, 1959; Watts, 1944). However, as discussed in this chapter, that position is not supported by clear and convincing evidence.

In those studies, children typically were presented with lists of proverbs out of context and were then asked to explain their meanings. For example, Richardson and Church (1959) read seven different proverbs to children ages 7 through 12 years ($N = 64$) and wrote down their explanations. They also tested adolescents and adults ($N = 30$) in this manner for purposes of comparison. Examples of proverbs used in their study were, "You can't teach an old dog new tricks," "Every cloud has a silver lining," and "All that glitters is not gold." Their results showed that explanations of the younger children were primarily literal and situationally specific. For example, an 8-year-old explained the "dog" proverb by saying, "Well, there's an old dog, and you're trying to get him to sit up or something, and he won't sit up for you." Moreover, a 9-year-old explained the "cloud" proverb by saying, "Maybe it's a man that has a silver lining in his coat." Although explanations gradually became more general and figurative as children got older (e.g., "It means it's futile to try to change old habits" for the "dog" proverb), the 12-year-olds still had difficulty with many of the proverbs, and even the adolescents and adults sometimes offered immature explanations.

Similar findings were reported by Watts (1944), who examined proverb understanding in children ages 11 through 14 years. Watts, however, constructed a multiple-choice task in which children read a list of proverbs (e.g., "Empty vessels make the most sound") followed by four alternative interpretations. The choices always included one correct figurative interpretation (e.g., "The people who talk most are often the most ignorant") and three foils. Although accuracy improved with the child's age, not even the oldest children had mastered the task.

Gorham (1956) developed a multiple-choice task very similar to Watts' (1944), which included 40 proverbs, each followed by four alternative interpretations. The task was administered to students at every level from fifth grade through the senior year of college ($N = 651$). The results of the study showed a low level of understanding for the youngest students but steady improvement with increasing grade level: mean accuracy scores ranged from 33% for the fifth graders to 81% for the college seniors. Holden (1978) later administered Gorham's task to students in Grades 5, 7, and 9 (ages 10 through 15; $N = 79$) and obtained similar results for those three grade levels: 28%, 47%, and 55% accuracy, respectively.

Factors That May Affect the Difficulty of Proverbs

Before embracing the conclusion that proverb understanding is limited before adolescence, it is important to consider certain factors that may have confounded the difficulty of the tasks just described. First, asking children to explain proverbs is a metalinguistic task that may underestimate their level of understanding. Children have some understanding of other types of figurative language several years before they can fully explain those meanings (Ackerman, 1982b; Dent, 1984; Gardner, 1974; Winner, Engel, & Gardner, 1980; Winner, Rosenstiel, & Gardner, 1976). This also may be true of proverbs.

Another factor to consider is that although the multiple-choice tasks developed by Watts (1944) and Gorham (1956) avoided this metalinguistic issue, they may have been confusing to the students because the foils often included at least one alternative that was literally correct. For example, in Gorham's task, the proverb "Rome was not built in a day" was followed by the literal alternative, "It took a number of years," in addition to the figurative alternative, "Great things come about slowly." However, at no point did either task specify clearly that nonliteral interpretations were expected of the students.

Proverb Understanding in Young Children

Evidence in conflict with the view that young children are unable to understand proverbs was provided by Honeck, Sowry, and Voegtle (1978), who questioned the validity of examining children's proverb comprehension through explanation tasks. Noting that children often display discrepancies between their comprehension and production of language, those investigators designed a task whereby children could point to pictures to indicate their understanding of proverbs. Honeck et al. were also concerned with confounding factors related to the proverbs themselves, such as syntactic and semantic complexity. Therefore, they developed a list of 10 proverbs that had relatively simple syntactic structure and whose content words were familiar to young children. An example of such a proverb was, "Bees give honey from their mouths and stings from their tails," which could be translated as, "A thing can be both good and bad at the same time." For each proverb, two pictures were provided, one illustrating the correct figurative interpretation and the other illustrating an incorrect interpretation (foil). Neither picture contained items that represented the literal meanings of the words in the proverbs. For example, the "bee" proverb was correctly illustrated by a girl roasting a hot dog over a camp fire while the fire was burning her slacks. The foil showed another girl opening a present as a ball was about to strike her.

Children from three age groups, 7, 8, and 9 years ($N = 60$), participated in the study. In presenting the task, the examiner first showed the child the two pictures and told the child to study them carefully. Ten seconds later, the examiner read the corresponding proverb and asked the child to point to the picture that meant the same thing. Practice trials were given prior to the test items to ensure that the child understood the procedures. The findings indicated above-chance performance for all three age groups but no differences as a function of age. Overall accuracy for the three groups combined was 68%.

Although task demands were carefully controlled by Honeck et al. (1978), it is noteworthy that not even the 9-year-olds showed evidence of having mastered the proverbs, a result left unexplained by the authors. This is an important finding and suggests that the gradual improvement in proverb understanding during adolescence that has been observed in other studies (Billow, 1975; Douglas & Peel, 1979; Gorham, 1956; Holden, 1978; Piaget, 1926; Richardson & Church, 1959; Watts, 1944) may not be due entirely to an increasing ability to deal with confounding factors. However, this point does not detract from the importance of this study in providing evidence of proverb understanding in children of an age range that other researchers either had not examined or for which they had found mostly literal interpretations.

Resnick (1982) also documented proverb understanding in younger children. In his investigation, students from Grades 3 through 7 (ages 8 through 13 years; $N = 438$) were presented with 10 different proverbs that contained simple vocabulary and depicted familiar situations (e.g., "If you cut down the forest, you will catch the wolf,"

"Don't plant thorns if you walk barefoot"). Understanding of each proverb was assessed using three different multiple-choice tasks, "Story Matching," "Proverb Matching," and "Paraphrase." For Story Matching, a short story followed by four different proverbs was presented, and the child was asked to choose the proverb that best completed the story. For Proverb Matching, the child chose a proverb that had the same meaning as the target proverb. For Paraphrase, each proverb was followed by four different interpretations from which to choose. Each child also was administered an analogies task as a measure of general intelligence. This task consisted of 10 analogy problems from the Cognitive Abilities Test (Thorndike & Hagen, 1971).

Results showed that Story Matching was the easiest task, that Paraphrase was the most difficult, and that Proverb Matching was intermediate in difficulty. Resnick (1982) suggested that Story Matching was easiest because the stories provided contextual support for the proverbs. It was also shown that even the youngest children performed above the level of chance and that proverb understanding steadily improved with increasing grade level. Combining the three different proverbs tasks, mean accuracy scores obtained by the students in Grades 3, 4, 5, 6, and 7, respectively, were 45%, 58%, 65%, 74%, and 89%. Correlation coefficients were calculated between the analogies task and each of the three proverbs tasks for the subjects as a whole. All were significant and indicated moderately strong relationships. Resnick concluded that intelligence plays an important role in proverb understanding, but that a student's grade level is an even more important factor.

Proverbs Compared to Other Types of Figurative Language

Another approach to studying the development of proverb understanding has been to compare the difficulty of proverbs with other types of figurative language. For example, in the Douglas and Peel (1979) study of idiom understanding described in Chapter 8, the same children from Grades 1, 3, 5, and 7 were also asked to explain six different proverbs presented within brief story contexts (e.g., "The teacher said, 'You can go to recess after the test, because sweet is pleasure after pain'"). The results indicated that, although proverb explanations steadily improved with increasing grade level, they were consistently more literal than idiom explanations at all four grade levels.

As another example, Billow (1975) compared children's understanding of proverbs and metaphors. In his investigation, 9-, 11-, and 13-year-olds were asked to explain the meanings of 12 proverbs (e.g., "There is many a slip between cup and lip") and 24 metaphors (e.g., "Hair is spaghetti"). The results of the study showed that proverbs were considerably more difficult to explain than metaphors for all three age groups. Although proverb explanations improved as subject age increased, they remained quite literal before adolescence, a finding that was consistent with other proverb studies that employed explanation tasks (e.g., Douglas & Peel, 1979; Lutzer, 1988; Piaget, 1926; Richardson & Church, 1959).

Piaget (1926) contended that proverb understanding requires advanced cognitive processes acquired during the stage of formal operational thought. However, research that examined the cognitive prerequisites hypothesis in relation to proverb understanding (e.g., Billow, 1975; Holden, 1978) has not provided convincing evidence in support of it. However, it has been shown that proverb understanding in adolescents is at least correlated to performance on various Piagetian tasks of formal operational thinking, especially those that involve syllogistic reasoning and mathematical probability (Holden, 1978).

Although the sources of proverb difficulty remain to be identified with certainty, the syntactic and semantic complexity (e.g., "To teach a fool is as easy as to cure a corpse," "A bad compromise is better than a good battle") of proverbs undoubtedly contributes. In addition, proverbs often express meanings that require world experience to be fully appreciated (e.g., "The bread of strangers can be very hard"). It is also possible that proverbs require greater analytical effort from the interpreter. For example, many proverbs are similar to metaphors in that they involve a comparison of entities that are normally viewed as distinct. The comparison provided in proverbs is more elusive than that provided in metaphors, however, because proverbs usually contain more than one vehicle and never state the topics. In fact, the topics of a proverb are variable and can only be found in the context in which the figurative statement occurred. These points are illustrated by the situation in which a fourth-grade teacher leaves her normally obedient classroom for five minutes only to return to chaos and remarks, "When the cat's away, the mice will play!" Here, the two topics *teacher* and *students* are being likened to the vehicles *cat* and *mice*, respectively, but they are not contained in the proverb itself. The same proverb with different topics might be just as appropriate if uttered by a track coach who assigns his runners a 10-mile workout but shortly finds them frolicking at the beach.

The reported difficulty of proverbs also seems to be a function of the methods used to examine students' understanding. Although context is necessary for the full appreciation of a proverb, few investigators have considered its importance. In most studies, proverb understanding has been examined by presenting students with lists of proverbs out of context and asking them to come up with their own explanations of the proverbs or to choose the best explanation of each from a set of answer choices also lacking contextual information (e.g., Billow, 1975; Gorham, 1956; Holden, 1978; Piaget, 1926; Richardson & Church, 1959; Watts, 1944). Presenting proverbs in isolation, however, ignores the fact that proverbs typically occur in conversations, lectures, or stories where linguistic and nonlinguistic contextual information may facilitate understanding. Therefore, tasks that present proverbs out of context may underestimate a child's understanding of the expressions in natural settings (Nippold, Martin, & Erskine, 1988). Explanation tasks may also underestimate understanding.

The Role of Context

Research has shown that when receptive tasks are used to assess comprehension of other types of figurative language, such as idioms and metaphors, students demonstrate an understanding of those expressions several years before they can adequately explain their meanings (Ackerman, 1982; Dent, 1984; Gardner, 1974; Winner et al., 1976, 1980). Nippold et al. (1988) suggested that a task involving contextual support and a nonspoken response mode would be a better method of assessing proverb understanding than a task where proverbs are presented out of context and the student must explain their meanings. They designed a proverbs task incorporating those features and presented it to students from Grades 4, 6, 8, and 10 (ages 9 through 16; N = 240). To determine if performance on a non-Piagetian reasoning task was related to proverb understanding, they also gave a perceptual analogies task to all students.

The proverbs task consisted of 30 items presented in a written multiple-choice format. The individual proverbs were borrowed from a variety of sources (Chambers, 1979; Gorham, 1956; Hoffman & Honeck, 1980; Honeck et al., 1978; Piaget, 1926; Reston, 1985; Watts, 1944) and represented different levels of familiarity as well as semantic and syntactic complexity. For each test item, a proverb was used by a named individual and was followed by four different contextual descriptions, for example:

▶ The teacher said, "The new broom sweeps clean."

   a. The new principal likes to coach the basketball team.

   b. The new principal likes to eat lunch with the students.

   c. The new principal fired all of the old teachers.*

   d. The new principal likes to have spelling contests every week.

Students were asked to select the context in which it was most appropriate to use the proverb. In writing the response alternatives for each test item, care was taken to ensure that none could be literally true and therefore misleading. An attempt also was made to write about situations thought to be meaningful to students in Grades 4 through 10, and to use relatively simple vocabulary and sentence structure so that proverb understanding would not be hampered by reading difficulties. The proverbs task was written at about the fourth-grade level (Fry, 1972). As a further safeguard against possible reading and vocabulary confounds, students were told before the testing began that they should ask the examiner about any words they could not read or did not understand. The Figure Analogies subtest from the nonverbal battery of the *Lorge-Thorndike Intelligence Tests* (Lorge & Thorndike, 1957) served as the perceptual reasoning task. This task contains 30 perceptual analogies expressing the relationship "A is to B as C is to D"; three designs (A, B, and C) are presented in a row and a fourth (D) is left to be inferred. Each test item is followed by five answer choices, only one of which best completes the analogy.

Results showed that the perceptual reasoning task was more difficult than the proverbs task, but that performance on both tasks steadily improved with increasing grade level. On the proverbs task, students in Grades 4, 6, 8, and 10, respectively, obtained mean accuracy scores of 67%, 77%, 83%, and 85%. On the reasoning task, scores of 61%, 70%, 76%, and 81% were obtained by the groups, respectively. With chance performance equal to 25% on the proverbs task and 20% on the reasoning task, even the youngest students, the fourth graders, performed well above the level of chance on both tasks. Correlations between proverb understanding and perceptual analogical reasoning were significant for each of the four grades. It is also important to note that proverb understanding in this investigation was markedly better than in other studies where explanation tasks were employed or proverbs were presented out of context (Billow, 1975; Gorham, 1956; Richardson & Church, 1959; Watts, 1944).

The Role of Concreteness and Familiarity

In the Nippold et al. (1988) study, the proverbs themselves varied widely in difficulty. For example, 95% of the 240 students understood "Barking dogs seldom bite," but only 46% of them understood "The squeaky wheel gets the oil." Nippold and Haq (1996) hypothesized that the concreteness and the familiarity of proverbs would affect their ease of understanding. To test that hypothesis, they designed a multiple-choice comprehension task that contained 32 proverbs. There were eight proverbs that represented each of four different types: concrete–familiar (e.g., "A leopard cannot change its spots"); concrete–unfamiliar (e.g., "Scalded cats fear even cold water"); abstract–familiar (e.g., "Two wrongs don't make a right"); and abstract–unfamiliar (e.g., "A wonder lasts but nine days"). Each proverb contained two nouns. The nouns referred to tangible items in the concrete proverbs and to intangible items in the abstract proverbs. The familiarity level of the proverbs had been determined through a prior experiment in which adolescents ($N = 40$) and adults ($N = 40$) had been presented with a list of 107 proverbs in random order. They were asked to rate each expression for the frequency with which they had heard or read it before, using a 5-point Likert scale (1 = never; 5 = many times; note that the 1 to 5 Likert scale is the reverse of that used for the idiom familiarity scale in Chapter 8.) The results showed that the adolescents and adults did not differ in rating the proverbs for familiarity. Hence, the ratings for the two groups were combined when selecting proverbs for the main experiment. The entire set of ratings for all 107 proverbs from both groups is reported in Appendix 9.1. These ratings may be useful to other researchers in figurative language.

In the proverb comprehension task, each expression was presented in the context of a short paragraph, followed by four possible interpretations. Students read the stories and the answer choices silently. They were then asked to choose the answer that best explained the meaning of the proverb. One of the problems on the task was as follows:

▶ While eating a hot dog at a party one night, Rachel spilled mustard on her black velvet slacks. She was upset and complained about how her favorite slacks had been ruined. Her father offered to buy Rachel a new pair of slacks. Rachel's mother said, "Every cloud has a silver lining." What does it mean to say, *Every cloud has a silver lining?*

A. if you complain, you'll get what you want

B. people should save money for important things

C. spoiled children should not whine

D. there is something good in any bad situation (p. 176)*

The task, which was written at a fourth-grade reading level (Fry, 1972), was administered to students from Grades 5, 8, and 11 (ages 10 through 17 years; $N = 180$). Performance steadily improved as grade level increased, and overall accuracy scores of 55%, 76%, and 89% were obtained by the three groups, respectively. As predicted, the concrete proverbs were easier than the abstract, and the familiar proverbs were easier than the unfamiliar. The researchers contended that their findings concerning familiarity were consistent with the *language experience hypothesis*, the view that proverb understanding develops through meaningful exposure to the expressions. They also contended that, in addition to exposure, understanding develops through active analysis of the words contained in an expression, a view they called the *metasemantic hypothesis* of figurative language development.

In a subsequent experiment, Nippold, Hegel, Uhden, and Bustamante (1997a) modified the task employed by Nippold and Haq (1996) in an effort to make it more challenging. This was accomplished by including a greater proportion of low-familiarity proverbs in the task, but maintaining an equal number of concrete and abstract expressions. As in the previous study, the task contained 32 proverbs, and each was presented in a brief story context followed by a set of four alternative interpretations. The task was administered to adolescents from Grades 8, 10, and 12 (mean ages = 14, 16, and 18 years; $N = 150$) and to young adults (mean age = 25 years; $N = 50$) who were college students. Overall mean accuracy scores obtained by the four groups, respectively, were 71%, 73%, 81%, and 93%. As predicted, the concrete proverbs were easier to understand than the abstract for all four groups, results that provided further support for the metasemantic hypothesis. Out of 16 possible points per type, mean accuracy scores for the concrete and abstract proverbs, respectively, were as follows: Grade 8 = 12.18, 10.50; Grade 10 = 12.30, 11.16; Grade 12 = 13.62, 12.32; College = 15.12, 14.56. Thus, on this challenging task of proverb comprehension, students did not attain mastery (90%+) until young adulthood. It would be interesting to know if this reflects a plateau in the development of proverb understanding, or if further improvement occurs beyond young adulthood. In this study, the relationship between proverb comprehension and academic achievement was also examined. Recent scores for Reading and Mathematics obtained from the *Oregon Statewide Assessment Program* were available for 80% ($N = 40$) of the tenth-grade students. Correlation coefficients calculated between total raw scores on the proverb comprehension task and scaled scores on the two achievement tests were statistically significant (Reading = .55; Mathematics = .63), indicating that proverb comprehension in adolescents is associated with school success.

Proverb Understanding Through the Lifespan

To examine the possibility of further growth in proverb understanding during adulthood, Nippold, Uhden, and Schwarz (1997b) presented a proverb explanation task to individuals ranging in age from 13 through 79 years ($N = 353$). Two groups were comprised of adolescents, and six groups were comprised of adults drawn from every decade from the 20s through the 70s. Mean ages of the eight groups of subjects were as follows: 13, 16, 24, 33, 44, 53, 65, and 74 years. The task contained 24 different proverbs, each presented in a brief written story as in the two previous studies (Nippold & Haq, 1996; Nippold et al., 1997a). Half the proverbs were concrete (e.g., "A caged *bird* longs for the *clouds*"), half were abstract (e.g., "*Humility* often gains more than *pride*"), and all were of low familiarity as determined by Nippold and Haq (1996). Each participant read the problems silently and provided written explanations of the proverbs. An explanation response mode was employed in order to provide an even more challenging task of proverb understanding than the multiple-choice task employed by Nippold et al. (1997a). Each response was awarded 2, 1, or 0 points, depending on how well it captured the meaning of the proverb. Thus, it was possible to earn a total of 48 points. Performance on the task improved markedly during adolescence and into early adulthood. It reached a plateau during the 20s, remained stable during the 30s, 40s, and 50s, and began a slight decline during the 60s that continued into the 70s. Concrete proverbs were easier to explain than abstract for adolescents and young adults, but did not differ in difficulty for adults in their 30s and older. Thus, the metasemantic hypothesis was supported in relation to adolescents and young adults, which was consistent with Nippold et al. (1997a). No group reached a ceiling on the task, indicating that it was indeed challenging. Overall mean accuracy scores for each of the eight groups, from youngest to oldest, were as follows: 16.67, 25.30, 33.37, 31.95, 33.78, 31.88, 28.08, and 25.59.

It was unclear why performance began to decline in the 60s, because the six groups of adults did not differ in educational background as determined by number of years of formal education completed, and no participant in the study had any known problems in speech, language, or hearing. Nevertheless, educational background was found to be closely related to performance on the proverb explanation task; adults who had completed more years of formal education provided better explanations of the proverbs than did those with less education. In particular, adults in every decade from the 20s through the 70s who had completed at least four years of post-secondary formal education were especially proficient at explaining the proverbs.

Summary

From a life span perspective, proverb understanding begins in early childhood and continues unabated through adolescence and into early adulthood. The ability to explain proverbs remains stable through the middle years of adulthood, but begins a slight decline during the 60s that continues into the 70s. For school-age children and adolescents, proverb understanding is related to frequency of exposure such that low-familiarity expressions are more difficult than high-familiarity expressions, a finding that supports the language experience hypothesis of figurative language development. Proverb understanding in youth is also related to the concreteness of the nouns contained in an expression, a finding that is consistent with studies of the development of metaphor understanding (see Chapter 7). The fact that concrete expressions are easier to interpret than abstract expressions supports the metasemantic hypothesis. The greater visualization of concrete proverbs seems to facilitate a youth's ability to analyze the meanings of the words in the expression.

This chapter has also highlighted the contrast between two points of view regarding younger children's ability to understand proverbs. Some researchers (Billow, 1975; Gorham, 1956; Holden, 1978; Piaget, 1926; Richardson & Church, 1959; Watts, 1944) contended that proverb understanding was largely an adolescent attainment, but others (Honeck et al., 1978; Nippold et al., 1988; Nippold & Haq, 1996; Resnick, 1982) showed that it was possible well before the adolescent years. It appears that when task demands are simplified, younger children can understand proverbs reasonably well, a finding that is consistent with research in metaphors, similes, and idioms.

Also consistent with research into other types of figurative language, it appears that the active explanation of proverbs lags behind their passive understanding. Although the Piagetian cognitive prerequisite hypothesis has been examined in relation to proverbs, the results have not been supportive. Nevertheless, it has been shown that proverb understanding is related to general cognitive ability as measured by tasks of analogical and syllogistic reasoning (see Chapters 5 and 6), to school success as measured by academic achievement tests, and to the amount of formal education that a child, adolescent, or adult has completed.

Appendix 9.1
Mean Familiarity Ratings for 107 Proverbs*

	Adolescents	Adults
1. A bad broom leaves a dirty room.	1.40	1.10
2. A caged bird longs for the clouds.	1.55	1.30
3. A drowning man grabs at a straw.	1.48	2.53
4. A forced kindness deserves no thanks.	1.50	1.38
5. A golden key opens every door.	2.38	1.58
6. A good sailor likes a rough sea.	1.55	1.13
7. A leopard cannot change its spots.	3.20	4.18
8. A little bait catches a large fish.	1.85	1.90
9. A little spark can kindle a great fire.	2.93	2.38
10. A mouse may help a lion.	1.93	1.50
11. A peacock should look at its legs.	1.13	1.03
12. A rolling stone gathers no moss.	2.50	4.75
13. A small leak will sink a great ship.	2.50	2.63
14. A still river never finds the ocean.	1.55	1.18
15. A still tongue makes a wise head.	2.18	1.65
16. A tree is known by its fruit.	2.33	3.18
17. A wonder lasts but nine days.	1.13	1.25
18. All bread is not baked in one oven.	1.85	1.20
19. An optimistic attitude is half of success.	1.85	1.95
20. Anger is never without reason.	2.13	1.65
21. Big fish eat little fish.	3.00	2.70
22. Big trees grow from little acorns.	1.85	3.35
23. Blame is safer than praise.	1.20	1.53
24. Blood is thicker than water.	4.48	4.78
25. Cleanliness is next to godliness.	2.93	4.85
26. Clothes do not make the man.	4.08	4.25
27. Courage is always safer than cowardice.	1.95	1.23
28. Crooked logs make a straight fire.	1.18	1.00
29. Democracy is better than tyranny.	2.30	2.30
30. Envy is destroyed by true friendship.	2.00	1.18
31. Even a blind hen sometimes finds a grain.	1.53	1.25
32. Even a monkey will fall from a tree.	1.70	1.13
33. Every bird is known by its feathers.	1.60	1.90
34. Every bird likes its own nest best.	1.98	1.75
35. Every bird must hatch its own eggs.	1.78	1.10
36. Every cloud has a silver lining.	3.85	4.90
37. Every horse thinks its own pack heaviest.	1.88	1.30
38. Every oak must be an acorn.	1.75	2.45
39. Expectation is better than realization.	1.85	1.63
40. Falling raindrops will wear through a stone.	1.40	1.33
41. Fine feathers make fine birds.	2.00	1.45

(continues)

Appendix 9.1. Continued

	Adolescents	Adults
42. Foresight is better than hindsight.	2.78	3.95
43. Forgiveness is better than revenge.	2.63	2.30
44. Gentle persuasion is better than force.	2.25	2.43
45. Gentleness skillfully subdues wrath.	1.63	1.13
46. Good fences make good neighbors.	1.88	3.43
47. Goodness is better than beauty.	2.35	2.28
48. Gratitude is a heavy burden.	1.80	1.43
49. Great events have small beginnings.	2.55	2.70
50. Great trees keep down the little trees.	1.40	1.15
51. Half a loaf is better than no bread.	2.18	2.73
52. Harmony seldom makes a headline.	1.65	1.13
53. Humility often gains more than pride.	1.90	1.53
54. In idleness there is perpetual despair.	1.23	1.20
55. Intelligence is worth more than richness.	2.30	1.83
56. Knowledge is better than wealth.	3.38	2.15
57. Little by little the bird builds its nest.	1.68	1.68
58. Little pitchers have big ears.	1.50	2.60
59. Little sticks kindle large fires.	2.03	1.78
60. Little streams make mighty rivers.	2.68	2.98
61. Loose teeth are better than no teeth.	1.55	1.25
62. Many eyes are upon the king.	1.65	1.40
63. Misfortunes may come in spite of watchfulness.	1.43	1.18
64. Newborn calves don't fear tigers.	1.10	1.00
65. No garden is without its weeds.	2.40	2.25
66. Of idleness comes no goodness.	1.55	1.83
67. One rotten apple spoils the barrel.	3.60	4.40
68. One saddle is enough for one horse.	1.30	1.03
69. One stone does not make a wall.	1.75	1.50
70. Patience is the best virtue.	4.25	4.08
71. Persistence will accomplish more than force.	2.38	2.10
72. Quality is better than quantity.	4.48	4.58
73. Quarreling sparrows do not fear man.	1.10	1.00
74. Scalded cats fear even cold water.	1.75	1.10
75. Shared sorrow is half sorrow.	1.58	1.63
76. Sleeping cats catch no mice.	2.43	2.18
77. Sleeping foxes catch no poultry.	1.58	1.45
78. Small fish mingle with big fish.	1.38	1.30
79. Sorrow is born of excessive joy.	1.25	1.33
80. Sour grapes can never make sweet wine.	2.38	2.00
81. Success is first a dream.	2.48	1.75
82. The apple never falls far from the tree.	3.53	3.53
83. The bad workman always blames his tools.	1.85	2.03
84. The bait hides the hook.	2.18	1.30

(continues)

Appendix 9.1. *Continued*

	Adolescents	Adults
85. The cat plays with the mouse.	3.33	2.30
86. The chickens give advice to the hen.	1.33	1.05
87. The crying baby gets the milk.	2.58	2.58
88. The early bird catches the worm.	4.65	4.95
89. The end justifies the means.	3.25	4.88
90. The pen is mightier than the sword.	3.83	4.75
91. The pot calls the kettle black.	2.80	4.43
92. The pretty shoe often pinches the foot.	1.90	1.40
93. The reddest apple has a worm in it.	2.50	1.55
94. The restless sleeper blames the bed.	1.50	1.25
95. The saddest dog sometimes wags its tail.	1.53	1.15
96. The squeaking wheel gets the grease.	2.63	4.88
97. The tongue is more powerful than the sword.	2.88	3.35
98. The tongue is sharper than the sword.	3.55	3.63
99. The tongue wounds more than the arrow.	2.53	2.08
100. The truth is better than a lie.	4.03	3.43
101. The twigs are rarely better than the trunk.	1.10	1.20
102. There is no glory without sacrifice.	3.13	2.55
103. Tigers and deer do not stroll together.	1.33	1.03
104. Too many cooks spoil the broth.	2.33	4.73
105. Too much bed makes a dull head.	1.95	1.63
106. Two captains will sink a ship.	1.73	1.35
107. Two wrongs don't make a right.	4.95	4.98
Mean (M)	2.22	2.24
Standard Deviation (SD)	.88	1.22
Range	1.10–4.95	1.00–4.98

*Familiarity is a measure of how often one has heard or read the proverb before:
1 = never; 2 = once; 3 = a few times; 4 = several times; 5 = many times.

(Note that this scale is the reverse of the idiom familiarity scale in Chapter 8.)

Acknowledgments

Portions of this chapter appeared in the following article:

Nippold, M.A. (1985). Comprehension of figurative language in youth. *Topics in Language Disorders*, 5(3), 1–20.

Used with permission of Aspen Publishers.

C   H   A   P   T   E   R

AMBIGUITY AND SARCASM

*"Mine is a long and sad tale!" said the mouse, turning to Alice and sighing.
"It is a long tail, certainly," said Alice, looking with wonder at the mouse's
tail, "but why do you call it sad?"*

—Lewis Carroll, *Alice's Adventures in Wonderland*
(Fromkin & Rodman, 1988, p. 210)

Metalinguistic awareness, the ability to consciously reflect on the nature of language, is called upon when words are used in unique or unexpected ways. This occurs when an individual encounters ambiguity or sarcasm, two aspects of language that express complex and multi-dimensional meanings. This chapter discusses the changes that occur in the understanding of ambiguity and sarcasm during the school-age and adolescent years.

Ambiguity

The humor in riddles, jokes, and comic strips often stems from linguistic ambiguity (e.g., Q: "What did the short tree say to the tall tree?" A: "I'm stumped"; Q: "Can the match box?" A: "No, but the tin can"), a phenomenon that can also serve as an attention-capturing device in newspaper headlines (e.g., "Bike sales ride on all-terrain cycles," "Storm damage stumps tree surgeons"), bumper stickers (e.g., "You can't hug your kids with nuclear arms"), and advertisements (e.g., ad for Ford Tempo cars: "Designed to move you"). To understand these types of ambiguous messages, an individual must know the double meanings of words and appreciate the linguistic contexts in which they occur. Nonlinguistic information may also be required. For example, a full understanding of the newspaper headline "Night owls flock back to Hoots" requires knowledge that Hoots was a 24-hour restaurant in Eugene, Oregon where students could study all night. Similarly, appreciating the full meaning of the headline, "Store's counterculture to end" requires knowledge that when a downtown Woolworth's store closed, people who visited the lunch counter on a daily basis lost an important social network.

Developmental studies have examined the understanding of linguistic ambiguity in three different domains: (1) isolated *sentences* (e.g., "It's too hot to eat"); (2) *humor* (e.g., Q: "Why did the hungry man go into the lamp store?" A: "Because he wanted a light snack"); and (3) *advertisements* (e.g., "Grounds for owning a Subaru") (Brodzinsky, Feuer, & Owens, 1977; Keil, 1980; Kessel, 1970; Muus & Hoag, 1980; Nippold, Cuyler, & Braunbeck-Price, 1988; Shultz, 1974; Shultz & Horibe, 1974; Shultz & Pilon, 1973; Spector, 1996; Wiig, Gilbert, & Christian, 1978).

Sentences

Four different types of sentential ambiguity have been examined in terms of their relative difficulty: *phonological* (e.g., "I have enough for eight tea/eighty cups"), *lexical* (e.g., "The lady wiped the glasses"), *surface-structure* (e.g., "He fed her // dog biscuits" versus "He fed her dog // biscuits"), and *deep-structure* (e.g., "The duck is ready to eat"). The double meaning of a phonological ambiguity results from varying the pronunciation of one or more words in the sentence. For a lexical ambiguity, however, the double meaning results from a word or phrase having two different meanings. A surface-structure ambiguity is a sentence where the double meaning results from variations in intonational patterns, primarily in stress and juncture. A deep-structure ambiguity contains a noun that serves as an agent in one meaning but as an object in the other meaning (Nippold et al., 1988).

Research with adults (MacKay & Bever, 1967) had shown that when persons were asked to interpret different types of ambiguous sentences, the two meanings of lexical ambiguities were detected faster than those of surface-structure ambiguities, which were detected faster than those of deep-structure ambiguities. Phonological ambiguities were not presented. On the assumption that response latency reflects processing complexity, these findings led many investigators (e.g., Brodzinsky et al., 1977; Keil, 1980; Kessel, 1970; Shultz & Pilon, 1973; Wiig et al., 1978) to predict that children's understanding of sentential ambiguity would mirror this pattern developmentally such that lexical ambiguities would be understood earlier than surface-structure ambiguities, which in turn would be understood earlier than deep-structure ambiguities. However, research evidence has only partially supported that prediction.

For example, Kessel (1970) examined the understanding of sentential ambiguity in children ages 6, 7, 8, 9, and 11 years ($N = 50$). The task consisted of 12 sentences, with four representing each of the following three types of ambiguity: lexical, surface-structure, and deep-structure. For each sentence, the child was shown four pictures, two illustrating the correct interpretations and two illustrating foils. For example, pictures accompanying the sentence, "The eating of the chicken was sloppy" showed (1) a chicken eating grain sloppily, (2) a chicken eating grain neatly, (3) a boy and girl eating chicken sloppily, and (4) a boy and girl eating chicken neatly. The examiner read each sentence aloud two times and asked the child to choose the pictures that went with it. The child was then asked to explain those choices. The purpose of the questioning was to assess the child's depth of understanding and to control for random guessing. Because each of the four surface-structure ambiguities could be spoken with two different intonational patterns corresponding to different interpretations, the examiner used a different vocal intonational pattern for the two readings of each of those sentences, for example, "He fed her dog // *biscuits*" versus "He fed her // *dog* biscuits." To receive full credit for a sentence, the child had to select the correct pictures and provide acceptable explanations of each.

As predicted, the lexical ambiguities were easier to understand than the other two types. However, the surface- and deep-structure ambiguities were about equal in difficulty, which was inconsistent with Kessel's prediction. Although most 6- and 7-year-olds understood both meanings of the lexical ambiguities, few detected the dual meanings of the surface- or deep-structure ambiguities. In fact, it was not until age 11 that children consistently understood the latter two types. Qualitative changes were also evident from their explanations. For example, the 11-year-olds were able to target the ambiguous elements in a sentence more readily than any of the younger groups.

Using different procedures from Kessel's, Shultz and Pilon (1973) examined the understanding of ambiguous sentences in children ages 6, 9, 12, and 15 years ($N = 112$). The experiment contained phonological, lexical, surface-structure, and deep-structure ambiguities, with six sentences per type. For each sentence, understanding was assessed first with a paraphrase task and then with a picture task. For the paraphrase task, the child listened to a sentence and then explained what it meant. If only one meaning was explained, the examiner prompted the child by asking if the sentence meant anything else. For the picture task, two pictures illustrating the correct meanings of the sentence were presented and the examiner asked the child to point to the picture or pictures that illustrated the sentence. As an example, one picture for the sentence, "He saw a man eating fish" showed a ferocious shark and another showed a man at a table eating fish. If only one picture was chosen, the examiner prompted the child by asking if the sentence meant anything else. The child was then asked to explain the picture choices. For both the paraphrase and picture tasks, a sentence was credited only if the child could explain both meanings adequately.

Results showed that the picture task elicited more correct responses than the paraphrase task. On both tasks, understanding of the four ambiguity types steadily improved as subject age increased, with phonological ambiguities easier than lexical, and lexical easier than surface- and deep-structure, which were equally difficult to understand. Although the phonological and lexical ambiguities were nearly mastered by age 15, the surface- and deep-structure ambiguities were infrequently understood before age 12 and continued to challenge even the 15-year-olds. Despite procedural variations, Shultz and Pilon's (1973) results were consistent with Kessel's (1970) in showing that lexical ambiguities were easier than the two syntactic types, and that surface- and deep-structure ambiguities were equally difficult.

Using the same procedures as Shultz and Pilon (1973), Brodzinsky et al. (1977) examined children's understanding of linguistic ambiguity in relation to their problem-solving styles. Children ages 10 and 13 years old ($N = 96$) participated in the study. The *Matching Familiar Figures Test* (MFFT) (Kagan, Rosman, Day, Albert, & Phillips, 1964) was administered to establish each child's problem-solving style. This is a task that measures speed and accuracy in matching identical pictures and yields four different response patterns: slow-accurate ("reflective"), fast-inaccurate ("impulsive"), slow-inaccurate, and fast-accurate. In the present study, it was predicted that impulsive children, known to perform quick and cursory analyses of stimuli, would be less successful in understanding both meanings of ambiguous sentences than reflective children, known to be more systematic in their analyses. However, it was also predicted that the prompting procedures employed in the Shultz and Pilon (1973) experiment ("Does it mean anything else?") would eliminate any differences between the reflective and impulsive children by encouraging a closer analysis of the sentences.

Results showed that on both the paraphrase and picture tasks, the reflective children spontaneously understood a greater number of double meanings than the impulsive or slow-inaccurate children. Fast-accurate children performed between these two extremes. However, the impulsive and slow-inaccurate children performed as well as the reflective children after prompting had occurred. This pattern was particularly strong for the 10-year-olds in relation to the surface- and deep-structure ambiguities. Consistent with Shultz and Pilon (1973), it was also shown that phonological ambiguities were easier to understand than lexical, that lexical were easier to understand than deep- and surface-structure, and that the two syntactic types were equally difficult. Not surprisingly, the 13-year-olds were more successful than the 10-year-olds at spontaneously explaining the double meanings of the sentences and pictures. Combining the problem-solving styles and ambiguity types, mean accuracy scores on the spontaneous paraphrase task (before prompting) were 40% and 23% for the 13- and 10-year-olds, respectively. On the picture task, those scores were 73% and 54%, respectively. It was also reported that the understanding of linguistic ambiguity was positively correlated to intelligence test scores for the children in this study.

Wiig et al. (1978) examined accuracy and speed in relation to the understanding of ambiguous sentences. The subjects in their study were ages 5, 7, 10, 12, and 18 years ($N = 50$). Each subject was administered a picture-pointing task that contained eight lexical, five surface-structure, and three deep-structure ambiguities. Unlike in previous studies, some of the lexical ambiguities in this task had both a literal and an idiomatic interpretation rather than two literal interpretations only. These included, "She did not press the suit," "This restaurant even serves crabs," and "The man kept the watch." In addition, some of the lexical ambiguities were also deep-structure ambiguities (e.g., "This restaurant even serves crabs"). Each ambiguous sentence was accompanied by four picture choices, two illustrating the correct meanings and two representing foils. For example, the pictures for the lexical ambiguity, "He is drawing a gun" were (1) a man drawing a picture of a gun, (2) a cowboy drawing a gun from his holster, (3) a man throwing a gun, and (4) a man holding a smoking gun. The examiner read each sentence aloud and the subject pointed to the picture(s) that expressed the appropriate meaning(s). Each pointing response was timed with a stopwatch. Subjects were not required to explain their picture choices.

Consistent with previous studies, the number of correct responses increased as a function of age, and mean accuracy scores obtained by the groups of 5-, 7-, 10-, 12-, and 18-year-olds, respectively, were 14%, 36%, 46%, 58%, and 59%. However, in contrast to previous studies, no ambiguity type was found to be easier than any other type. This may be due to the fact that some of the lexical ambiguities had idiomatic interpretations, and thus were not typical examples of this sentence type. The researchers also reported that few changes occurred in speed of response time as a function of subject age or ambiguity type.

In an examination of the psychological bases of ambiguity, Keil (1980) predicted that children's competence with linguistic ambiguity would be related to their competence with nonlinguistic ambiguity. Pictures that could be interpreted in two different ways served as the nonlinguistic stimuli. For example, a sketch of a ladder could also be viewed as a railroad track, and a sketch of a horse's head could also be viewed as a seal if the ears were thought of as flippers and the nostrils as eyes. The ambiguous sentences in this study consisted of 24 lexical and 24 syntactic (12 surface- and 12 deep-structure). All sentences were presented on audiotape. Because lexical ambiguities tend to be easier to understand than syntactic, it was also predicted that lexical ambiguities would be more closely related to easier "symbolic" pictorial ambiguities (e.g., the ladder-railroad track picture), and that syntactic ambiguities would be more closely related to more difficult "structural" pictorial ambiguities (e.g., the horse-seal picture). Twelve symbolic and twelve structural pictorial ambiguities were presented. Children who were ages 6, 8, 10, and 13 years (N = 72) participated. They were told that all sentences and pictures would have two meanings, which they should explain. To receive credit, both meanings of a sentence or picture had to be expressed.

Despite Keil's (1980) predictions, no picture-sentence correlations reached significance for any age group. Thus, it was concluded that sentential and pictorial ambiguities have different psychological bases. Consistent with previous studies, however, the syntactic sentences were more difficult than the lexical, and the deep- and surface-structure ambiguities were equally difficult to understand. Although the 13-year-olds understood the sentences and pictures better than any of the younger groups, even the oldest children remained challenged by the two tasks.

Summary

Developmental studies have shown that the ability to identify and explain sentential ambiguity steadily improves during the school-age and adolescent years. In general, phonological ambiguities are easier than lexical, and lexical are easier than surface- or deep-structure ambiguities, which are about equal in difficulty. However, it appears that ambiguous sentences of any particular type can vary widely in difficulty. For example, certain lexical ambiguities that have both a literal and an idiomatic interpretation (e.g., "She did not press the suit") are more difficult than certain deep-structure ambiguities that have two literal interpretations only (e.g., "The duck is ready to eat"). Studies have also shown that children's competence with ambiguous sentences is enhanced by picture cues, and that competence is related to intelligence and to problem-solving style. It is noteworthy that similar findings regarding intelligence and problem-solving style have been documented with respect to verbal analogical reasoning (see Chapter 5).

However, it should be emphasized that the studies just discussed presented children and adolescents with sentences out of context, sentences that would not be ambiguous during ongoing discourse because of linguistic and nonlinguistic information provided by natural settings (Van Kleeck, 1984). For example, if people were discussing the menu at a new seafood restaurant, the comment, "This restaurant even serves crabs" would not be ambiguous. Therefore, studies of sentential ambiguity provide little information about students' understanding of language that is truly ambiguous in natural settings. Jokes and riddles, however, are humorous forms of language that occur in social situations where an understanding of the double meanings of words and phrases is often required (Shultz, 1974; Shultz & Horibe, 1974). Students' performance in these settings provides insight into their competence with "real world" language.

Humor

An understanding of humor is interwoven with linguistic and cognitive development, abstract reasoning ability, and factual knowledge (Masten, 1986; McGhee, 1979; Prentice & Fathman, 1975; Zigler, Levine, & Gould, 1966). It also is associated with academic achievement, leadership, creativity, and a reflective problem-solving style (Brodzinsky, 1977; Damico & Purkey, 1978; Masten, 1986). Spontaneous humor expressed by school-age children and adolescents promotes peer acceptance, self-esteem, and personal adjustment and provides a socially acceptable way of releasing stress and tension associated with dating, sexuality, and bodily changes (Damico & Purkey, 1978; Masten, 1986; Ransohoff, 1975). Therefore, the topic of humor development in school-age children and adolescents must be taken seriously.

Jokes

Children's understanding of humor based on linguistic ambiguity has been investigated by a small number of researchers. The first known study in this area was conducted by Shultz and Horibe (1974), who examined children's understanding of jokes that were based upon the four major types of ambiguity: phonological, lexical,

Table 10.1
Types of Jokes Used by Shultz and Horibe

Phonological:

Speaker A:	"Waiter, what's this?"
Speaker B:	"That's bean soup, ma'am."
Speaker A:	"I'm not interested in what it's been. I'm asking what it is now."

Lexical:

| Speaker A: | "Order! Order in the court!" |
| Speaker B: | "Ham and cheese on rye, please, Your Honor." |

Surface-Structure:

| Speaker A: | "I saw a man eating shark in the aquarium." |
| Speaker B: | "That's nothing. I saw a man eating herring in the restaurant." |

Deep-Structure:

| Speaker A: | "Call me a cab." |
| Speaker B: | "You're a cab." |

Note. Adapted from "Development of the Appreciation of Verbal Jokes" by T. R. Shultz and F. Horibe, 1974, *Developmental Psychology, 10,* p. 14.

surface-structure, and deep-structure. Jokes of each type are contained in Table 10.1. The humor in each joke resulted from the incongruity between two sentences and its subsequent resolution. For example, in the lexical ambiguity, "Order! Order in the court!" "Ham and cheese on rye, please, Your Honor," *order* first implies a request for quiet but then implies a request for food. Resolution of this incongruity requires knowledge of two distinct meanings of *order*, and the ability to consider both meanings simultaneously. In Shultz and Horibe's study, the task contained six jokes of each of the four types. Each joke was presented audibly in the form of a tape-recorded dialogue and visually in written form. Children who were ages 6, 8, 10, and 12 years ($N = 120$) were asked to explain what was funny about the jokes. Results showed that the ability to target the critical ambiguous elements improved as subject age increased. Moreover, jokes based on phonological ambiguity were generally easiest, followed successively by surface-structure, lexical, and deep-structure ambiguities, results that were inconsistent with studies of sentential ambiguity.

Muus and Hoag (1980) conducted a study that examined adolescents' understanding of jokes based on lexical and syntactic ambiguity. In their study, a group of 14- and 15-year-old adolescents ($N = 38$) were asked to explain the humor involved in jokes similar to those employed by Shultz and Horibe (1974). Ten lexical and 10 syntactic ambiguities were presented in written form, and explanations were scored

Table 10.2
Types of Riddles Used by Shultz

Phonological:

Question: "Why did the cookie cry?"
Answer: "Because its mother had been a wafer so long."

Lexical:

Question: "Why did the farmer name his hog Ink?"
Answer: "Because he kept running out of the pen."

Surface-Structure:

Question: "Tell me how long cows should be milked."
Answer: "They should be milked the same as short ones, of course."

Deep-Structure:

Question: "What animal can jump as high as a tree?"
Answer: "All animals. Trees cannot jump."

Note. Adapted from "Development of the Appreciation of Riddles" by T. R. Shultz, 1974, *Child Development*, 45, p. 101.

in terms of the number of legitimate meanings expressed. The adolescents obtained an overall accuracy score of 83%, with lexical and syntactic ambiguities equally easy to explain. Thus, it appears that by middle adolescence, young people are quite adept at understanding jokes involving linguistic ambiguity. Muus and Hoag also reported that adolescents in their study who had performed better on a Piagetian task of formal operational thinking also performed better on the ambiguity task, compared to age-matched students with lower cognitive performance. This finding supported the view that cognition plays a role in the understanding of humor.

Riddles

Children's understanding of riddles has also been examined in terms of the four major types of ambiguity. Like jokes, riddles express incongruity that is resolvable through an understanding of ambiguous elements. Riddles differ from jokes, however, by employing a question and answer format (e.g., Q: "Where does a walnut stay the night?" A: "In the Nutcracker Suite"; Q: "Why can't a bicycle stand up by itself? A: Because it's two-tired"). Shultz (1974) examined the understanding of riddles in children who were ages 6, 8, 10, and 12 years (N = 120). The task consisted of six riddles of each of the four types, as shown in Table 10.2. Each riddle was presented audibly and in written form, and children were asked to explain the humor in

Table 10.3
Types of Jokes and Riddles Used by Spector, With the Idioms Italicized

---

Jokes:

1.	Joe:	"I would like to become a space engineer."
	Jeff:	"Do you think you can pass the test?"
	Joe:	"Sure. I *took up space* in school."
2.	Sarah:	"Do you think it's possible to communicate with fish?"
	Rachel:	"You might try *dropping them a line*."
3.	Moe:	"I'd like to *give you a piece of my mind*."
	Flo:	"Are you sure you can spare it?"

Riddles:

1.	Q:	Why did Snoopy want to quit the comic strip?
	A:	He was tired of *working for Peanuts*.
2.	Q:	Which sport is the quietest?
	A:	Bowling. You can *hear a pin drop*.
3.	Q:	Why didn't the mother dog wake her puppies for school?
	A:	She believed in *letting sleeping dogs lie*.

Note. Adapted from "Children's Comprehension of Idioms in the Context of Humor" by C. C. Spector, 1996, *Language, Speech, and Hearing Services in Schools, 27*, p. 313.

each. As with the Shultz and Horibe (1974) study on jokes, the children's performance steadily improved as a function of increasing age. In contrast with Shultz and Horibe, however, lexical riddles were easiest to understand, and phonological, surface-structure, and deep-structure riddles were about equal in difficulty. This finding is inconsistent with studies of sentential ambiguity, which showed that phonological ambiguities were easiest to understand (Brodzinsky et al., 1977; Shultz & Pilon, 1973). However, this finding is consistent with the view that ambiguities of any type can vary widely in difficulty.

Idioms

Recently, Spector (1996) examined children's ability to detect and explain idioms that occurred in the context of humor. Students from Grades 3, 4, and 5 (ages 8 through 11 years) ($N = 90$) were presented with a test booklet that contained 12 jokes and riddles that were borrowed from children's books and magazines. Examples of the test items are contained in Table 10.3. The examiner read each item aloud as the students followed along in their booklets. For each item, students were asked to underline the idiom and then write an explanation of the figurative meaning of the expression. A practice item was as follows: "I can tell my pet owl is sick because he doesn't give a hoot" (p. 309). In order to grasp the humor in this sentence, the child would need to understand the nonliteral meaning of the idiom *doesn't give a hoot* in addition to its more obvious literal meaning. Recognizing that the expression has a double meaning would be necessary for a full appreciation of the joke. An acceptable explanation of the figurative meaning would be something like, "It means the owl doesn't care about anything" (p. 309). A maximum of 12 points could be earned for detection and 12 for explanation of the idioms.

Results indicated that detection was easier than explanation for all three groups. Although performance improved as a function of increasing subject age, not even the oldest children had mastered the task. Mean raw scores for detection and explanation, respectively, were as follows: Grade 3 = 6.43, 3.95; Grade 4 = 7.67, 5.38; Grade 5 = 10.27, 7.08. Although the fifth graders were able to detect the presence of idioms with 86% accuracy, their ability to explain the idioms lagged behind at 59% accuracy. This suggests that gaining a full appreciation of jokes and riddles containing idioms is a gradual process that remains incomplete by late childhood. Performance can be expected to improve considerably during adolescence.

Adolescence

However, little is actually known about the development of humor in adolescents, and it is unclear to what extent performance in this area improves beyond age 15. In view of the studies on sentential ambiguity, improvements might be expected to occur throughout the adolescent years, especially in relation to riddles involving more advanced vocabulary (Q: "How did Shakespeare find out everything?" A: "A little bard told him"), world knowledge (Q: "What did the Cyclops say to Ulysses?" A: "Watch your step. I've got my eye on you"), or idiomatic meanings (Q: "What should you do if you have insomnia?" A: "Don't lose any sleep over it"). However, McGhee (1979) reported that adolescence is a time when humor based on ambiguity is no longer considered funny because of its simplistic nature. Adolescents are often bored by memorized jokes and riddles and prefer more sophisticated forms of humor where abstract themes (e.g., irony) are involved and greater cognitive challenges are presented. Humor expressed in the form of witty remarks and spontaneous anecdotes is also enjoyed by adolescents, especially when social or sexual conflicts are highlighted (Ransohoff, 1975; Wolfenstein, 1978). However, adolescence is also a time when preferences for humor become more individualistic (Laing, 1939), a phenomenon that is consistent with the increasing individualism that occurs in other aspects of later language development (see Chapter 1).

Summary

Studies of humor development have not made any consistent findings with regard to the four different types of linguistic ambiguity, a pattern that contrasts with studies on isolated sentences. Nevertheless, the two domains are consistent in reporting that the understanding of ambiguity improves as students get older. Less is known about the development of humor during adolescence, but it appears that growth continues at least through the middle years.

Table 10.4
Examples of Ambiguous Advertisements Used by Nippold, Cuyler, and Braunbeck-Price

1. Here's an ad for Ford Tempo cars. It says, "Designed to move you."
   (picture shows Ford Tempo car driving down highway)
   Acceptable answers:
   (1) transportation move
   (2) emotion move
2. Here's an ad for Diaparene Corn Starch Baby Powder. It says, "The absorbing facts about cornstarch."
   (picture shows container of Diaparene)
   Acceptable answers:
   (1) absorbs moisture
   (2) interesting, engrossing
3. Here's an ad for some new dinners from Stouffer's foods. It says, "Introducing the Upper Crusts. Two sensational new entrees from Stouffer's."
   (picture shows top-crusted meat dishes served on elegant table setting)
   Acceptable answers:
   (1) pie crusts
   (2) wealthy social class

Note. Adapted from "Explanation of Ambiguous Advertisements: A Developmental Study with Children and Adolescents" by M. A. Nippold, J. S. Cuyler, and R. Braunbeck-Price, 1988, *Journal of Speech and Hearing Research, 31*, p. 473.

Advertisements

As with jokes and riddles, advertisements that play on the double meanings of words and phrases require an understanding of linguistic ambiguity in natural settings. Children's understanding of ambiguous ads reflects their metalinguistic development and their competence with "real world" language experiences. It is therefore an important topic for research.

Nippold et al. (1988) examined students' explanations of ambiguous advertisements. Students who were ages 9, 12, 15, and 18 years old ($N = 40$) were individually administered the "Ambiguous Ads Task." This task required the students to explain the meanings of 18 different advertisements. The ads had been taken from magazines, newspapers, and brochures, and each represented a common product or service. Examples of the ads are provided in Table 10.4. Each ad displayed a picture of the product and a main caption. Fourteen ads had two different meanings, and four were foils having only one meaning each. The ambiguous ads were all considered to be lexical ambiguities, and each contained a word or phrase that had a physical and a psychological meaning. The physical meaning pertained to a concrete object or activity, whereas the psychological meaning pertained to a concept, mental state, or other abstract entity. For example, an ad for Subaru cars displayed a station wagon driving on various types of rugged terrain and a caption that read "Grounds for owning a Subaru." To present a test item, the examiner displayed the ad, read the main caption aloud, and asked the student to explain what it meant. If only one meaning were explained, the examiner asked the student if it meant anything else. Responses to the four foil items were not scored.

Results of the study showed steady improvement with increasing age: mean accuracy scores for the 9-, 12-, 15-, and 18-year-olds, respectively, were 33%, 64%, 71%, and 84%. The greatest improvement occurred between the ages of 9 and 12, perhaps reflecting the transition into formal operational thinking, the stage of cognitive development when abstract reasoning comes into fruition (see Chapters 5 and 6). Performance improved beyond the age of 12, but at a slower pace. Qualitative analyses indicated that the explanations of the youngest students often were incomplete or overly general. For example, for the Diaparene ad (see Table 10.4, item 2), one 9-year-old simply responded, "It's for powdering babies." As students got older, however, their explanations became more complete and specific. For example, one 18-year-old explained the Diaparene ad as follows:

> By absorbing, they mean the interesting or appealing facts about cornstarch. The facts that perhaps you didn't know before. But at the same time, they mean absorbing, as in naturally absorbing . . . the cornstarch keeps your baby dry.

However, even the 18-year-olds had not completely mastered the task and sometimes struggled to express themselves. For example, another 18-year-old responded to that same ad as follows:

> Absorbing . . . I don't know how to explain it. It kind of has a double meaning . . . Well, something . . . It's kind of like the facts about cornstarch, like here's what it's going to do, if that makes any sense. I can't really describe it.

The results also showed that accuracy was greater in response to the physical meanings of the ads than to the psychological, particularly for the 9-year-olds. Perhaps this was due to the fact that the pictures provided clearer visual cues for the physical meanings. For example, for the Stouffer's ad (Table 10.4, item 3), the picture showed top-crusted dinners being served. In contrast, the visual cues for the psychological meanings of the ads were much more subtle (e.g., an elegant table setting for the Stouffer's ad). The fact that some of the psychological meanings were idiomatic (e.g., in his eyes, the upper crusts, swing of things, looks like a million) also may have contributed to the greater difficulty of the psychological meanings, because idiomatic meanings are more difficult to understand than literal (see Chapter 8). This discrepancy between the physical and psychological meanings of the ads was also consistent with Asch and Nerlove (1960), who found that the physical meanings of double-function terms are understood several years before their psychological meanings. As discussed in Chapter 2, double-function terms are words such as *bright*, *sweet*, and *warm* that have a related physical and psychological meaning. It is interesting that, in the present study, six of the ads contained ambiguous words that were actually double-function terms (i.e., *move, delivers, absorbing, appetite, support*, and *deliver*).

Summary

Students' performance on the Ambiguous Ads Task (Nippold et al., 1988) was consistent with developmental studies of linguistic ambiguity involving isolated sentences, jokes, and riddles in showing steady improvement during the school-age and adolescent years. However, all of the ambiguous ads in the Nippold study were lexically based. Therefore, no statement can be made concerning the extent to which ads that contain phonological or syntactic ambiguities might challenge students of this age range. It should also be emphasized that not even the 18-year-olds had completely mastered the Ambiguous Ads Task. This suggests that growth in the understanding of ambiguous ads may continue to improve into adulthood, as it does in relation to other types of multiple-meaning stimuli such as metaphors, similes, idioms, and proverbs (see Chapters 7, 8, and 9).

Sarcasm

As with ambiguity, sarcasm expresses complex meanings that can be interpreted in a variety of ways. Understanding sarcasm requires a listener to recognize a discrepancy between what is said and what is meant, and to realize the speaker's purpose in making a comment (Demorest, Silberstein, Gardner, & Winner, 1983; Winner, 1988). As with ambiguity, it also requires a person to have knowledge of relevant background information, to be aware of critical context cues, and to pay attention to patterns of vocal intonation ("Now I've seen *everything*!").

Consider the situation where a young boy drops spaghetti on his lap, and an older brother says, "My, how graceful you are!," using prolonged vowels and exaggerated variations in pitch. A person observing the situation must recognize that the older boy's comment should not be taken literally, and indeed that he intends just the opposite of what his words say. The observer also must realize that the brother's ultimate purpose in commenting is to tease the younger boy.

Studies have shown that while preschoolers have difficulty understanding sarcasm, comprehension gradually improves during the school-age years (Ackerman, 1982a, 1986; Capelli, Nakagawa, & Madden, 1990; Demorest, Meyer, Phelps, Gardner, & Winner, 1984; Demorest et al., 1983; Winner, 1988). For example, Demorest et al. (1983) examined the understanding of sarcasm in children ages 6, 8, and 11 years ($N = 72$). Each child listened to a short story that ended with a sarcastic remark, such as the following:

Jane's family was cleaning up the house and Jane had to clean up her bedroom. It was crowded with toys and boxes and clothes all piled on top of each other. Jane started by taking everything out of her drawers. She tossed it all on her bedroom floor and soon the room was a complete mess. Jane's sister looked at the room and said to her: "Your room looks like it's totally clean now." (p. 123)

The stories were accompanied by colorful pictures that helped to maintain the child's attention and interest. After listening to a story, the child was asked to explain what was meant by the final sentence (e.g., "What did her sister mean when she said, 'Your room looks like it's totally clean now'?") and further to explain why the speaker had made that comment (e.g., "Why did she say that?") (p. 125). According to the authors an acceptable response to the first question, which probed the child's ability to recognize the discrepancy between what was said and what was meant, would be, "She meant that her room was a mess" (p. 125). For the second question, which probed the child's understanding of the speaker's purpose, an acceptable response would be, "She said it to tease Jane, or to make fun of her" (p. 125).

The results indicated that 6-year-olds generally failed to recognize both the discrepancy and the speaker's purpose, that 8-year-olds recognized the discrepancy but not the purpose, and that 11-year-olds recognized both elements, thereby demonstrating the most advanced understanding of sarcasm. Interestingly, when children misinterpreted a speaker's purpose they often thought that the speaker either was trying to make the listener feel good or had simply misperceived the situation.

The importance of context and intonational cues to the understanding of sarcasm was demonstrated by Capelli et al. (1990). In their study, children from Grades 3 and 6, who were ages 8 and 11 years, respectively ($N = 64$), and a group of college students ($N = 80$) listened to a series of tape-recorded stories concerning the interactions of some children. Four different versions of each story were constructed by varying two factors: the story context (either sarcastic or neutral), and the vocal intonation (sarcastic or neutral) employed by one of the characters in the story. For example, the following story contains context cues that support a *sarcastic* interpretation:

Dick and Wendy were playing catch with a football at recess. Wendy threw out a long pass, and Dick was running full speed for it, when he slipped in the mud. His feet flew out from under him and he landed flat on his bottom. The ball bounced off his head and landed next to him in the mud. "Oooh, nice catch," said Wendy. (p. 1836)

The same story presented with *neutral* context cues was as follows:

Dick and Wendy were playing catch with a football at recess. Wendy threw out a long pass, and Dick went running full speed for it. He jumped in the air and then had to fall over backwards to catch it. "Oooh, nice catch," said Wendy. (p. 1836)

For each contextual variation, the final sentence (e.g., "Oooh, nice catch") was spoken with either a sarcastic or a neutral vocal intonation. When produced sarcastically, the speaker used a "mocking" tone, with prolonged vowels and exaggerated pitch. In sum, each story was presented in four different ways: (1) sarcastic context with sarcastic intonation; (2) sarcastic context with neutral intonation; (3) neutral context with sarcastic intonation; and (4) neutral context with neutral intonation. Types 1, 2, and 3 were appropriately interpreted as "sarcastic," and Type 4 was appropriately interpreted as "sincere." Of the three sarcastic versions, Type 1, offering two different kinds of cues, was expected to provide the greatest support for a correct interpretation. Each student was presented with eight different stories, two for each of the four types. Thus, there were six stories that were sarcastic and two that were sincere. After a story was presented, the student was asked a series of questions concerning its meaning. Questions were designed to determine how well the student attended to both types of cues, contextual and intonational, in correctly interpreting a speaker's intention as sarcastic or sincere.

Results showed that stories presented in a neutral context with neutral intonation ("sincere") were well understood by all groups of students. Moreover, the ability to interpret the three types of stories expressing sarcasm improved with each successive group: combining the three types, mean accuracy scores of 63%, 79%, and 93%, respectively, were obtained by students in Grades 3, 6, and college. Interestingly, stories that expressed sarcasm through context cues only (Type 2) were more difficult for both groups of children to understand than were those that expressed sarcasm through intonational cues only (Type 3) or through both context and intonational cues (Type 1). However, the ability to interpret sarcasm solely on the basis of context cues did improve as a function of age, with the sixth graders outperforming the third graders on Type 2 stories. For the adults, however, all three types of sarcastic stories were well understood.

In sum, the findings of Capelli et al. (1990) show that, although children depend on both types of cues to interpret sarcasm, intonational cues play an especially important role and the use of story context cues improves as children get older. Other types of context cues besides linguistic may also play a role in children's interpretation of sarcasm, especially in naturalistic settings. For example, Milosky (1994) suggested that children might attend to nonverbal cues such as a speaker's use of facial expressions (e.g., eye rolling) and hand gestures (e.g., slapping the forehead) to enhance their detection of sarcasm. She also suggested that children's knowledge of the relationship between two persons might enhance their ability to detect sarcasm. For example, if it is known that two people are antagonistic toward each other, children are more likely to interpret one person's comment to the other ("Thanks a lot!") as sarcastic than if the two are known to be supportive friends.

Summary

Studies have shown that sarcasm is difficult for preschool children to understand and that young school-age children heavily depend upon a speaker's vocal intonation and perhaps other nonlinguistic and experiential cues to understand sarcasm. As they mature, however, children show an increasing ability to attend to relevant context cues that are primarily linguistic. Although little is known about the ability of adolescents to interpret sarcasm, it is likely that progress occurs during this developmental period as well, given the superior performance of young adults compared to preadolescents on tasks of sarcasm detection (e.g., Capelli et al., 1990). Future research should examine the development of sarcasm during adolescence in terms of a variety of linguistic (e.g., lexical, syntactic, pragmatic) and nonlinguistic (e.g., intonational, facial, gestural) factors. However, it is important to remember that, in natural settings, even adults do not always perform consistently well in the use and understanding of sarcasm. For example, as listeners, we frequently ask for clarification (e.g., "Are you serious?") following another's attempt at sarcasm, especially when an utterance is delivered without the appropriate intonational, facial, or gestural cues or when we lack enough background knowledge to infer the speaker's intention accurately.

Conclusions

Although the ability to understand ambiguity and sarcasm steadily improves as students mature, certain tasks remain challenging. For example, in the case of ambiguity, difficulties arise even for college students when idiomatic or unfamiliar word meanings are involved (e.g., "This restaurant even serves *crabs*," "*In his eyes*, only Johnson's baby shampoo . . ."). Although this has not been examined in relation to sarcasm, it seems likely that when idiomatic expressions are used sarcastically (e.g., describing a team's weakest player an "an awesome athlete"), this would add complexity to the task of interpreting the speaker's intention, particularly in the absence of intonational cues and relevant background information. This issue seems ripe for research. Additionally, although research has shown that skill with ambiguity is associated with high intelligence, academic achievement, and a reflective problem-solving style, similar studies involving sarcasm have not yet been conducted, but also would be worthwhile.

Studies where ambiguity occurs in naturalistic contexts (e.g., jokes, riddles, and advertisements) have yielded interesting findings concerning the development of communicative competence in specific discourse settings during the school-age and adolescent years. Similar studies could be conducted in relation to sarcasm. In addition, the spontaneous production of utterances containing ambiguity and sarcasm in children and adolescents could be examined, particularly during peer interactions where humorous stories or anecdotes are exchanged.

Acknowledgments

Portions of this chapter appeared in the following publication:

Nippold, M. A. (1988). Linguistic ambiguity. In M. A. Nippold (Ed.), *Later language development: Ages nine through nineteen* (pp. 211–223). Austin, TX: PRO-ED.

Used with permission of PRO-ED.

CHAPTER

SYNTACTIC ATTAINMENTS

"Syntax is the way in which words are arranged to show relationships of meaning within (and sometimes between) sentences. The term comes from syntaxis, *the Greek word for* arrangement."

—Crystal (1987, p. 94)

Ironically, the subtle and protracted nature of later language development becomes particularly obvious upon examining spoken and written syntax. Considerable growth in syntax beyond the preschool years is evidenced at both the *intrasentential* and *intersentential* levels (Karmiloff-Smith, 1986). Intrasentential growth occurs at the level of the individual sentence, whereas intersentential growth refers to changes that occur in joining sentences. Syntactic attainments that occur during the school-age and adolescent years are addressed in this chapter, highlighting those closely related to academic success.

Intrasentential Growth

Basic English sentences can be *simple, compound, complex,* or *compound-complex.* Whereas a *simple sentence* consists of one independent clause (e.g., "It's sunny today"), a *compound sentence* contains at least two independent clauses joined by a coordinating conjunction such as *so* or *but* (e.g., "It's sunny today, so we'll go on a picnic"). A *complex sentence* contains one independent clause and at least one dependent clause joined by a subordinating conjunction such as *if* or *when* (e.g., "We'll go on a picnic if it's sunny today"). Sentences that contain an independent clause and a nonfinite verb phrase such as an infinitive (e.g., "We're going on a hike *to find* arrowheads"),

157

Table 11.1
Mean Number of Words Per C-Unit in Spoken
and Written Language Samples Obtained
in Loban's Longitudinal Study

Grade (Age)		Spoken	Written*
1	(6 through 7)	6.88	——
3	(8 through 9)	7.62	7.60
6	(11 through 12)	9.82	9.04
9	(14 through 15)	10.96	10.05
12	(17 through 18)	11.70	13.27

Note. Adapted from *Language Development: Kindergarten Through Grade Twelve* (Research Report No. 18), p. 35, by W. Loban, 1976, Urbana, IL: National Council of Teachers of English.

*Written language samples were not available for Grade 1.

participle (e.g., "*Running swiftly*, Uta won the Boston Marathon"), or gerund (e.g., "*Hiking in the mountains* is her passion") are also complex. A *compound-complex sentence* contains at least two independent clauses and at least one dependent clause (e.g., "It was raining when we arrived, but soon the sun came out") (Blake & Madden, 1994; Crews, 1977; Quirk & Greenbaum, 1973). As school-age children and adolescents mature, they show increasingly sophisticated use of spoken and written sentences, particularly of those that are complex and compound-complex (Hass & Wepman, 1974; Hunt, 1965, 1970; Loban, 1976; Scott, 1988b).

Sentence Length

Numerous investigators have charted the growth that occurs in sentence length during the school-age and adolescent years by counting the mean number of words in *communication units* (C-units) or *terminable units* (T-units) in spoken or written language samples (e.g., Chappell, 1980; Hunt, 1965, 1970; Klecan-Aker & Hedrick, 1985; Loban, 1976; Morris & Crump, 1982; O'Donnell, Griffin, & Norris, 1967; Savage & Fallis, 1988). Defined by Loban, C-units and T-units both consist of an independent clause and any modifiers such as a dependent clause (e.g., "A frightening storm came up while we were on the river"). The only difference between C-units and T-units is that C-units can also include incomplete sentences when used to answer questions (e.g., "for five years" would be a C-unit when used to answer the question, "How long have you lived in Oregon?"). When counting T-units, incomplete sentences are excluded. Collectively, the studies have documented small but regular increases in sentence length during the school-age and adolescent years. This pattern is depicted in Table 11.1, which reports the mean number of words per C-unit for spoken and written language samples for students at Grades 1, 3, 6, 9, and 12 in Loban's longitu-

Table 11.2
MLUs Obtained by Leadholm and Miller
(1992) for Children in Two Speaking Modes
($N = 167$)

Age	Conversation	Narration
5.4	5.71	6.06
7.1	5.92	7.32
9.1	6.50	8.80
11.1	7.62	9.83
13.0	6.99	9.32

Note. Adapted from *Language Sample Analysis: The Wisconsin Guide* (pp. 95–108) by B. J. Leadholm and J. F. Miller, 1992, Madison, WI: Wisconsin Department of Public Instruction.

dinal study. The data were obtained from the "random group" ($N = 35$) and represent a mix of students with high, average, and low levels of language proficiency.

More recently, Leadholm and Miller (1992) collected spontaneous language samples from children ages 3 through 13 years ($N = 266$) in two different speaking modes, conversation and narration. Unlike Loban (1976), they analyzed their samples in terms of *mean length of utterance* (MLU) in morphemes and included all incomplete sentences in addition to complete sentences. Leadholm and Miller found that the average length of utterance gradually increased as a function of age, and that children tended to produce longer utterances when speaking in the narrative mode than in the conversational mode. This general pattern can be discerned from Table 11.2, which reports the MLUs that were obtained in the two discourse modes from children in the study who were ages 5, 7, 9, 11, and 13 years ($N = 167$).

Like Leadholm and Miller (1992), other investigators have also found that sentence length can vary greatly in relation to discourse mode. Crowhurst and Piche (1979) examined compositions written by students in Grades 6 and 10 (ages 11 and 15 years, respectively) ($N = 240$). At each grade level, 40 students were assigned to write in one of three different modes—narrative, descriptive, or persuasive—and each student wrote six compositions for each mode over a period of several weeks. To elicit the compositions, students were shown pictures (e.g., a whale performing in a show) and were asked to "write an exciting story" for the narrative mode and to "describe the picture" for the descriptive mode. For the persuasive mode, they were shown the same picture and asked to take a position about a controversy (e.g., whether or not whales should be trained to perform in shows) and defend their stance.

Results indicated that at both grade levels, the mean number of words per T-unit was highest in the persuasive mode (Grade 6 = 11.75; Grade 10 = 14.26), lowest in the narrative mode (Grade 6 = 10.13; Grade 10 = 11.15), and intermediate in the descriptive mode (Grade 6 = 10.45; Grade 10 = 12.81). They also found that the persuasive and descriptive modes were more sensitive to developmental growth in T-unit length than the narrative mode.

Crowhurst (1980) replicated this study with students in Grades 6, 10, and 12 (ages 12, 16, and 18 years, respectively) (N = 240). Procedures employed in the previous study (Crowhurst & Piche, 1979) were used again with the exception that students wrote compositions in only two modes, persuasive and narrative. At every grade level, students produced a greater mean number of words per T-unit when writing in the persuasive mode than in the narrative mode. For the persuasive and narrative modes, respectively, those means were as follows: Grade 6 = 13.78, 10.60; Grade 10 = 15.17, 12.48; Grade 12 = 16.06, 12.51. It was also found that the persuasive mode was more sensitive to developmental growth than the narrative mode, particularly in the oldest students. Whereas in the persuasive mode, significant growth occurred with each successive grade level, in the narrative mode, no improvement occurred beyond Grade 10. Nevertheless, the differences in mean T-unit length that occurred between modes at each of the three grade levels (Grades 6 = 3.18; Grade 10 = 2.69; Grade 12 = 3.55) were actually greater than the differences that occurred between the youngest and oldest groups for either the persuasive (2.28) or the narrative (1.91) mode.

Crowhurst (1980) concluded that, given the wide variability in performance that can occur across modes of written discourse, it is important to obtain and refer to separate sets of normative data for the various modes when attempting to determine if students are making adequate progress in syntactic development. Given the findings of Leadholm and Miller (1992) that children's MLUs were greater during story re-telling than in conversation, the same cautions should pertain to spoken discourse as well.

Low-Frequency Syntactic Structures

It is interesting to consider *how* sentences change as they lengthen during the school-age and adolescent years. One way in which sentence length increases is through the use of *low-frequency syntactic structures*. Scott (1988b) and Scott and Stokes (1995) reported that as students mature, *noun phrases* are expanded through the use of structures such as appositives, elaborated subjects, and postmodification via prepositional phrases, nonfinite verbs, and relative clauses. *Verb phrases* are expanded through structures such as modal auxiliary verbs, the perfect aspect, and the passive voice. Examples of these low-frequency structures are contained in Table 11.3. Scott (1988b) also reported that, as students mature, they are more likely to produce complex sentences that contain other uncommon structures, such as *clefting*, which serves to focus attention on particular elements of a sentence (Quirk & Greenbaum, 1973) (e.g., "*It was early in the race* when she began to feel ill," derived from the shorter and simpler version, "She began to feel ill early in the race"). The tendency to combine low-frequency structures is also characteristic of more mature language users (Scott &

Table 11.3
Examples of Low-Frequency Syntactic Structures

Noun phrase expansion through the use of:

Appositives, e.g., Margaret *the corporate attorney* bought a town house.

Elaborated subjects, e.g., *Dogs such as collies, cocker spaniels, and golden retrievers* were at the show.

Postmodification via prepositional phrase, e.g., They knew the Italian cyclist *in the lead pack* would win the race.

Postmodification via nonfinite verb, e.g., The next runner *to compete* would anchor the relay.

Postmodification via relative clause, e.g., Some birds *that dive for their food* are extremely colorful

Verb phrase expansion through the use of:

Modal auxiliary verbs, e.g., We *should* have gone skating.

The perfect aspect, e.g., She *had been working* all day.

The passive voice, e.g., The house *was carefully designed* by a famous architect.

Note. Adapted from "Spoken and Written Syntax" (p. 49–95) by C. M. Scott, 1988, in M. A. Nippold (Ed.) *Later Language Development: Ages Nine Through Nineteen*, Austin, TX: PRO-ED; and "Measures of Syntax in School-Age Children and Adolescents" by C. M. Scott and S. L. Stokes, 1995, *Language, Speech, and Hearing Services in Schools*, 26, (p. 309–319).

Erwin, 1992), as when a sentence contains clefting, an appositive, a relative clause, and the passive voice (e.g., "It was Rosa, the favorite, who was passed by Uta on Heartbreak Hill"). By using low-frequency structures, the number of words per clause increases, along with the density of information expressed.

Subordination, Coordination, and Correlation

In addition to the use of low-frequency syntactic structures, sentence length increases through the use of *subordinating, coordinating,* and *correlative conjunctions.* All three types of conjunctions serve to join ideas within sentences, and are therefore called *intrasentential cohesion devices.* A *subordinating conjunction* (e.g., *when, although, unless*) introduces a dependent clause (e.g., "when the bell rang"), which must be attached to an independent clause (e.g., "the children ran outside") (e.g., "When the bell rang, the children ran outside"). The dependent clause is said to be *embedded* within the larger independent clause (Langacker, 1973). Although an independent clause can stand alone as a sentence, a dependent clause cannot. In contrast, a *coordinating conjunction* (e.g., *and, but, so*) joins two independent clauses (e.g., "Mary likes purple and Jack likes green") or smaller units within a sentence such as nouns (e.g., "Jeff bought apples *and* pears"), verbs (e.g., "Jake will swim *and* run"), adjectives (e.g., "Jane is tall *and* slim"), and adverbs (e.g., "The dog waited quietly *and* calmly"). *Correlative*

Table 11.4

Examples of Subordinating, Coordinating, and Correlative Conjunctions

Subordinating conjunctions:

after	Thad bought ice cream *after* he left the dance.
although	*Although* the exam was difficult, we passed.
as	*As* the music began, the couple walked outside.
as if	The child looked around *as if* she were lost.
because	I bought an umbrella *because* my old one broke.
before	We stayed in Verona *before* we went to Venice.
even if	She'll be happy *even if* she doesn't win.
if	We'll buy a road map *if* we rent a car.
since	They're going home *since* it's already midnight.
unless	We'll share our lunch *unless* you don't like tacos.
until	The band practiced their song *until* the bell rang.
when	*When* the cat came in, she jumped on the sofa.
whenever	They go out to breakfast *whenever* Grandma visits.
wherever	We'll buy postcards *wherever* we go.
whereas	A beaver is large *whereas* a marmot is small.
while	I listened to music *while* I wrote a letter.

Coordinating conjunctions:

and	Henry likes chess *and* David likes checkers.
but	Tony wanted a hamburger *but* got a hot dog.
for	Tim studied hard, *for* he wanted a good grade.
nor	Jack did not see Robert *nor* Tom.
or	The couple will cook dinner *or* go out.
so	Jane won two tickets, *so* she invited Alice.
yet	Kim finished the exam quickly *yet* made few errors.

Correlative conjunctions:

both . . . and	Jennifer would like *both* pie *and* cake for dessert.
either . . . or	I'll take *either* chocolate *or* vanilla ice cream.
neither . . . nor	*Neither* Dan *nor* Jim will plant squash this year.
not only . . . but also	Mary wants *not only* corn *but also* tomatoes.

Note. Adapted from *Facets: Writing Skills in Context* by S. M. Blake and J. Madden, 1994, New York: Macmillan; *The Random House Handbook* (2nd ed.), by F. Crews, 1977, New York: Random House; and *A Concise Grammar of Contemporary English*, by R. Quirk and S. Greenbaum, 1973, New York: Harcourt Brace Jovanovich.

conjunctions (e.g., *both, either, neither*) signal that two items, joined by a coordinating conjunction, are related symmetrically (e.g., "*Both* London *and* Paris are exciting cities"; "*Neither* silver *nor* crystal were found in the cave"). Table 11.4 contains additional examples of each type of conjunction.

Studies of syntactic development have documented gradual improvement in students' knowledge and use of subordinating and coordinating conjunctions. In contrast, little attention has been devoted specifically to correlative conjunctions. However, when used correctly, these words can enhance clarity and limit redundancy in communication, two hallmarks of linguistic sophistication, particularly in the written mode. Given that correlative conjunctions are not often heard in the speech of preschool children, skill in using these words can be expected to improve during the school-age and adolescent years. Their development should be investigated further.

In an early investigation, Katz and Brent (1968) examined students' knowledge of the conjunctions *but* and *although*. Students in Grades 1 and 6 ($N = 43$) and college sophomores ($N = 41$) participated in the study. A paired-sentences task was presented where a correct and an incorrect usage of each conjunction occurred. For the conjunction *but*, the sentences were, "Jimmie went to school, but he felt sick" and "Jimmie went to school, but he felt fine" (p. 503). For *although*, the sentences were, "The meal was good, although the pie was bad" and "The meal was good, although the pie was good" (p. 503). Students listened to each pair and were asked to select the sentence that sounded better. Correct usage of *but* was identified by 19% of the first graders, 68% of the sixth graders, and 98% of the college students; correct usage of *although* was identified by 14% of the first graders, 68% of the sixth graders, and 100% of college students. The results showed that *but* and *although* are difficult for first graders, but that knowledge of these words improves during the school-age and adolescent years.

Robertson (1968) examined the development of conjunctions that frequently occurred in fourth through sixth grade reading textbooks, including coordinating (e.g., *and, but, for*) and subordinating (e.g., *although, because, if, when*) conjunctions. Students in Grades 4, 5, and 6 ($N = 402$) were given a task designed by the researcher called the *Connectives Reading Test*. The task consisted of 150 multiple-choice items. Test items were sentences taken directly from the students' reading textbooks. Each item was presented in the form of an incomplete sentence containing a conjunction (e.g., "He held the rod and . . .") followed by four choices of ways to complete the sentence; only one choice expressed an appropriate meaning and was grammatically correct (e.g., "the horse jumped over it"). Students were asked to choose the best alternative.

Performance on the *Connectives Reading Test* improved as a function of age; mean accuracy scores of 57%, 66%, and 75% were obtained by the students in Grades 4, 5, and 6, respectively. However, because the sentences had been considered "grade appropriate," Robertson (1968) interpreted the results as poor and suggested that the failure to understand conjunctions could contribute to reading problems in upper elementary grade students. Therefore, she argued that textbook writers should consider more closely the comprehension skills of students at various grade levels. She also recommended that teachers directly teach the meanings of conjunctions in written language.

Also in Robertson's (1968) study, a standardized measure of academic achievement, the *Sequential Tests of Educational Progress*, was administered and scores in the areas of reading, writing, and listening were available. Correlation coefficients calculated between each of those subtests and the *Connectives Reading Test* were significant and positive. Those findings further supported the view that knowledge of conjunctions is important for the development of literacy and that educators should pay close attention to children's understanding of these words. This view was also expressed by McClure and Geva (1983), who reported that even eighth-grade students lacked a full understanding of the cohesive properties of the conjunctions *but* and *although*. In addition to teaching directly the meanings of conjunctions, Geva and Ryan (1985) emphasized the importance of training students to attend more closely to conjunctions as they occur in written expository texts. Support for their view was based on research they had conducted with fifth- and seventh-grade students that showed that comprehension of written text was enhanced when the conjunctions were underlined and capitalized.

Dependent clauses that contain subordinating conjunctions appear in the speech of preschool children (Scott, 1988a). However, their frequency of use gradually increases throughout childhood and adolescence in both spoken and written contexts. In his longitudinal study, Loban (1976) reported that for students in Grades 1, 3, 6, 9, and 12, respectively, the mean number of dependent clauses per C-unit was .16, .22, .37, .43, and .58 in spoken language. For Grades 6, 9, and 12, respectively, those means were .29, .47, and .60 in written language. Written language data were not available for Grades 1 and 3. Loban also examined the proportion of different types of dependent clauses that occurred in students' spoken and written language samples, including *nominal* (e.g., "Jim was surprised *that he lost the race*"), *adverbial* (e.g., "*When he passed the German*, Pedro took the lead"), and *adjectival* or *relative* (e.g., "The poet, *who was sitting by the fire*, was inspired"). Although all types were used, nominal clauses tended to predominate in spoken language, and adverbial tended to predominate in written language. This is consistent with the point made by Scott and Stokes (1995) that left-branching structures, such as adverbial clauses, can be difficult to process, and typically occur in more sophisticated, formal language contexts such as academic writing.

Loban (1976) noted, however, that certain types of verb phrases, when used in place of dependent clauses, suggest even greater syntactic sophistication because of their conciseness of expression. Examples include *participial phrases* (e.g., "*Passing the German*, Pedro took the lead"), *infinitive phrases* (e.g., "Jim was surprised *to lose the race*"), and *gerund phrases* (e.g., "*Sitting by the fire* inspired the poet"). The greater sophistication of concise verb phrases supports the view that increased sentence length does not always imply increased syntactic maturity in spoken and written language (Scott, 1988b).

Other investigators have also shown that the acquisition of conjunctions is a gradual process. Flores d'Arcais (1978) examined Dutch children's understanding of a variety of conjunctions. In one experiment, understanding of the intrasentential conjunctions *because* (*omdat*), *since* (*doordat*), *so that* (*zodat*), and *before* (*voordat*) was examined using a judgment task where students were asked to decide if pairs of sentences were equivalent in meaning. Children who were ages 7, 8, 10, and 12 years ($N = 80$) were tested. The task consisted of 12 pairs of complex sentences where the members of each pair were identical except for the conjunction (e.g., "The dog barks *because* the cat approaches," "The dog barks *so that* the cat approaches") (p. 138). Each of the four conjunctions was paired with each of the other three. An additional four pairs of sentences ("dummy pairs") were presented as foils for a total of 32 sentences in the task. The child read each pair of sentences aloud and was asked to decide if the second sentence could be used "to tell another child about the event described in the first sentence" (p. 138). Results showed that the 7- and 8-year-olds had great difficulty distinguishing between many of the conjunctions. Although the 10-year-olds outperformed the two younger groups, they made more incorrect judgments than the 12-year-olds, particularly in distinguishing the following pairs of conjunctions: *because-before*, *because-so that*, and *before-since*. However, even the 12-year-olds had not completely mastered all of the distinctions.

In a second experiment, Flores d'Arcais (1978) examined Dutch children's understanding of the intrasentential conjunctions *because*, *before*, and *so that* using a written, multiple-choice task. Groups of children ages 8, 10, and 12 years ($N = 60$) were tested. The task consisted of nine short stories. Each was followed by a choice of three sentences, only one of which best paraphrased the story. Three stories were presented in random order for each of the three conjunctions. The examiner read each test item aloud and then asked the child to choose the sentence that best expressed the meaning of the story. An example of a test item for *because* was as follows:

▶ The dog is sitting in the garden. At a certain moment, a cat arrives. The dog sees the cat. He then begins to bark.

1. The dog barks *because* the cat arrives.
2. The dog barks *before* the cat arrives.
3. The dog barks *so that* the cat arrives. (p. 143)

Performance improved with each successive age group, but even the 12-year-olds had some difficulty with the task. For all three groups, *so that* was the most difficult conjunction, *because* was easiest, and *before* was intermediate in difficulty.

To examine further the development of conjunctions, Flores d'Arcais (1978) designed a sorting task that involved 20 common Dutch conjunctions. This time, children ages 8, 10, and 12 years and a control group of adults ($N = 80$) were tested. Each subject was given a stack of 20 cards, randomly ordered. A different conjunction had been typed on each card, and the subject was asked to sort the cards into different piles having similar meanings. The underlying assumption of this experiment was that greater knowledge of the conjunctions would be reflected in a stronger tendency to sort the words into clusters that expressed three distinct meanings: causal (e.g., *because, since, so that*), temporal (e.g., *after, before, until*), and conditional (e.g., *provided that, unless, although, in case*). Although the adults could do this accurately, the 8- and 10-year-olds showed little awareness of the semantic clusters and the 12-year-olds performed only slightly better than the 10-year-olds.

In discussing the experiments, Flores d'Arcais (1978) concluded that a full understanding of conjunctions is acquired gradually and continues to develop beyond age 12. However, because of the metalinguistic demands of the three experiments just described, the investigator cautioned that poor performance on such tasks does not necessarily imply that a child will fail to understand conjunctions in other, more natural situations where contextual information may facilitate performance.

Wing and Scholnick (1981) examined children's understanding of concepts expressed by five different subordinating conjunctions: *because, although, if + indicative* (e.g., "*If* the bag *has* a red tag, it's mine"), *if + subjunctive* (e.g., "*If* Jim *had won* the race, he would have told us"), and *unless. Because* and *although* express belief about a proposition, *if + indicative* and *unless* express uncertainty, and *if + subjunctive* expresses disbelief. They predicted that conjunctions expressing uncertainty would be more difficult to understand than conjunctions expressing belief or disbelief. Students from Grades 1, 3, and 5 ($N = 90$) participated in the study. Understanding of the concepts was assessed using a judgment task that involved a set of 25 sentences; five for each of the conjunctions under investigation. The following examples were provided:

▶ 1. This is a monkey *because* it has two hands.
2. This is a monkey *although* it has a trunk.
3. This is a monkey *if* it has two hands.
4. These would be monkeys *if* they had two hands.
5. This is a monkey *unless* it has a trunk. (p. 352)

The child was told that an astronaut was studying some animals on a new planet and was reporting his observations back to earth. However, the astronaut was not always sure of his observations because the animals were unfamiliar and the atmosphere was cloudy. The child was asked to determine if the astronaut was expressing belief, disbelief, or uncertainty in his statements about the animals. Immediately after the astronaut made a statement (e.g., "This is a monkey if it has two hands"), the child was questioned about the astronaut's beliefs concerning three things: the truth of the main clause (e.g., "Does he believe this is a monkey?"), the truth of the subordinate clause (e.g., "Does he believe it has two hands?"), and the entailment relation between the clauses (e.g., "Does he believe most monkeys have two hands?") (p. 354). For each question, the child was expected to respond *Yes, No,* or *He's not sure.* Correct responses to the first two questions were each worth one-half point, and a correct response to the third question was worth one point. Thus, it was possible to earn a maximum of 50 points for the entire task. Performance steadily increased with each successive grade level, and mean raw scores of 29.80 (60%), 33.35 (67%), and 37.02 (74%) were obtained by the students in Grades 1, 3, and 5, respectively. From easiest to most difficult, the five conjunctions were ordered as follows: *because, although, if + subjunctive, if + indicative,* and *unless.* At each grade level, statements expressing belief (*because, although*) were easiest. At Grades 3 and 5, statements expressing disbelief (*if + subjunctive*) were easier than those expressing uncertainty (*if + indicative, unless*); however, at Grade 1, statements expressing disbelief and uncertainty were equally difficult.

McClure and Steffensen (1985) examined the ability of children and adolescents to use the subordinating conjunctions *because* and *even though,* and the coordinating conjunctions *and* and *but* in writing. Students in Grades 3, 6, and 9 (ages 8 through 15 years) (*N* = 96) performed a written sentence completion task in which 24 sentences were presented. Each sentence began with an independent clause followed by one of the four targeted conjunctions. The student was asked to complete the sentence so that it made sense. Six problems were presented for each of the four conjunctions. Examples of each type were as follows:

▶ He bought a TV *because* . . .
The puppy is tired *even though* . . .
Dad is hungry *and* . . .
Sam gets good grades in school *but* . . .

Across conjunctions, mean accuracy scores for students in Grades 3, 6, and 9, respectively, were 64%, 84%, and 85%, indicating that performance improved as grade level increased. In general, accuracy was greater with the conjunctions *but, and,* and *because* than with *even though,* particularly for the two youngest groups. Although performance on *but, and,* and *because* reached a plateau by Grade 6, performance on *even though* improved to Grade 9. However, even the oldest students sometimes experienced difficulty with *even though,* producing sentences such as, "The puppy is tired even though *it's been playing all day*" (p. 231). It was also found that, at every grade level, performance on the sentence completion task was significantly correlated to performance on the Vocabulary, Comprehension, and Total Reading subtests of the *Stanford Achievement Test* (Madden, Gardner, Rudman, Karlsen, & Merwin, 1973), indicating that skill in using subordinating and coordinating conjunctions, an important syntactic attainment, is also related to literacy acquisition.

Using a story retelling task, Savage and Fallis (1988) examined the development of subordinating and coordinating conjunctions in spoken language. Students in Grades 6 and 9 (ages 12 and 15 years) (*N* = 120) participated. Each student listened to a story read aloud by an examiner and then was asked to retell the story. The story, "A Car for John," was fairly sophisticated in terms of its syntactic and semantic elements, containing many long and complex sentences, low-frequency syntactic structures, subordinating and coordinating conjunctions, and abstract words. This served to stimulate the use of those elements if students were indeed capable of using them. For example, a portion of the story was as follows:

> John, who was almost 16, wanted to buy a car, but his father, Mr. Lawrence, felt that his son was too young for such a purchase. Nevertheless, he made some concessions and indicated to John that he could get a car under the following conditions. Firstly, John would have to pay for the vehicle and all of the expenses attached to owning a car on his own. Secondly, he would have to maintain his B+ average at school; and finally, John would have to adhere strictly to the curfew rules outlined by his father. Otherwise, the car keys would be taken away. (Appendix 1A)

Each student was audio-recorded while retelling the story to the examiner. Each recording was then transcribed and analyzed for a number of features. Relevant to this discussion was the finding that subordinating and coordinating conjunctions both increased in frequency as a function of grade level. For Grades 6 and 9, respectively, students produced an average of 7.2 and 10.8 subordinating conjunctions, and an average of 4.6 and 7.2 coordinating conjunctions per narrative.

This outcome was consistent with other studies of syntactic development in school-age children and adolescents. For example, Chappell (1980), who also presented a sophisticated story retelling task, found that between Grades 4 and 7 (ages 9 through 13 years) (N = 240), the use of subordinating and coordinating conjunctions increased in students' spoken language samples.

Intersentential Growth

Growth in syntax during the school-age and adolescent years can also be charted in the use and understanding of linguistic devices that join sentences to produce cohesive discourse. Two types of intersentential cohesion devices that have been examined include adverbial conjuncts and lexical cohesion.

Adverbial Conjuncts

Adverbial conjuncts such as *moreover, consequently,* and *furthermore* are a type of intersentential cohesion device used to link clauses or sentences on the basis of some logical relationship (Quirk & Greenbaum, 1973). A list of adverbial conjuncts that can be expected to develop as children and adolescents mature is contained in Table 11.5. These words often occur in literate contexts such as textbooks, essays, lectures, and debates at the high school and college levels. Some of the more common adverbial conjuncts also occur in less formal contexts, such as casual conversations where they can be used to signal transitions into new or related topics (e.g., *anyway, by the way*) (Mentis, 1994) or a difference of opinion (e.g., *even so, on the other hand*). Skill in using these devices is important for academic success and conversational dexterity.

Table 11.5
Examples of Adverbial Conjuncts

accordingly	additionally	afterward
alternatively	anyway	apparently
besides	coincidentally	consequently
contrastively	conversely	finally
fortunately	furthermore	happily
hence	however	indeed
instead	ironically	likewise
meanwhile	moreover	namely
nevertheless	nonetheless	notably
otherwise	overall	predictably
rather	regretfully	sadly
similarly	still	subsequently
surprisingly	then	therefore
thus	traditionally	typically

Note. Adapted from *Facets: Writing Skills in Context* by S. M. Blake and J. Madden, 1994, New York: Macmillan; *The Random House Handbook* (2nd ed.), by F. Crews, 1977, New York: Random House; and *A Concise Grammar of Contemporary English*, by R. Quirk and S. Greenbaum, 1973, New York: Harcourt Brace Jovanovich.

Scott (1984) examined adverbial conjuncts in the spontaneous conversations of children ages 6, 8, 10, and 12 years ($N = 114$). Her research showed that adverbial conjuncts were used infrequently during this age range and were confined mainly to a small set of the more common ones (e.g., *then*, *so*, *though*). Although the 10- and 12-year-olds used a greater number and variety of adverbial conjuncts than the 6- and 8-year-olds, even the oldest children showed limited spontaneous usage compared to a control group of adults. Scott suggested that growth in using these words must occur during adolescence.

In another study, Scott and Rush (1985) examined the development of adverbial conjuncts in children ages 7, 9, and 13 years ($N = 11$). Children were asked to perform various formal tasks such as retelling stories that contained adverbial conjuncts (e.g., *however*, *then*), making judgments about the grammaticality of sentences containing those words (e.g., "It was her birthday; *however*, she had a nice cake"), and supplying the appropriate adverbial conjunct to complete a sentence (e.g., "He has been sick; _____ he would have been at school"). On all tasks, children showed greater accuracy with the more common adverbial conjuncts (e.g., *so*, *then*) than the less common ones (e.g., *hence*, *nevertheless*). Although the older children were more accurate than the younger ones, none of the children performed the tasks perfectly.

Nippold, Schwarz, and Undlin (1992) examined the use and understanding of ten different adverbial conjuncts (*therefore*, *however*, *consequently*, *rather*, *nevertheless*, *furthermore, moreover, conversely, contrastively, similarly*) in adolescents and young adults. Thirty students in each of four age groups participated. Mean ages of the groups were 12, 15, 19, and 23 years (Groups 1, 2, 3, and 4, respectively). A writing task was first administered, which required the student to create a sentence using each of the ten adverbial conjuncts. Each problem consisted of one completed sentence followed by an adverbial conjunct, for example:

▶ Father told Crystal that she had to complete all of her homework before she could go skating. Furthermore, _____. (p. 116)

A sentence was judged correct if it expressed an appropriate meaning, was semantically consistent with the previous sentence, and was grammatically correct (e.g., "Furthermore, she had to clean her room and wash the dishes"). Immediately following the writing task, a reading task was administered, which examined comprehension of the same set of adverbial conjuncts. Each problem required the student to read a paragraph and select the most appropriate conjunct to begin the final sentence. An example of a problem for *nevertheless* was as follows:

▶ The Vikings came from Norway, Sweden, and Denmark. They turned to the sea because they did not have very rich land. The Vikings built good ships but they had no compasses or modern instruments on board to guide them. _____ , they sailed all over Europe to explore and conquer new lands.

A. Nevertheless
B. Conversely
C. Rather
D. Moreover (p. 117)

Performance on both tasks steadily improved with increasing subject age. Students found the writing task more difficult than the reading task. Mean accuracy scores obtained by Groups 1, 2, 3, and 4, respectively, were as follows: 45%, 50%; 50%, 64% on writing; 79%, 85%; 85%, 94% on reading. Analysis of the written responses indicated that as subject age increased, instances of ungrammatical and inappropriate sentences steadily declined. For example, responses such as the following, produced by a 12-year-old, never occurred among the 23-year-olds: "Furthermore, "Crystal decided to leaves without doing it anyways." It was also found that the easier conjuncts (e.g., *however*) tended to occur more often in textbooks written for school-age children and adolescents than the more difficult ones (e.g., *conversely*). This suggests that competence with adverbial conjuncts has much to do with the amount of meaningful exposure a student receives to these words in formal academic contexts. However, in interpreting this study, it should be noted that the two oldest groups were college or university students. Because of the scholarly nature of adverbial conjuncts, some adolescents and adults may never master this cohesion device, especially if their formal educations are limited to high school.

Lexical Cohesion

Research has also shown that certain lexical cohesion devices such as *synonyms* and *collocation* are used across sentences in written language with increasing frequency during the school-age and adolescent years (Crowhurst, 1987). According to Halliday and Hasan (1976), a synonym or near-synonym can be used as a cohesion device to refer to a previously mentioned item. In the example below, *contest* is used in one sentence to refer back to *tournament* used in the previous sentence:

> The fraternity was staging a tennis tournament over the weekend. Organizers were working diligently to prepare for the contest, as it was expected to draw many competitors.

The use of synonyms minimizes redundancy and provides variety while maintaining cohesion across sentences.

In contrast, collocation occurs when words commonly associated with one another co-occur in a passage of text. Examples of collocation from Halliday and Hasan (1976, pp. 285–286) include contrasts (*boys, girls*) and antonyms (*wet, dry*), and words that bear a categorical (*table, chair*), superordinate (*dollar, penny*), part-whole (*lid, box*), or sequential (*Tuesday, Thursday*) relationship to one another. When words that are related by physical (*door, window*) or topical (*sunshine, cloud, rain*) proximity co-occur, this also constitutes collocation. According to Halliday and Hasan, words used in collocation "will generate a cohesive force if they occur in adjacent sentences" (p. 286). In the sentences below, *girls* collocates with *boy*:

> Why does this little boy wriggle all the time? Girls don't wriggle. (p. 285)

Developmental increases in the use of these two types of lexical cohesion devices, synonyms and collocation, were demonstrated by Crowhurst (1987). In Crowhurst's study, students from Grades 6, 10, and 12 ($N = 140$) wrote compositions in two different modes, persuasive and narrative. The same procedures that were described previously for the studies by Crowhurst (1980) and Crowhurst and Piche (1979) were employed to administer the task. Each composition was later examined in terms of the types of cohesive ties that were used across T-unit boundaries.

The results indicated that the frequency of synonyms and collocation both increased in relation to grade level. Grade 12 outperformed Grades 10 and 6 on synonyms, and Grades 12 and 10 outperformed Grade 6 on collocation. The superior performance of the older students was attributed to them having more diverse knowledge of words and a greater tendency to elaborate upon their ideas. In this study, discourse mode had little effect on the specific lexical cohesion devices that were used, with the exception that students in Grade 12 used collocation more often when writing in the narrative mode than in the persuasive mode.

The Role of Context

Caution must be exercised when interpreting the literature on intrasentential and intersentential syntactic development. In each of the developmental studies discussed in this chapter, formal, experimenter-generated tasks were employed such as having children and adolescents tell or write stories, argue a point of view, construct particular types of sentences, or converse with an adult. Different results would undoubtedly occur in more spontaneous settings as when young people talk among themselves and have their own personal goals for communicating.

An interesting example of context-specific syntactic simplification can be seen when school-age children engage in spontaneous play behaviors such as "sportscasting." Hoyle (1991) audio-recorded her 8-year-old son and his friends while they were playing a computer game of basketball. During the game, the boys traded off the role of a professional sports announcer, offering play-by-play accounts of the action and other commentary. During a live game, professional sports announcers speak rapidly, frequently, and with exaggerated prosodic patterns in order to keep the crowd informed and interested, resulting in utterances that are short and to the point (e.g., "Jones to the line . . . and it's good! Six for the Blazers!"). Although superficially simple, language used in this manner requires many linguistic skills such the ability to call up names quickly and accurately, to articulate thoughts clearly and precisely, to maintain the flow of discourse, and to infer the needs of the crowd.

The children in Hoyle's (1991) study were remarkably adept at sportscasting, producing utterances that, under other circumstances, would be considered quite impoverished and ungrammatical, given their ages. For example, the simple present tense predominated (e.g., "Bird makes a bad shot!" "Celtics have the ball"), one- and two-word utterances were common (e.g., "Bird" "Comes in" "Shoots" "Misses!"), and normally obligatory sentential elements were omitted because of their low-information value (e.g., "Takes a shot" = subject omission; "McHale to Bird" = main verb omission; "The Doctor driving in" = auxiliary verb omission), adjustments that professional sports announcers make routinely.

Similarly, there is evidence that adolescents simplify their syntax in certain spontaneous communicative contexts. In a study of adolescent conversational patterns, Eckert (1990) audio-recorded the after-school conversations of eleventh-grade girls (ages 16 through 17) ($N = 6$) who were discussing boys, dating, and popularity. The girls were all described as "good students" who were active in a variety of social groups.

An analysis of a published transcript from that study indicated that one of the more talkative girls, Carol, produced a mean C-unit of only 7.86 words, a figure that differs markedly from the mean for her grade level (11.17 words) and is closest to Loban's (1976) mean C-unit for spoken language in average third-grade students (7.62 words). Although it is unknown how Carol would perform on a more formal language sampling task, the discrepancy between her mean C-unit and the mean for her grade level is consistent with Scott's (1988b) point that syntactic structure in older children and adolescents is greatly affected by contextual factors. This discrepancy also emphasizes the need to examine the language skills of school-age children and adolescents in a variety of formal and informal contexts and to not adhere rigidly to published norms for sentence length when judging the adequacy of a student's syntactic development.

Maze Behavior

In Loban's (1976) longitudinal study of language development, which extended from kindergarten through twelfth grade ($N = 211$), students with lower overall language proficiency tended to show more false starts, hesitations, and revisions or "mazes" in their spoken language samples than students with average or superior language proficiency. This suggests that excessive maze behavior in a school-age child or adolescent may signal difficulty in formulating sentences and inadequate syntactic development. However, this factor must be interpreted cautiously (see Dollaghan & Campbell, 1992). Other researchers have reported that maze behavior may be common in the speech of children with normal language development, especially when they are attempting to formulate long, complex utterances (Leadholm & Miller, 1992; MacLachlan & Chapman, 1988; Miller, Freiberg, Rolland, & Reeves, 1992). Moreover, in Eckert's (1990) study of adolescent conversations, several girls displayed frequent maze behavior (and grammatical errors) when talking with peers:

> It was at a party earlier this year like . . . November . . . like was it . . . late about . . . late October early November and um everybody's in real good mood from the party OK? (p. 103)

Given the girls' reported academic and social success, it would be inappropriate to assume that maze behavior always signals a deficiency in language development, particularly when it occurs in spontaneous conversations with peers. It has also been reported that mature speakers sometimes display excessive maze behavior. This is apparent in the following example from Scott (1988b) of an educated adult discussing a legal issue on the radio:

> Well . . . there's . . . there's no . . . uh . . . the only limit I see to this type of . . . first of all . . . uh you have to understand ev . . . even in this court in this . . . uh urban area . . . about 65 percent of the defendants uh . . . go to probation . . . uh . . . the others generally go to jail. (pp. 52–53)

These reports indicate that hesitations, false starts, and revisions in the speech of school-age children, adolescents, and adults must be interpreted cautiously.

Conclusions

As young people mature, their sentences gradually increase in length, complexity, and informational density, and they are able to produce discourse that is more logical and cohesive across sentences (Crowhurst, 1987; McCutchen & Perfetti, 1982). Reports have indicated that syntactic development in school-age children and adolescents results, in large part, from regular and frequent opportunities to read and write in literate ways. As Perera (1992) explained, "reading and writing are not just very useful practical skills; they are also powerful agents in the process of language development" (p. 186). By reading a variety of written materials such as books, articles, and poems, students are exposed to low-frequency syntactic structures they might not otherwise encounter in casual spoken language. Subsequently, through formal writing, students have the opportunity to practice using the newly encountered structures. According to Perera (1986), writing is an ideal mode for the acquisition of complex structures "because it allows the language user to deliberate, to review and to correct, without pressure from conversational partners" (p. 518).

Through regular and frequent reading and writing, a great deal of syntactic sophistication can be attained by early adulthood. Nevertheless, it should not be assumed that all aspects of syntax are mastered by then or that mature language users are always coherent and free of grammatical errors, false starts, hesitations, and revisions. Although college students tend to have higher language skills than individuals with only a high school education (Menyuk, 1977), even well-educated adults sometimes have difficulty with certain syntactic structures. For example, in casual conversation college graduates sometimes make grammatical errors as when they substitute an irregular past tense verb for the past participle (e.g., "He should have *stole* the ball") or use a plural instead of a singular pronoun (e.g., "The owner should give *their* consent").

It is also important to recognize that syntactic complexity in school-age children and adolescents can vary greatly in relation to the discourse mode and the context of communication. For example, Crowhurst (1980) reported that T-unit length was significantly longer in students' persuasive writing than in their narrative writing, and Leadholm and Miller (1992) found that children produced longer MLUs when talking in a narrative mode than in a conversational mode. Moreover, Hoyle (1991) found that school-age children produced extremely simple utterances when spontaneously engaging in "sportscasting" during play. Similarly, informal observation indicates that school-age children and adolescents employ more complex syntax when communicating for serious purposes, such as writing compositions for their teachers, applying for scholarships, giving book reports in class, or competing on the debate team. In contrast, they communicate in simpler ways when engaging in tasks that are more relaxed and frivolous such as writing notes to friends, explaining to a toddler how to play a game, or talking about their day. This ability to talk and write differently in varied contexts seems itself to be a major attainment.

Acknowledgments

Portions of this chapter appeared in the following publications:

Nippold, M. A. (1988). The literate lexicon. In M. A. Nippold (Ed.), *Later language development: Ages nine through nineteen* (pp. 29–47). Austin, TX: PRO-ED.

Nippold, M. A. (1993). Developmental markers in adolescent language: Syntax, semantics, and pragmatics. *Language, Speech, and Hearing Services in Schools, 24*, 21–28.

Nippold, M. A., Schwarz, I. E., & Undlin, R. A. (1992). Use and understanding of adverbial conjuncts: A developmental study of adolescents and young adults. *Journal of Speech and Hearing Research, 35*, 108–118.

Used with permission of PRO-ED and the American Speech-Language-Hearing Association.

C H A P T E R

CONVERSATION AND NARRATION

There was a time when I would have told anyone who asked to run with me that I had already run—when that was not true. Now I look forward to running with people. I need people to talk to. I need people to listen to. I need people to be with.

—George Sheehan (Henderson, 1995, p. 108)

Conversation and narration are modes of spoken discourse used to obtain or share information; to entertain, humor, and comfort others; to boast, compete, and dominate (McDowell, 1985); and to establish, build, and maintain friendships and other key relationships. Whereas *conversation* is essentially a dialogue between people, *narration* is a monologue in which a particular event, condition, or experience is described. In natural communication, conversations are often interspersed with narratives as when people tell stories about what happened to themselves or to others, seeking empathic or epistemic responses from their listeners. Both modes of discourse help people of all ages interpret and order their world and achieve feelings of solidarity (Rawlins, 1992). The development of a sense of solidarity through conversation is reflected in the earlier quoted words of George Sheehan, long distance runner and medical doctor. When confronted with his own terminal illness, George came to recognize the value of talking and listening to others with genuine interest and sincerity. Meaningful communication with our fellow human beings is important throughout the life span.

Conversation and narration both require a speaker to call upon a variety of cognitive, linguistic, metalinguistic, and pragmatic competencies. Despite these demands, most children, upon entering kindergarten, can easily converse with others (Brinton

177

Table 12.1
Areas in Which Gradual Improvements Occur in Conversation and Narration as School-Age Children and Adolescents Mature (Ages 5 through 18+ years)

Conversation:

1. Stays on topic longer
2. Has extended dialogues with others
3. Makes greater number of relevant and factually based comments
4. Shifts gracefully from one topic to another
5. Adjusts the content and style of speech to the thoughts and feelings of the listener

Narration:

1. Produces longer stories with more details and better organization
2. Produces stories with a greater number of episodes
3. Produces a greater number of complete episodes
4. Embeds smaller episodes within larger episodes (subplotting)
5. Achieves greater cohesion across episodes
6. Says more about the characters' emotions, thoughts, and plans
7. Makes more effort to entertain and engage the listener

& Fujiki, 1984) and can produce many types of narratives in their spontaneous speech (Preece, 1987). Nevertheless, competence with both modes of discourse gradually improves well beyond school entry. In this chapter, major developments that are known to occur during the school-age and adolescent years are described. The major focus is on the production of spoken communication, emphasizing one-to-one and small group settings. The interface between conversation and narration is highlighted. Table 12.1 lists the major attainments that occur in conversation and narration during the school-age and adolescent years.

Conversation

Beyond the preschool years, growth in conversation is characterized by gradual refinements in the ability to stay on topic, to have extended dialogues, to make relevant and factually based comments, to shift gracefully from one topic to another, and to adjust the content and style of one's own speech in relation to the thoughts and feelings of others (Brinton & Fujiki, 1984; Dorval & Eckerman, 1984; Mentis, 1991, 1994). However, there is a great deal of variability in children and adolescents at any particular age level, making it difficult to identify and describe "normal" conversational skills. Therefore, as with many aspects of later language development, such as the use of advanced syntax, it is necessary to examine students of widely separated age groups in order to document significant growth in conversational skills.

Brinton and Fujiki (1984) examined the development of conversation in two groups of school-age children, ages 5 and 9 years, and one group of young adults ($N = 36$). At each age level, six dyads of same-sex peers were audio- and video-recorded as they spontaneously conversed while sitting at a table. For each dyad, 15 minutes of conversation were examined for instances of topic introduction, reintroduction, and maintenance. Topic maintenance was said to occur when at least one relevant utterance was produced by a speaker following the introduction or reintroduction of a topic by the other speaker. The number of utterances produced per topic was also recorded as a measure of the length of topic maintenance. Topic shading was also examined, a behavior in which a speaker gracefully changes the topic of conversation by relating the new topic to some element of the old topic, as in the following example:

SPEAKER 1:   I'm going to Sarah's birthday party next weekend. She turns 10 on Saturday. (topic = Sarah's party)

SPEAKER 2:   Yeah, I'm invited too. Should be fun . . . (topic = Sarah's party)
Did you know there's a football game on Saturday? (topic = football game)

Results indicated that the two groups of children did not differ from each other in terms of the number of topics that were introduced, reintroduced, or maintained. In contrast, the adults produced significantly fewer topic introductions and reintroductions than the children, and the adults were able to maintain a greater proportion of those topics. For the 5- and 9-year-olds and the adults, respectively, the mean number of topic introductions were 23.50, 23.33, and 13.17; the mean number of topic reintroductions were 22.83, 20.50, and 6.00; and the mean percentage of topics maintained were 79%, 84%, and 96%. The adults also produced a greater number of utterances per topic than the children. For the 5- and 9-year-olds and the adults, respectively, the mean number of utterances per topic were 5.08, 6.34, and 10.69. The two groups of children did not differ statistically on this variable. However, they did differ in the *types* of utterances they used to maintain topic; whereas the 5-year-olds often repeated what they had already said, the 9-year-olds produced a greater variety of novel utterances. All groups shaded topics, but the adults did so more often than the children. For the 5- and 9-year-olds and the adults, respectively, the mean number of topic shadings were 4.83, 6.00, and 10.50.

The findings of this study suggest that development of the ability to stay on topic and to shift gracefully from one topic to another is a gradual process that continues well beyond middle childhood. However, Brinton and Fujiki (1984) emphasized that there were large differences within age groups on most of the factors they examined. For example, there were adults who moved quickly from one topic to another, and there were 5-year-olds who stayed on topic for a considerable length of time. They suggested that differences in interpersonal style and personality may affect the types of conversational behaviors displayed, and that the findings represent developmental trends rather than definite patterns of "normalcy" at any particular age.

Using similar procedures, Schober-Peterson and Johnson (1993) also found wide differences in the structure and content of children's conversations. In their study, 10 dyads of normally achieving third-grade students (ages 8 through 9 years) were audio- and video-recorded while conversing spontaneously for 20 minutes. The conversations were transcribed and analyzed for factors such as the number of different topics initiated and the presence of topic progressions. A topic progression consisted of a series of linked topics that related to a larger theme, such as candy bars (topics = how many bars were sold, where they were sold, why they were sold, etc.).

Although 58 different topics were produced on average, the number ranged from a low of 21 to a high of 82, demonstrating considerable variability across dyads. Similarly, an average of 11 topic progressions occurred, ranging from a low of 5 to a high of 15. It would be interesting to replicate this study with dyads of younger and older students to examine possible developmental patterns in topic initiation and progression. Given the large amount of variability in this study for third-grade students, it would be most informative to compare students of widely separated ages such as kindergartners compared with students in Grades 4, 8, and 12.

In any case, other researchers have examined the development of conversation by comparing students of widely separated age levels. Dorval and Eckerman (1984) compared students in Grades 2, 5, 9, 12, and late college (ages 7 through 8, 10 through 11, 14 through 15, 17 through 18 years, and early 20s, respectively). Five groups of 6 acquainted peers (3 males, 3 females) were formed at each level. Each group met regularly for 12 weeks, and the eighth meeting of each group was audio-recorded, transcribed, and analyzed for various types of conversational behaviors.

The major finding was that conversational coherence gradually improved as age increased, particularly during adolescence and young adulthood. This was accomplished by the use of focused turns, factually related utterances, perspective-related utterances, and smooth transitions between topics, coupled with a decline in unrelated or marginally related utterances, and abrupt topic switches. Focused turns consisted of exchanges where a speaker asked a question and another answered, or where a speaker agreed with the immediately preceding utterance of another. Factually related utterances added new information to the topic at hand, and perspective-related utterances expressed awareness of the thoughts, feelings, and motives of others. Topic transitions were accomplished by waiting for a pause in the conversation before moving on. The following dialogue between two young adults illustrates the use of focused turns, as well as factually and perspective-related utterances (Dorval & Eckerman, 1984, p. 11):

SPEAKER 1:   I . . . got . . . a small problem. Um . . . simply . . . um . . . after you study all day, don't have anything to do. Especially this summer. [4-second pause.] Just can't get it together . . . lonely.

SPEAKER 2: You miss somebody?

SPEAKER 1: Well . . . um . . . like that's part of it. Ronny's back in New York. I'm
here alone.

SPEAKER 2: You have seemed down lately. Got to shake off the blues.

Future Research

Mentis (1994) and Scott (1984) suggested that the use of adverbial conjuncts (*mean-while, anyway, then, so, incidentally*) and related phrases ("before I forget," "that reminds me") to shift gracefully from one topic of conversation to another can be expected to improve during the adolescent years (see Chapter 11). Although the use of these words in written contexts improves during adolescence (Nippold, Schwarz, & Undlin, 1992), their use specifically as topic transition devices has not been investigated during this age range. Given Dorval and Eckerman's (1984) findings concerning growth in topic transitions during this age range, it would be worthwhile to study this issue in greater depth, focusing on these and other linguistic devices in conversation.

Other topics for research could include detailed examinations of the content of conversations. In view of Piaget's hypotheses concerning formal operational reasoning and its close relationship to abstract thought (Brainerd, 1978), students should be capable of increasingly sophisticated philosophical discussions as they move through adolescence. Although this is often assumed to be the case, little data are available to support this view. Analyses of the content of adolescents' conversations in academic and social contexts could be informative.

Narration

Narrative ability is often called upon in school settings when teachers ask students to describe current or historical events, to retell folk tales, to generate imaginative stories, or to report their observations during a science experiment. Skill at performing such tasks influences teachers' judgments of students' intellectual and academic capacities (Crais & Lorch, 1994; Garnett, 1986). Narrative ability is also called upon in social settings as when children and adolescents describe what happened to themselves or to others, or when they exchange jokes or humorous anecdotes as a means of gaining peer group acceptance (Eder, 1988).

Narration is thought to be a more challenging and sophisticated mode of discourse than conversation. As MacLachlan and Chapman (1988) explained, narration "demands more complex syntax, offers less discourse support, and poses more organization problems than conversation" (pp. 2–3). Moreover, effective storytelling requires one to be guided by sets of internal organizational rules called story grammar (Mandler & Johnson, 1977; Stein & Glenn, 1979). *Story grammar* consists of certain key elements such as the *setting*, which introduces the main characters and the time and location in which the story takes place. It also consists of one or more *episodes*, which involve an event or problem faced by a character; an *attempt* to resolve the problem; and an outcome or *consequence* of that attempt (Liles, 1993). Despite the difficulty of narratives, young school-age children already know a great deal about this discourse mode and can produce many different types of narratives in their spontaneous conversations.

In a naturalistic investigation, Preece (1987) audio-recorded the spontaneous conversations of three young children, two girls and a boy, while they were being driven to and from kindergarten. Each child was 5 years old at the beginning of the study. The children's conversations were recorded several times per week during the school year, transcribed verbatim, and analyzed. All three children regularly and frequently produced a wide variety of narratives when talking with each other. Typically, their narratives contained the essential elements of a good story, such as a description of the setting, characters, main events, and outcome, and the stories were told enthusiastically in an effort to maintain the listener's attention. *Personal anecdotes*, which involved the telling of an event that had happened to the speaker, were the most common type of narrative, followed by *vicarious anecdotes*, in which the child told about an event that had happened to someone else or to an animal. Examples of these two types of narratives from Preece (1987) are as follows:

Personal anecdote:

HEATHER: I'm gonna tell you what happened to me this morning . . . I'm gonna tell you what happened to me, Bron. Um, I was playin' on the monkey bars. A boy came along with a big, huge, giant spider in his hand. (Heather laughs.)

BRONWYN: Real?

HEATHER: Yeah! No, it wasn't real, it was a play one, it was a colored one, it was a big, black spider he had in his hand. And he was chasing me with it . . . A big, black spider. (Heather giggles.) (p. 358)

Vicarious anecdote:

BRONWYN: Ya know what? . . . guys, once I . . . I . . . once I knew this dog, and you know what? His name is Brandy. And you know what? He got sprayed by um a skunk.

ADULT: Yes . . . he did, didn't he.

BRONWYN: And then, what did they have to get it off with? (rising intonation, voice animated) Tomato juice!! (p. 359)

Other types of spontaneous narratives produced by the children included the retelling of familiar stories from books, television, movies, and plays, and the telling of fantasies about people and events the child made up. When a child attempted to retell a familiar story, such as *Snow White*, accuracy was demanded by the others, and, if certain details were missed, another child would retell the story in a more elaborate fashion. Over time, children seemed to improve their own retellings of familiar stories. Occasionally, children told outlandish stories about themselves or others to see if they could "trick" their friends into believing something that was untrue. These "cons" seemed to be produced simply for the sake of entertainment. Collaborative narratives were also produced where children worked together to tell stories or describe events.

Given this level of narrative ability in kindergartners, it is reasonable to ask if any notable improvements occur as children move through the school-age years. The answer is yes—a number of important changes do happen. For example, reports have indicated that as children mature, their stories gradually become longer, more detailed, and better organized, that their stories contain a greater number of episodes; that episodes are more likely to be complete and to be embedded within larger episodes (subplotting); that cohesion across episodes increases through the use of syntactic devices such as conjunctions; that more is said about the characters' emotions, thoughts, and plans; and that more effort is made to entertain and engage the listener (Bamberg & Damrad-Frye, 1991; Botvin & Sutton-Smith, 1977; Crais & Lorch, 1994; Garnett, 1986; Johnson, 1995; Kemper, 1984; Kernan, 1977; Liles, 1987, 1993; McCartney & Nelson, 1981; Page & Stewart, 1985; Roth & Spekman, 1986; Stein & Glenn, 1979; Weaver & Dickinson, 1982; Westby, 1984).

Whereas Preece (1987) employed a naturalistic approach to examine narrative ability, other researchers have employed more formal and structured approaches. For example, Stein and Glenn (1979) conducted a classic experiment using a story retelling task. Six- and 10-year-old children ($N = 48$) listened to folk tales that were told by an examiner. Before a story was told, the child was instructed to listen carefully so as to be able to tell it back to the examiner in exactly the same way. Each story included statements from each of the major story grammar categories, including the setting (e.g., "Once there was a little boy who lived in a hot country"), initiating events (e.g., "Then she gave him a pat of butter to take to his mother's house"), internal responses (e.g., "The little boy wanted to be very careful with the butter"), attempts (e.g., "so he put it on top of his head"), direct consequences (e.g., "and when he got home, the butter had all melted"), and reactions (e.g., "His mother told him he was a silly boy") (p. 78).

The children's story retellings were audio-recorded and analyzed for the number of idea units that were accurately recalled, accuracy in sequencing the events, and for the extent to which information was mentioned from each of the story grammar categories. Results indicated that the older group recalled a greater proportion of total idea units than the younger group. For example, on one of the stories, *Epaminondas*, the mean proportion of total idea units recalled was .65 and .47 for the 10- and 6-year-olds, respectively. Both groups were successful at retelling the events in the proper sequence, and they did not differ on this variable. In terms of story grammar analyses, the groups performed similarly on all categories except internal responses, where the older children accurately recalled more information than the younger ones.

The tendency for older individuals to say more about the emotions, thoughts, and plans of story characters has also been demonstrated by other researchers. For example, Bamberg and Damrad-Frye (1991) presented 5- and 9-year-old children and 20-year-old adults (N = 36) with a wordless picture book, *Frog, Where are You?* Each subject was asked to tell a story to the examiner based on the events depicted in the 24 pages of the book. The pictures feature a young boy, his dog, and a pet frog. Upon awakening one morning, the boy discovers the frog is missing, so he and the dog set out to find their friend. During the search, they encounter many problems, but in the end, the frog is found and everyone is happy again.

Not surprisingly, the stories told by the adults were longer than those of the children. Whereas the 20-year-olds produced an average of 79.25 clauses per story, the 5- and 9-year-olds, respectively, produced an average of only 47.58 and 46.08 clauses per story. Controlling for differences in story length, the adults were more likely to mention the thoughts, feelings, and emotions of the characters through the use of words such as *happy, sad,* and *scared.* Of the total clauses produced by the adults, 20% referred to mental states, contrasting with only 4% and 7% for the 5- and 9-year-olds, respectively. The authors suggested that this difference reflected adults' greater awareness of other peoples' minds. It should be noted that similar findings have been made in relation to conversational skills, as discussed earlier (Dorval & Eckerman, 1984).

Other types of tasks have also been used to study narrative development. For example, Kernan (1977) conducted a study in which African-American girls told stories about themselves to African-American women they knew well. Girls from three different age groups participated: 7 through 8 years, 10 through 11 years, and 13 through 14 years. The stories were prompted by a series of questions that focused on the girls' personal experiences (e.g., "Were you ever really frightened?" p. 92). Of particular interest was the finding that, as the girls got older, they showed a greater effort to engage and entertain their listener. This was accomplished, for example, by repeating certain ideas in a dramatic way, exaggerating for effect, and emphasizing key words. This is illustrated in the story below, told by a 13-year-old girl:

> An *girl,* you know, *half* of the cake was gone. I was so *mad* I almost cried, girl. I say "Mama, I told you Tommy was gonna eat all that cake." I mean, Tommy had him a *big, giant* piece, girl. That cake was *gone.* (pp. 98, 101)

Moreover, older girls were more likely to mention their own feelings and attitudes about a situation than younger girls (e.g., "I was so scared" p. 101), a result consistent with other studies indicating that, as children grow older, they are more likely to mention the thoughts and reactions of story characters (Bamberg & Damrad-Frye, 1991; Stein & Glenn, 1979).

Using a story-generating task, Botvin and Sutton-Smith (1977) examined developmental changes in the structural complexity of narratives. Children ranging in age from 3 through 12 years ($N = 80$) were asked individually to make up an imaginative story and to tell it to the examiner. The stories were audio-recorded and later analyzed for overall length, and the presence of plot units (episodes) and plots within plots (embedding of episodes).

Their results indicated gradual increases in story length, the number of episodes, and the use of embedding during this age range. Typically, at 3 through 4 years, children produced short, simple stories characterized by a listing of unrelated events (e.g., "The little duck went swimming. Then the crab came . . ." p. 379). At 5 through 6 years, longer stories were produced containing a sequence of events organized around a simple theme. For example, one child told about a girl who goes walking in the woods, gets lost, but safely returns home with the assistance of a friendly owl. At 7 through 9 years, stories contained even greater use of organized plots along with an increase in story length; and at 10 through 12 years, children were producing longer, more complex stories containing minor plots embedded within major plots. For example, one child told about a farmer who goes searching for a lost calf (major plot). During the search, the farmer is chased by an angry bear (minor plot). The manner in which the farmer escapes harm is described in detail before the original problem is resolved and the calf is found. The researchers speculated that older children are better able to coordinate minor plots within major plots, a phenomenon called *hierarchical organization*, because of greater memory capacity.

Roth and Spekman (1986) conducted a similar experiment but included young adolescents in addition to older, school-age children. Normally achieving students who were ages 8 through 9, 10 through 11, and 12 through 13 years ($N = 48$) were asked individually to make up an imaginative story and to tell it to the examiner. The stories were audio-recorded and subsequently analyzed for structural complexity. Compared to the two younger groups, the oldest group produced a greater proportion of episodes that were complete. A complete episode was defined as one that included at least three key elements: an initiating event or response that prompts a character to do something (e.g., a young boy goes shopping with his mother in a large department store but soon becomes separated from her), an attempt to address a problem (e.g., the boy walks around the store to try to find his mother), and a direct consequence or resolution (e.g., a security guard finds the boy and takes him to the "lost and found" area where his mother is waiting). For the 12- and 13-year-olds, 69% of the episodes were complete compared to 56% for the 10- and 11-year-olds, and 50% for the 8- and 9-year-olds. It was also reported that the oldest group used a greater proportion of embedded episodes (12 through 13 years = 17%) than the two younger groups (8 through 9 years = 5%; 10 through 11 years = 7%). An embedded episode occurred when a subplot was introduced within an episode before the main problem was resolved (e.g., while looking for his mother, the boy wanders into the toy area and begins playing with a train, a tractor, and some farm animals). Like Botvin and Sutton-Smith (1977), Roth and Spekman speculated that improvements in the use of episodic embedding may have resulted from the older students' superior ability to plan and organize, which requires greater memory capacity.

Nevertheless, despite the success of the oldest group in this study, the 12- and 13-year-olds, it would not be appropriate to conclude that the development of narrative ability is complete by early adolescence. The possibility of further growth during adolescence is suggested by the fact that 31% of the episodes produced by this group were incomplete. It is also suggested by the fact that embedding failed to occur in 83% of the episodes that this group produced. Additional research should be conducted to examine possible changes in these and other aspects of narrative ability beyond early adolescence. Without this research, we will remain unaware of any improvements that might occur during middle and late adolescence and into adulthood, and of the cognitive and linguistic factors that might precipitate that growth.

Development in the ability to join episodes through the appropriate use of conjunctions was reported by Liles (1987) in a study of children ages 7 through 10 years ($N = 20$). Each child watched a movie, an adventure story, with an examiner. Following the movie, the child was asked to tell the story to another adult who had not seen the movie. The stories were audio-recorded and later transcribed and analyzed for the presence of episodes (complete and incomplete) and the use of conjunctions both within and across episodes. Conjunctions that expressed additive (e.g., *and, also*), temporal (*meanwhile, next*), causal (*so, therefore*), and adversative (*yet, but*) relations as defined by Halliday and Hasan (1976) were of interest. No developmental changes occurred in the use of conjunctions *within* episodes; however, the use of conjunctions *across* episodes to create cohesive discourse did increase in relation to age. It was also found that the frequency of complete episodes increased, a result that was consistent with other developmental studies that examined this age range (e.g., Roth & Spekman, 1986).

The results concerning the use of conjunctions to achieve coherence across episodes are consistent with the views of Mentis (1994) and Scott (1984) that students gradually acquire skill in using adverbial conjuncts (e.g., *anyway, meanwhile, incidentally*) and related phrases (e.g., "before I forget," "that reminds me") as transition devices to signal new topics of conversation. Their use as cohesion devices in storytelling during adolescence should be examined further.

As mentioned above, collaborative narratives, where two or more speakers work together to tell a story, occur in the spontaneous conversations of kindergarten children (Preece, 1987). According to Eder (1988), they also occur in the conversations of adolescents where they can serve important social functions such as strengthening peer relationships, achieving group solidarity, and influencing individuals' perceptions of people and events. Eder conducted a study of the spontaneous lunchtime conversations of small groups of adolescent girls, most of whom were eighth-grade students (13 through 14 years old). Relevant background information was collected on the girls, including shared activities, friendships, and popularity within the group. Conversations were audio-recorded, transcribed, and analyzed for the types of strategies the speakers employed.

A common finding was that a speaker, often a popular girl, would enter into an ongoing narrative to support and validate the story. This in turn would elevate the status of the main narrator within the group. This reportedly occurred in the narrative cited below, where a less popular girl, Faye, is talking about her weekend that was spent with the most popular group member, Carol. When Carol joins in, her comments add plausibility to the story and contribute to the group's interest and enjoyment of it, which reflects favorably on Faye:

FAYE: What else did we do? Oooh! . . . . There's this *great* big catfish 'bout this big (gestures) and it was real fat, about this fat, you know . . . (gestures). And it was in—and we were rowing on the boat—we saw it and it was dead, you know . . . and we put it in the boat and it 'bout stunk us out and uh . . .

CAROL: (comes up to the table) Uh! You had that fish, that catfish—Oh!

FAYE: It was great big and we were gonna tell our brothers how we caught it! . . . Oo, and its eyes were all, it looked like an albino fish. It was about this big (gestures) and it stunk us out, didn't it?

CAROL: What?

FAYE: We were sitting there oaring . . . Carol goes, "Trade me places so you can be back here by this thing."

CAROL: It was *gross*. I had to pick it up.

FAYE: It weighed about twenty pounds.

CAROL: It did. It was so full of water. (p. 228)

In that same investigation, Eder (1988) also reported that, when several girls collaborated on a story, they still were able to maintain a sense of cohesion. On one occasion when they were discussing a conflict they had had with their choir director, they accomplished this through the repetition of certain key words and phrases (e.g., "she goes . . ."), by finishing each others' sentences, repeating what another had said (e.g., "Good night"), imitating each others' intonational patterns, and speaking the same words simultaneously as if they were one person. Some of these behaviors are illustrated in the excerpt below (// = the next speaker begins talking):

K: We didn't want to sing it to begin with . . . We just // sang so everybody'd stop

M: sang

K: so everybody'd stop naggin' at // us.

M: gripin' at us.

K: I just loved that one time when she goes, "I have nothing else to say to you girls. Good *night*." (said in a high voice) (laughter)

M: She goes out that door and goes, "*Good night!*" (in a high voice) (laughs)

K: It's a good thing she didn't hear what we said after she got out the door . . . You would of

M: Oh God . . .

K: She probably heard that. It was awfully loud. (p. 231)

The ability to maintain cohesion in this manner was thought to result from the fact that the girls had all shared the experience that was being recalled and had interpreted it similarly.

Future Research

Eder's (1988) results concerning the use of collaborative storytelling within conversations suggest that this may be a common pattern during adolescence. Researchers should examine this pattern in greater depth, comparing groups of older and younger students. Investigations of narrative development should also attempt to explain more fully *how* change comes about. Most developmental studies have attempted to identify growth in the structure and content of children's stories, primarily asking questions of *what* and *when*. More attention should now be directed to questions concerning the underlying processes. For example, it is possible that growth occurs as a result of repeated exposure to storytelling in formal and informal settings, enabling a child or adolescent to abstract the key features of a coherent and engaging tale. This would be similar to the manner in which other aspects of later language development unfold (e.g., knowledge of subtle word meanings). However, little attention has been directed toward this process in relation to narrative ability. According to American folk wisdom, "A tale grows better in the telling." Not surprisingly, reports have indicated that children's stories improve with subsequent retellings (Preece, 1987). This suggests that growth in narrative ability also results from repeated opportunities to tell stories and to receive feedback from others. However, little data are available to support this hypothesis. It is clear that further study of the development of narrative ability in school-age children and adolescents is in order.

C H A P T E R

PERSUASION AND NEGOTIATION

"Gentle persuasion often succeeds where forcefulness fails."

—Anonymous

An important aspect of pragmatic development in school-age children and adolescents is the use of reasoned discourse in interpersonal contexts. As young people mature, they show increasing levels of social perspective-taking, bargaining, cooperation, and compromise as they engage in two major types of reasoned discourse, persuasion and negotiation.

Persuasion involves the use of argumentation to convince another person to perform an act or to accept a point of view desired by the persuader. *Negotiation*, a distinct but related ability, involves communication to resolve conflicts and to achieve goals in mutually acceptable ways. Competence with both types of discourse is important for personal satisfaction and social success. This chapter discusses the ability of school-age children and adolescents to persuade and negotiate in interpersonal contexts. The developmental literature is reviewed, and suggestions for future research are offered. Table 13.1 contains an overview of the major attainments that occur in persuasion and negotiation as children and adolescents mature.

Persuasion

Persuasion, a powerful pragmatic ability, is the use of communication "to influence the acts, beliefs, attitudes, and values of others" (Freeley, 1993, p. 8). A variety of strategies may be used to persuade others, ranging from the highly emotional and manipulative appeals found in political campaigns and advertisements for consumer

Table 13.1

Areas in Which Gradual Improvements Occur in Persuasion and Negotiation as School-Age Children and Adolescents Mature (Ages 5 through 18+ years)

Persuasion:

1. Adjusts to listener characteristics (e.g., age, authority, familiarity)
2. States advantages to the listener as a reason to comply
3. Anticipates and replies to counterarguments
4. Uses positive strategies such as politeness and bargaining
5. Gives up negative strategies such as whining and begging
6. Generates a large number and variety of different arguments
7. Controls the discourse assertively

Negotiation:

1. Takes the social perspective of another
2. Shows awareness of the needs, thoughts, and feelings of others
3. Reasons with words (verbal reasoning)
4. Uses cooperative and collaborative strategies
5. Shows concern for group welfare
6. Shows concern for long-term implications of conflict
7. Shows willingness to compromise

Note. Adapted from "Persuasive Talk in Social Contexts: Development, Assessment, and Intervention," by M. A. Nippold, 1994, *Topics in Language Disorders, 14*(3), p. 2.

products, to the truthful and logical arguments found in scholarly philosophical debates (Makau, 1990).

Tapping a wide variety of linguistic, cognitive, and social competencies, persuasion can occur in spoken or written form. Spoken persuasion, the focus of this chapter, is a distinct type of discourse that requires the speaker to adjust the style of communication to relevant interpersonal and situational factors. For example, a kindergartner may successfully persuade a friend to share an attractive toy through a simple request (e.g., "Can I play with that?"), but a high school student, seeking to persuade the senior class to support a paper recycling program, may need to present some informative skits to achieve success. Faced with additional challenges, a young adult who seeks on-the-job training with a prestigious law firm may need to offer a series of cogent arguments to persuade a potential employer. In contemporary society, skillful persuasion can lead to personal satisfaction and professional success. Deficiencies in this area may lead to frustration and low self-esteem.

Hypothetical Tasks

Most researchers employed hypothetical role-playing tasks to examine the development of spoken persuasion. For example, in an early investigation, Wood, Weinstein, and Parker (1967) examined the strategies used by young elementary school-age children to convince others to change their minds. Children from kindergarten, and Grades 1, 2, and 3 (ages 5, 6, 7, and 8 years, respectively) (N = 16 per group) participated. Each child was interviewed individually about three hypothetical but familiar situations. Children were asked what they would say to get their teachers to allow their class to go swimming, to get their mothers to allow them to watch a particular television show, and to get a friend to vote a particular way at school.

Results showed that as grade level increased, children were more likely to use positive, listener-oriented strategies such as bargaining and politeness and less likely to use negative strategies such as nagging and begging. Positive strategies were used 15% of the time by kindergartners and 48% of the time by third-grade students.

Other studies have demonstrated gradual improvement in spoken persuasion beyond the third grade. For example, Flavell, Botkin, Fry, Wright, and Jarvis (1968) examined persuasion in girls from Grades 3, 7, and 11 (N = 20 per group). Each child participated in two role-playing tasks. In one task, the girl was shown a photograph of a man, handed a necktie, and told to try to sell the necktie to the man. In the other task, she was told to imagine that her father was present and to try to convince him to buy her a television set. In both situations, the girl was urged to say everything she could think of to influence the listener.

Results showed that the two oldest groups were able to generate a greater number of different arguments than the youngest group. For the two tasks combined, the mean number of different arguments provided by the third-, seventh-, and eleventh-grade girls, respectively, was 3.35, 7.65, and 8.05. Moreover, with each successive grade level, there was an increase in the frequency of arguments stating an advantage to the listener (e.g., "If I have my own TV set, I won't be bothering you and Mom when you're watching programs I don't like." p. 137). Persuasive effectiveness, a global judgment made by an independent listener, also increased with each successive grade level, and older students were better able to organize their arguments than younger ones. The researchers suggested that these improvements in persuasion reflected growth in social perspective-taking.

Similar findings were made by Finley and Humphreys (1974), who examined persuasion in girls who were ages 5, 9, and 13 years (N = 20 per group). Each girl participated in two role-playing tasks where the goal was to convince another person, who preferred to watch a television show, to play the girl's favorite game with her. The listener was the girl's mother in one task and her best friend in the other. Picture frames containing felt figures represented the two different listeners, and an unmarked box represented the game. In each task, the girl was urged to say and do everything she could think of to convince the listener to play the game. Consistent with Flavell et al. (1968), the older girls were able to generate a greater number of different arguments than the younger girls, and the older girls' arguments were more likely to offer an advantage to the listener.

Clark and Delia (1976) examined the development of persuasion in children from each of Grades 2 through 9 (ages 7 through 15 years) (N = 58 total). As in the three previous studies (Finley & Humphreys, 1974; Flavell et al., 1968; Wood et al., 1967), children were interviewed individually and were presented with hypothetical but familiar situations. In this investigation, they were told to try to convince their parents to buy them a particular present, to convince their mothers to allow them to host an overnight party, and to convince a stranger to keep a lost puppy they had found. Children were asked to pretend that the examiner was the listener and to say whatever they thought would yield the desired outcome.

In agreement with the three previous studies (Finley & Humphreys, 1974; Flavell et al., 1968; Wood et al., 1967), the responses of the older children reflected a greater ability to consider the perspective of the listener than did those of the younger children. For example, older children were more likely to point out certain advantages to the listener of granting the request (e.g., "If I were you and I lived alone, I'd like a good watchdog like this one" p. 1010). In contrast, younger children were more likely to phrase the request in terms of the advantages it offered themselves (e.g., "If I had a bike, I could get to school better" p. 1010). Children's ability to deal with counter-arguments also improved as a function of age. For example, older children were more likely to anticipate the types of objections a listener might have and to supply reasonable replies (e.g., "It doesn't cost too much to feed a dog if you buy the big bags of food" p. 1010). Older children also produced a greater number and variety of arguments for each situation than younger ones did. However, the puppy situation elicited the most sophisticated responses from both younger and older children. The researchers hypothesized that this situational difference resulted from the children's need to use higher-level strategies when the listener was a stranger (as in the puppy situation) rather than a parent (as in the other two situations) because the response of an unfamiliar person is less predictable than that of a familiar person. For example, a child who believes that a parent will object to a request may invest less effort trying to change the parent's mind, compared to the situation where the response of an adult is less certain.

The major findings of Clark and Delia (1976) were later replicated by Delia, Kline, and Burleson (1979) but with children and adolescents of a wider age range. Students from kindergarten and each of Grades 1 through 12 (ages 5 through 18 years) ($N = 211$) were administered two of the role-playing tasks used by Clark and Delia, the party and puppy situations.

Gradual improvement occurred on the tasks throughout this age range, and once again, the puppy situation elicited more sophisticated responses than the party situation. These researchers also believed that difficulty in predicting an unfamiliar listener's response led students to use higher-level strategies in the puppy situation than in the party situation.

However, the possible influence of other factors should also be considered, such as the outcome of a speaker's persuasive efforts, in this case, having a party or saving a puppy. For some children, the latter may be a more desirable goal and hence may motivate greater persuasive effort. It would be interesting to question children about the relative importance they assign to various persuasive situations used in research.

Nevertheless, additional support for the view that listener characteristics influence the types of persuasive strategies children use can be found in a study conducted by Piche, Rubin, and Michlin (1978). In their investigation, fifth- and ninth-grade students (N = 16 per group) were individually interviewed and told to pretend to try to sell newspaper subscriptions to four imaginary listeners. To determine how well a child could accommodate to others, the listeners varied systematically in authority and intimacy in relation to the child. Listeners included the child's same-sex parent (+ authority, + intimacy), a same-sex peer friend (− authority, + intimacy), a same sex peer stranger (− authority, − intimacy), and a same-sex unfamiliar teacher (+ authority, − intimacy).

Results showed that both groups of students made adjustments to different listeners in terms of both dimensions of interest—authority and intimacy. For example, both groups addressed more imperatives (e.g., "Oh please just buy it" p. 776) to low-authority than to high-authority listeners, and to intimate than to non intimate listeners. However, ninth graders were better able to accommodate to different listeners than fifth graders. For example, ninth graders addressed more personal appeals ("The kids in your class will really like reading it" p. 776) to intimate than to non-intimate listeners, a distinction that was rarely marked by fifth graders. Ninth graders also produced a greater variety of persuasive appeals than fifth graders, including a strategy of citing group standards as a reason to comply (e.g., "We ought to do things for each other" p. 776). These results indicate that listener characteristics do affect the types of strategies children employ to persuade others, and that older children use this information more than younger ones.

In addition to authority and intimacy, the age of the listener seems to affect the types of persuasive strategies children employ. Bragg, Ostrowski, and Finley (1973) designed a task where 10-year-old boys (N = 58), tested individually, were asked to play the role of a salesman who was supposed to convince three different "customers" to eat as many crackers as possible. The customers, who were actors rather than imaginary listeners, included a boy of the same age (age 10), a younger boy (age 7), and an older boy (age 13). Unknown to the salesman, each customer had been instructed by the examiner to accept only one cracker and then to politely refuse additional crackers.

Results showed that persuasive appeals directed to the younger boy were more aggressive than those directed to the peer or to the older boy. For example, the younger boy often was asked to explain why he would not eat the crackers (e.g., "What's wrong with these crackers?" p. 353) and often was told directly to comply (e.g., "Come on, eat the cracker" p. 354).

Motivational and Situational Factors

From the studies discussed so far, it is clear that gradual improvement in persuasion occurs throughout the school-age and adolescent years. It should be emphasized, however, that motivational and situational factors can affect the types of strategies that young people employ, and that speaker age is not always an accurate predictor of how a youth will perform.

For example, there is evidence from Ritter (1979) that even high school seniors do not always employ the most sophisticated strategies when trying to persuade others to do things for them. In Ritter's study, ninth- and twelfth-grade students (ages 14 and 17 years, respectively) ($N = 33$) were compared in their ability to perform a hypothetical, persuasive role-playing task. During individual interviews, students were asked what they would say to convince a friend to help them solicit pledges for a walkathon; the person receiving the most pledges would win a bicycle. Speaker responses were scored using a scale that reflected increasing levels of social perspective-taking. Out of 8 possible points, twelfth graders achieved a mean of 4.63 and ninth graders achieved a mean of 2.75. Although twelfth graders outperformed ninth graders, only 53% of the older group performed at the highest level on this task.

The surprisingly low performance of the seniors suggests that the development of persuasion is incomplete by age 17 and that further growth in this area occurs during adulthood. While this may be true, other factors could also explain these unexpected results. As Ritter (1979) pointed out, many of the students may not have been motivated to perform the task because most were from affluent families and probably already had bicycles. Therefore, the hypothetical nature of the task may have affected the outcome. Also, many of the students were reluctant to persuade their friends, not wanting to cause them discomfort (e.g., "I'd hate to put her on the spot" p. 51). Moreover, some students felt it was unnecessary to use elaborate persuasive techniques, believing their friends would grant a simple request for assistance.

Naturalistic Tasks

Limitations in using hypothetical rather than real situations in studies of persuasion were pointed out by Bearison and Gass (1979), who questioned the generalizability of results when nonnaturalistic contexts are employed. These researchers examined the performance of 10- and 11-year-old children ($N = 46$) under two persuasive conditions, hypothetical and actual. Each child was tested individually. Those in the hypothetical condition were asked to pretend that an adult would give them $2.00 if they could convince the adult to do so. No money was displayed. Children in the actual condition were shown envelopes containing $2.00 and told that they would receive an envelope if they could convince the examiner to give them one. Children's responses were scored using a 4-point scale, which reflected increasing levels of social perspective-taking.

Results showed that children in the actual condition obtained a higher mean score (2.29) than those in the hypothetical condition (1.90). This result was attributed to the greater motivational levels of children in the former condition.

By engaging children in more naturalistic tasks, one can also examine the outcome of their persuasive efforts. Jones (1985), for example, studied dyads of young school-age children during a competitive coloring game. Children from kindergarten, and Grades 2 and 4 (ages 5, 7, and 9, respectively) ($N = 109$) participated. Each child was paired with another child of the same age and gender. Members of a dyad were either friends or acquaintances. Children were given a color-by-number design and told that whoever colored more numbers would receive more prizes. There was only one crayon, however, and children were told that they should try to convince each other to share the crayon. Of interest was the manner in which friends versus acquaintances (1) persuaded each other to share the crayon and (2) responded to each other's persuasive efforts to obtain the crayon.

During this competitive activity, the most common type of persuasive appeal used by children of all ages was a simple request (e.g., "May I have it please?" p. 759) to both friends and acquaintances. However, children's responses to the persuasive efforts of their peers differed according to the relationship between the two children. When the persuader was a friend rather than an acquaintance, the child holding the crayon was more likely to grant the request; and when the child denied the request, friends received extended refusals (e.g., "I've got to color more to win" p. 759) more often than acquaintances, who received more terse rejections (e.g., "Never" p. 759). In denying a request, older children used delay tactics (e.g., "I'll give it to you later" p. 759) more often than younger ones, a way of placating the listener and controlling the interaction.

Given the findings of Bearison and Gass (1979) and Jones (1985), it would be interesting to explore the changes that may occur in the development of spoken persuasion when school-age children and adolescents interact in even more naturalistic contexts, where they actually generate the goals and initiate the exchange with individuals of their own choosing. Under such conditions, sophisticated behaviors might be observed, even among younger children. Support for this view is suggested by Erftmier and Dyson (1986), who reported on a six-year-old boy, Bruce, who was remarkably adept at persuading his mother to make Jello and popcorn for a play session with a friend, Elizabeth, and allowing him to sample the snacks. In the dialogue below, Bruce produces many arguments and even anticipates his mother's objections:

BRUCE: Well, see, they're gonna be for this afternoon in the army [a game he and Elizabeth like to play]. I'm getting ready for then 'cause when Liz gets home she needs a little snack 'cause she always says, "I'm hungry." So, this is gonna be for her evening snack.

MOTHER: So it all has to be made now?

BRUCE: We'll make the Jello first 'cause it takes longer and we can cook it shorter [meaning that Jello takes longer to congeal, but a shorter time than popcorn to "cook"].

MOTHER: Ok. [Mother tears open Jello package to begin the cooking.]

BRUCE: Let me taste it.

MOTHER: Why?

BRUCE: I've never tasted peach flavoring before. I just want to taste a little bit and I'm not gonna get a big chunk.

MOTHER: Ok. (pp. 91–92)

Nonverbal Vocalizations and Interactional Management Strategies

When school-age children and adolescents are observed in naturalistic conditions, additional aspects of persuasion that have not yet been studied from a developmental perspective could be examined. Two behaviors worthy of study include the use of nonverbal vocalizations and interactional management strategies. Erftmier and Dyson (1986) reported that these two behaviors played a prominent role in the persuasive interactions of elementary school students. They studied dyads of fourth graders (ages 9 and 10 years) ($N = 6$) matched for gender and dominance. Children were observed as they participated in persuasive role-playing tasks in a quiet room at school. Dyads chose their own tasks from a list of peer-oriented scenarios (e.g., Should girls be allowed to join a boy's baseball team?). Following a brief planning session, children acted out their scenarios.

Results showed that children skillfully used nonverbal vocalizations such as modifications in pitch, rate, volume, and stress to convey their attitudes and emotions to each other as they spoke (e.g., "So . . . What do you mean 'so what?' Ya can't, can't let us, let us, make us lose our, our team, our games 'n everything!" p. 105). Also, they successfully used interactional management strategies such as repeating their own utterances and ignoring the other child's questions and arguments in order to wear down the opponent and control the discourse (e.g., "I want girls . . . Forever, I want girls . . . I still want girls . . . I want girls" pp. 104–105). In fact, children who employed those two behaviors were more likely to "win" the dispute than those who employed other strategies, which, from an adult perspective, were more logical, reasonable, and convincing.

Summary

Developmental studies have shown that, as young people mature, their strategies of spoken persuasion become increasingly sophisticated and reflect a greater tendency to consider the perspective of the listener. Compared to young school-age children, older children and adolescents are more likely to use politeness and bargaining, to point out advantages to the listener, to anticipate and reply to counterarguments, and to modify their strategies based on listener characteristics such as age, authority, and familiarity in relation to themselves. Older children also possess a larger repertoire of strategies for persuading others than their younger counterparts and are more adept at refusing the persuasive appeals of their peers and at controlling the discourse. It is clear, however, that motivational and situational factors affect the types of persuasive strategies that young people employ and that speaker age cannot always be used to predict a youth's performance.

Future Research

Most studies that examined the development of spoken persuasion did so using hypothetical rather than naturalistic contexts. Thus, it is difficult to know what school-age children and adolescents of different ages actually do to persuade others in natural settings and to what extent they are successful in influencing others' behavior, particularly when the situation is self-emanating and genuinely important to the speaker. Studies should be conducted to examine the development of persuasive strategies used by children and adolescents in natural settings with different listeners such as peers, parents, and teachers.

Although adults often attempt to persuade others through emotional and manipulative strategies (Makau, 1990), little attention has been directed toward the use of such tactics by children and adolescents. Researchers may wish to track these strategies in young people to determine at what ages and under what conditions emotional versus logical appeals are employed. Nonverbal vocalizations and interactional management strategies could also be observed in conjunction with this research.

Another topic for future research concerns the ability of young people to critically analyze the persuasive appeals of another, such as a popular peer, politician, or corporation. For example, adolescents must learn to evaluate peer pressure to drink alcohol, a politician's promises to support higher education, and a tobacco company's advertisements encouraging them to smoke. Little is known about the developmental changes that may occur in the ability of children and adolescents to critically analyze the persuasive appeals of another and to respond assertively so that self-esteem and personal welfare are protected. The uncritical acceptance of emotional and manipulative persuasive appeals can have very negative consequences for young people. Research that addresses this topic could therefore prove to be most worthwhile.

Negotiation

Interpersonal conflicts inevitably arise in home, school, work, and community settings, and the manner in which those conflicts are resolved can have pivotal implications for future interactions between the persons involved. For example, if solutions are reached through thoughtful negotiation that considers the goals, motives, and emotions of all participants, the outcome can be positive. Alternatively, if conflicts are resolved hastily and without concern for the perspectives of others, the outcome may discourage future interactions among participants.

Hypothetical and Naturalistic Tasks

As with persuasion, developmental researchers have examined school-age children and adolescents during situations that call for interpersonal negotiation. Although the primary method of data collection has been hypothetical role-playing tasks, naturalistic procedures have occasionally been employed as well.

In one of the first studies that addressed this topic, Abrahami, Selman, and Stone (1981) examined the relationship between social understanding and the use of strategies to resolve social conflicts in second- through fifth-grade girls ($N = 24$). Social understanding was measured through a structured interview task that involved a friendship dilemma. The dilemma concerned a girl who had made plans to spend time with a close friend but then was asked by another girl to go to an ice skating show. After the dilemma was presented, the child was questioned about aspects of friendship such as its formation and termination, and the causes and consequences of jealousy. Only girls who scored at a high or a low level of social understanding were selected for the study. Following the interview, girls were assigned to one of four different groups ($N = 6$ per group) based on grade level and level of social understanding. The groups consisted of: (1) second and third graders with low social understanding; (2) second and third graders with high social understanding; (3) fourth and fifth graders with low social understanding; and (4) fourth and fifth graders with high social understanding.

Each group participated in 12, weekly, 90-minute sessions that involved supervised cooperative activities such as making puppets, building a stage, writing a script, and putting on a puppet show. After the 12 sessions were completed, an action strategies resolution interview was conducted where each child was questioned about seven different dilemmas that were based on conflicts that actually had occurred during the group sessions. For example, the following conflict was presented, which involves the violation of rules and norms:

> Suppose your group decided to clean up after group activities and one of the girls in the group didn't want to clean. What would you suggest your group do? (p. 153)

For each dilemma, the child's stated choice of action was scored using a scale of 0 to 3, where 0 involved physical force and no attempt to reason with the uncooperative child (e.g., "Kick her out of the group" p. 153) and 3 emphasized group welfare and attempts to reason (e.g., "Keep talking to her, and keep saying this and that until she helps because if you are not helping you are not being part of the group . . ." p. 153).

Results indicated that the older group with high social understanding (Group 4; mean score = 2.03) provided the most advanced solutions, followed by the younger group with high social understanding (Group 2; mean score = 1.71). Moreover, the older group with low social understanding (Group 3; mean score = 1.59) provided more advanced solutions than the younger group with low social understanding (Group 1; mean score = 0.83). These findings indicated that, although older children tended to provide more advanced solutions than younger ones, a child's level of social understanding was an important predictor of performance in addition to age. Because no group reached the highest level of social action resolution, further growth in this domain can be expected to occur beyond the school-age years.

During the weekly group sessions that occurred in the study just described (Abrahami et al., 1981), each child was also observed for 10-minute segments by a trained examiner, who made extensive notes concerning the child's social interactions with other group members. Reported by Selman, Schorin, Stone, and Phelps (1983), this study examined children's use of social negotiation strategies in a natural setting. Typed transcripts of the observations were analyzed for the degree to which the child's verbal and nonverbal behaviors reflected the development of social negotiation strategies. For example, during the crafts activities, children with more advanced negotiation strategies demonstrated greater awareness of others' needs (e.g., "OK, I'll take the tacks out for you" p. 91) and a desire to work cooperatively (e.g., "You color in the spots and I'll hold it for you" p. 91). In contrast, children with less advanced negotiation strategies demonstrated little awareness of others' needs (e.g., "I was here first" p. 91) and a desire to work independently (e.g., "Can I do my own?" p. 91).

Results indicated that the older children (Grades 4 and 5) used a greater percentage of high-level negotiation strategies (mean = 43%) than did the younger ones (Grades 2 and 3) (mean = 34%). However, both the older and younger children used a greater percentage of low-level strategies (older mean = 57%; younger mean = 66%) than high-level strategies. This continued use of low-level strategies indicates that the development of interpersonal negotiation remains incomplete in preadolescents.

It is not surprising, then, that research has shown that improvements occur in interpersonal negotiation during the adolescent years. For example, Selman, Beardslee, Schultz, Krupa, and Podorefsky (1986) examined the development of interpersonal negotiation strategies in three groups of students they described as younger (11 through 13 years), middle (14 through 16 years), and older (17 through 19 years) adolescents (N = 30 per group). The extent to which the students employed mutual collaboration to resolve interpersonal conflicts was explored using a structured interview task. Each student listened to eight hypothetical dilemmas read by an interviewer. Each dilemma involved a protagonist who either wanted something from a significant other (a peer or an adult) or reacted to the wants of the significant other in a personal or a work situation. For example, the following dilemma concerns a personal situation in which the protagonist desires something from the significant other, a peer:

> Dan and his girlfriend are out on a date together. Dan wants to start going out with other girls but he doesn't think his girlfriend would like that. (p. 459)

In contrast, the next example concerns a work situation in which the significant other, an adult, desires something from the protagonist:

> John works in a grocery store after school. He is only supposed to work for 10 hours a week, but his boss keeps asking him at the last minute to work really late on Friday nights. Even though his boss pays him for his extra time, John doesn't like to be asked to work at the last minute. (p. 459)

Following each dilemma, the interviewer questioned the student about the nature of the conflict, how best to handle it, why it should be handled that way, and the feelings that might develop in the participants. Questions probed the student's ability to resolve the conflict by considering the perspectives of both the protagonist and the significant other, and by working cooperatively to preserve the participants' relationship. Students' responses were scored using a scale of 0 to 3 (0 = least advanced; 3 = most advanced).

The results showed that this was indeed a challenging task and that not even the oldest students consistently provided Level 3 responses. Nevertheless, the older adolescents were most aware of the wants and feelings of the participants, showed the most concern for the long-term consequences of the conflict, and were most interested in resolving the conflict through compromise and mutual agreement. In contrast, the younger and middle adolescents were less aware of the participants' perspectives and were oriented more towards short-term, unilateral conflict resolutions. Thus, although interpersonal negotiation improves during adolescence, further growth seems likely during adulthood.

It was also found in this investigation that girls demonstrated slightly more advanced negotiation strategies than boys, a result that the researchers attributed to differences in social conditioning between boys and girls. In addition, for the adolescents as a whole, more advanced negotiation strategies were used when the significant other was a peer rather than an adult, and when the conflict occurred in a personal rather than a work situation. The researchers suggested that the latter findings may reflect an adolescent's own life experiences that usually involve more instances of negotiation with peers than with adults and more conflict resolution in personal than in work situations. No differences were found in the protagonist's negotiation position, in other words, whether or not the protagonist wanted something from another or was reacting to the wants of another.

In natural settings, it is unknown how adolescents of different ages would actually resolve the types of interpersonal conflicts posed by Selman and colleagues (1986). It is likely, however, that they would attempt to resolve the conflicts in mutually acceptable ways, particularly when the participants are older girls. This was suggested by Eckert's (1990) study of adolescent conversational patterns (see Chapter 11). She examined the spontaneous after-school conversations of eleventh-grade girls who were talking among themselves about boys, dating, and popularity, and she reported that the girls engaged in considerable interpersonal negotiation. For example, even though they disagreed initially about certain issues (e.g., whether or not to use a third party to introduce a potential couple), the girls expressed their views openly, encouraged each others' contribution to the discussion, and eventually reached a consensus before moving to another topic. According to Eckert, these spontaneous efforts to negotiate resulted from the girls' desire for peer acceptance, friendly interaction, and solidarity. Other reports have also indicated that girls tend to use language more cooperatively than boys during peer interaction and that boys tend to show more domination and control of their peers through interruptions, insults, and practical jokes (Cooper & Anderson-Inman, 1988). This suggests that boys may be less likely than girls to employ cooperative strategies to resolve interpersonal conflicts in natural settings. Researchers should examine this issue in greater depth with boys and girls of different ages.

Summary

The development of interpersonal negotiation has been investigated in school-age children and adolescents for many years. Structured interview tasks as well as direct observation of young people in natural settings have been employed to examine their ability to resolve social conflicts. Collectively, the studies indicate that, as children and adolescents mature, they show an increasing tendency to resolve conflicts in ways that reflect greater social perspective-taking, verbal reasoning, cooperation and collaboration with others, and concern for group welfare. They also show increasing concern for the long-term implications of a conflict and a willingness to compromise if necessary. Growth in conflict resolution is especially active during adolescence, a time when the peer group becomes more important and opportunities for social interaction expand.

Future Research

As with persuasion, little is known about the ability of young people to critically analyze the negotiation strategies employed by others. Researchers should examine the development of this ability, in both structured and natural settings. Methods employed by school-age children and adolescents to verify the accuracy of another's claims and to determine the extent to which those claims promote mutual welfare could be analyzed. Another area for research concerns the fact that even by late adolescence, the most advanced levels of interpersonal negotiation strategies are not consistently employed. This suggests that growth in negotiation may continue into adulthood. The use of negotiation strategies by young adults would be interesting to examine in both social and vocational settings.

Acknowledgments

Portions of this chapter appeared in the following publications:

Nippold, M. A. (1993). Developmental markers in adolescent language: Syntax, semantics, and pragmatics. *Language, Speech, and Hearing Services in Schools, 24*, 21–28.

Nippold, M. A. (1994). Persuasive talk in social contexts: Development, assessment, and intervention. *Topics in Language Disorders, 14*(3), 1–12.

Used with permission of the American Speech-Language-Hearing Association and Aspen Publishers.

REFERENCES

Abrahami, A., Selman, R. L., & Stone, C. (1981). A developmental assessment of children's verbal strategies for social action resolution. *Journal of Applied Developmental Psychology, 2,* 145–163.

Achenbach, T. M. (1969). Cue learning, associative responding, and school performance in children. *Developmental Psychology, 1,* 717–725.

Achenbach, T. M. (1970). Standardization of a research instrument for identifying associative responding in children. *Developmental Psychology, 2,* 283–291.

Ackerman, B. P. (1982a). Contextual integration and utterance interpretation: The ability of children and adults to interpret sarcastic utterances. *Child Development, 53,* 1075–1083.

Ackerman, B. P. (1982b). On comprehending idioms: Do children get the picture? *Journal of Experimental Child Psychology, 33,* 439–454.

Ackerman, B. P. (1986). Children's sensitivity to comprehension failure in interpreting a nonliteral use of an utterance. *Child Development, 57,* 485–497.

Al-Issa, I. (1969). The development of word definition in children. *Journal of Genetic Psychology, 114,* 25–28.

Andersen, E. S. (1975). Cups and glasses: Learning that boundaries are vague. *Journal of Child Language, 2,* 79–103.

Anglin, J. M. (1993). Vocabulary development: A morphological analysis. *Monographs of the Society for Research in Child Development, 58*(10), Serial No. 238.

Arlin, P. K. (1978, February). *Piagetian operations in the comprehension, preference, and production of metaphors.* Paper presented at the Annual International Interdisciplinary Conference on Piagetian Theory and the Helping Professions, Los Angeles, CA.

Armour-Thomas, E., & Allen, B. A. (1990). Componential analysis of analogical-reasoning performance of high and low achievers. *Psychology in the Schools, 27,* 269–275.

Arter, J. L. (1976). *The effects of metaphor on reading comprehension.* Unpublished doctoral dissertation, University of Illinois at Urbana-Champaign.

Asch, S. E., & Nerlove, H. (1960). The development of double-function terms in children: An exploratory investigation. In B. Kaplan & S. Wapner (Eds.), *Perspectives in psychological theory: Essays in honor of Heinz Werner* (pp. 47–60). New York: International Universities Press.

Astington, J. W., & Olson, D. R. (1987, April). *Literacy and schooling: Learning to talk about thought.* Paper presented at the Annual Meeting of the American Educational Research Association, Washington, D. C.

Badian, N. A. (1982). The prediction of good and poor reading before kindergarten entry: A 4-year follow-up. *Journal of Special Education, 16,* 309–318.

Baldwin, R. S., Luce, T. S., & Readence, J. E. (1982). The impact of subschemata on metaphorical processing. *Reading Research Quarterly, 17,* 528–543.

Bamberg, M., & Damrad-Frye, R. (1991). On the ability to provide evaluative comments: Further explorations of children's narrative competencies. *Journal of Child Language, 18,* 689–710.

Bashaw, W. L., & Anderson, H. E. (1968). Developmental study of the meaning of adverbial modifiers. *Journal of Educational Psychology, 59,* 111–118.

Bearison, D. J., & Gass, S. T. (1979). Hypothetical and practical reasoning: Children's persuasive appeals in different social contexts. *Child Development, 50,* 901–903.

Bell, A. (1984). Short and long term learning—experiments in diagnostic teaching design. *Proceedings of the Conference of the International Group for the Psychology of Mathematics Education.* Sydney, Australia.

Benelli, B., Arcuri, L., & Marchesini, G. (1988). Cognitive and linguistic factors in the development of word definitions. *Journal of Child Language, 15,* 619–635.

Bennett, R. A. (1981). *Types of literature.* Lexington, MA: Ginn.

Berry, M. F. (1969). *Language disorders of children: The bases and diagnoses.* Englewood Cliffs, NJ: Prentice-Hall.

Billow, R. M. (1975). A cognitive developmental study of metaphor comprehension. *Developmental Psychology, 11,* 415–423.

Billow, R. M. (1977). Metaphor: A review of the psychological literature. *Psychological Bulletin, 84,* 81–92.

Billow, R. M. (1981). Observing spontaneous metaphor in children. *Journal of Experimental Child Psychology, 31,* 430–445.

Binet, A., & Simon, T. (1905). Methodes nouvelles pour le diagnostic du niveau intellectuel des anormaux. *L'Annee Psychologique, 11,* 191–244.

Bjork, R. A., & Bjork, E. L. (1992). A new theory of disuse and an old theory of stimulus fluctuation. In A. F. Healy, S. M. Kosslyn, & R. M. Shiffrin (Eds.), *From learning processes to cognitive processes: Essays in honor of William K. Estes* (Vol. 2, pp. 35–67). Hillsdale, NJ: Erlbaum.

Blachman, B. (1984). Relationship of rapid naming ability and language analysis skills to kindergarten and first grade reading achievement. *Reading Research Quarterly, 13,* 223–253.

Blake, S. M., & Madden, J. (1994). *Facets: Writing skills in context.* New York: Macmillan.

Bloom, L. (1973). *One word at a time: The use of single-word utterances before syntax.* The Hague: Mouton.

Boswell, D. A. (1979). Metaphoric processing in the mature years. *Human Development, 22,* 373–384.

Botvin, G. J., & Sutton-Smith, B. (1977). The development of structural complexity in children's fantasy narratives. *Developmental Psychology, 13,* 377–388.

Boynton, M., & Kossan, N. E. (1981, October). *Children's metaphors: Making meaning.* Paper presented at the Sixth Annual Boston University Conference on Language Development, Boston, MA.

Bragg, B. W. E., Ostrowski, M. V., & Finley, G. E. (1973). The effects of birth order and age of target on use of persuasive techniques. *Child Development, 44,* 351–354.

Brainerd, C. J. (1978). *Piaget's theory of intelligence.* Englewood Cliffs, NJ: Prentice-Hall.

Brasseur, J., & Jimenez, B. C. (1989). Performance of university students on the Fullerton subtest of idioms. *Journal of Communication Disorders, 22,* 351–359.

Brinton, B., & Fujiki, M. (1984). Development of topic manipulation skills in discourse. *Journal of Speech and Hearing Research, 27,* 350–358.

Brinton, B., Fujiki, M., & Mackey, T. A. (1985). Elementary school age children's comprehension of specific idiomatic expressions. *Journal of Communication Disorders, 18,* 245–257.

Brodzinsky, D. M. (1977). The role of conceptual tempo and stimulus characteristics in children's humor development. *Developmental Psychology, 11,* 843–850.

Brodzinsky, D. M., Feuer, V., & Owens, J. (1977). Detection of linguistic ambiguity by reflective, impulsive, fast/accurate, and slow/inaccurate children. *Journal of Educational Psychology, 69,* 237–243.

Brooks, P. (1972). *The house of life: Rachel Carson at work.* Boston: Houghton Mifflin.

Brown, R. (1973). A first language: The early stages. Cambridge, MA: Harvard University Press.

Brown, S. J. (1965). The world of imagery: Metaphor and kindred imagery (pp. 226–240). New York: Haskell House.

Burke, D. M., MacKay, D. G., Worthley, J. S., & Wade, E. (1991). On the tip of the tongue: What causes word finding failures in young and older adults? Journal of Memory and Language, 30, 542–579.

Cacciari, C., & Levorato, M. C. (1989). How children understand idioms in discourse. Journal of Child Language, 16, 387–405.

Capelli, C. A., Nakagawa, N., & Madden, C. M. (1990). How children understand sarcasm: The role of context and intonation. Child Development, 61, 1824–1841.

Carnine, D., Kameenui, E. J., & Coyle, G. (1984). Utilization of contextual information in determining the meaning of unfamiliar words. Reading Research Quarterly, 19, 188–204.

Carroll, J. B., Davies, P., & Richman, D. (1971). American heritage word frequency book. Boston, MA: Houghton-Mifflin.

Carson, R. (1962). Silent spring. Boston: Houghton Mifflin.

Carson, R. (1965). The sense of wonder. New York: Harper & Row.

Cashen, A. S. (1989). Analogical processing skills in three modalities in fifth, eighth, and eleventh graders. Unpublished master's thesis, Western Michigan University, Kalamazoo, MI.

Chambers, J. W. (1979, March). Proverb comprehension with pictorial and verbal scenarios. Paper presented at the Biennial Meeting of the Society for Research in Child Development, San Francisco, CA.

Chapman, R. L. (1988). The dictionary of American slang. London, England: Pan Books.

Chappell, G. E. (1980). Oral language performance of upper elementary school students obtained via story reformulation. Language, Speech, and Hearing Services in Schools, 11, 236–250.

Chukovsky, K. (1968). From two to five. Berkeley, CA: University of California Press.

Cirrin, F. (1983). Lexical access in children and adults. Developmental Psychology, 19, 452–460.

Clark, E. (1973). What's in a word? On the child's acquisition of semantics in his first language. In T. Moore (Ed.), Cognitive development and the acquisition of language (pp. 65–110). New York: Academic Press.

Clark, E., Gardner, M. K., Brown, G., & Howell, R. J. (1990). Changes in analogical reasoning in adulthood. Experimental Aging Research, 16, 95–99.

Clark, R. A., & Delia, J. G. (1976). The development of functional persuasive skills in childhood and early adolescence. Child Development, 47, 1008–1014.

Cliff, N. (1959). Adverbs as multipliers. Psychological Review, 66, 26–44.

Cometa, M. S., & Eson, M. E. (1978). Logical operations and metaphor interpretation: A Piagetian model. Child Development, 49, 649–659.

Coon, G. E., Cramer, B. B., Fillmer, H. T., Lefcourt, A., Martin, J., & Thompson, N. C. (1980). American book English. New York: Litton Educational Publishing.

Cooper, D. C., & Anderson-Inman, L. (1988). Language and socialization. In M. A. Nippold (Ed.), Later language development: Ages nine through nineteen (pp. 225–245). Austin, TX: PRO-ED.

Crais, E. R. (1990). World knowledge to word knowledge. Topics in Language Disorders, 10(3), 45–62.

Crais, E. R., & Lorch, N. (1994). Oral narratives in school-age children. Topics in Language Disorders, 14(3), 13–28.

Crews, F. (1977). The Random House handbook (2nd ed.). New York: Random House.

Crowhurst, M. (1980). Syntactic complexity in narration and argument at three grade levels. Canadian Journal of Education, 5, 6–13.

Crowhurst, M. (1987). Cohesion in argument and narration at three grade levels. *Research in the Teaching of English, 21*, 185–201.

Crowhurst, M., & Piche, G. L. (1979). Audience and mode of discourse effects on syntactic complexity in writing at two grade levels. *Research in the Teaching of English, 13*, 101–109.

Crystal, D. (1987). *The Cambridge encyclopedia of language.* Cambridge, England: Cambridge University Press.

Crystal, D. (1988). *The English Language.* London, England: Penguin.

Dale, E., & Eichholz, G. (1960). *Children's knowledge of words: An interim report.* Columbus, OH: Bureau of Educational Research and Service, Ohio State University.

Damico, S. B., & Purkey, W. W. (1978). Class clowns: A study of middle school students. *American Educational Research Journal, 15*, 391–398.

Davidson, J. E. (1986). The role of insight in giftedness. In R. J. Sternberg & J. E. Davidson (Eds.), *Conceptions of giftedness* (pp. 201–222). Cambridge, England: Cambridge University Press.

Delia, J. G., Kline, S. L., & Burleson, B. R. (1979). The development of persuasive communication strategies in kindergartners through twelfth-graders. *Communication Monographs, 46*, 241–256.

Demorest, A., Meyer, C., Phelps, E., Gardner, H., & Winner, E. (1984). Words speak louder than actions: Understanding deliberately false remarks. *Child Development, 55*, 1527–1534.

Demorest, A., Silberstein, L., Gardner, H., & Winner, E. (1983). Telling it as it isn't: Children's understanding of figurative language. *British Journal of Developmental Psychology, 1*, 121–134.

Denckla, M., & Rudel, R. (1974). Rapid "automatized" naming of pictured objects, colors, letters and numbers by normal children. *Cortex, 10*, 186–202.

Denckla, M. B., & Rudel, R. G. (1976a). Naming of object-drawings by dyslexic and other learning-disabled children. *Brain and Language, 3*, 1–15.

Denckla, M. B., & Rudel, R. (1976b). Rapid 'automatized' naming (R.A.N.): Dyslexia differentiated from other learning disabilities. *Neuropsychologia, 14*, 471–479.

Dennis, M. (1992). Word finding in children and adolescents with a history of brain injury. *Topics in Language Disorders, 13*(1), 66–82.

Dent, C. H. (1984). The developmental importance of motion information in perceiving and describing metaphoric similarity. *Child Development, 55*, 1607–1613.

DeVries, M. A. (1991). *The complete word book.* Englewood Cliffs, NJ: Prentice Hall.

Dias, M. G., & Harris, P. L. (1988). The effect of make-believe play on deductive reasoning. *British Journal of Developmental Psychology, 6*, 207–221.

Dias, M. G., & Harris, P. L. (1990). The influence of the imagination on reasoning by young children. *British Journal of Developmental Psychology, 8*, 305–318.

Dollaghan, C. A., & Campbell, T. F. (1992). A procedure for classifying disruptions in spontaneous language samples. *Topics in Language Disorders, 12*(2), 56–68.

Donahue, M., & Bryan, T. (1984). Communicative skills and peer relations of learning disabled adolescents. *Topics in Language Disorders, 4*(2), 10–21.

Dorval, B., & Eckerman, C. (1984). Developmental trends in the quality of conversation achieved by small groups of acquainted peers. *Monographs of the Society for Research in Child Development, 49*, (2, Serial No. 206).

Douglas, J. D., & Peel, B. (1979). The development of metaphor and proverb translation in children grades 1 through 7. *Journal of Educational Research, 73*, 116–119.

Duffy, G. G., & Roehler, L. R. (1981). *Building reading skills: Level 4.* Evanston, IL: McDougal, Littel, & Company.

Dunn, L. M., & Dunn, L. M. (1981). *Peabody picture vocabulary test-revised.* Circle Pines, MN: American Guidance Service.

Dunn, L. M., & Markwardt, F. C. (1970). *Peabody individual achievement test.* Circle Pines, MN: American Guidance Service.

Durkin, K., Crowther, R., & Shire, B. (1986). Children's processing of polysemous vocabulary in school. In K. Durkin (Ed.), *Language development in the school years* (pp. 77–94). Cambridge, MA: Brookline.

Durkin, K., Crowther, R., Shire, B., Riem, R., & Nash, P. (1985). Polysemy in mathematical and musical education. *Applied Linguistics, 6,* 147–161.

Durost, W. N. (1959). *Metropolitan achievement tests.* New York: Harcourt, Brace, and World.

Durr, W. K., LePere, J. M., Pescosolido, J., Bean, R. M., & Glaser, N. A. (1981a). *Practice book: Awards.* Boston: Houghton Mifflin.

Durr, W. K., LePere, J. M., Pescosolido, J., Bean, R. M., & Glaser, N. A. (1981b). *Teacher's guide: Awards.* Boston: Houghton Mifflin.

Eckert, P. (1990). Cooperative competition in adolescent "girl talk." *Discourse Processes, 13,* 91–122.

Eder, D. (1988). Building cohesion through collaborative narration. *Social Psychology Quarterly, 51,* 225–235.

Education for All Handicapped Children Act of 1975, 20 U.S.C. §1400 *et seq.*

Edwards, P. (1975). The effect of idioms on children's reading and understanding of prose. In B. Smith Schulwitz (Ed.), *Teachers, tangibles, techniques: Comprehension of content in reading* (pp. 37–46). Newark, DE: International Reading Association.

Eller, W., & Hester, K. B. (1980a). *Reflections.* River Forest, IL: Laidlaw.

Eller, W., & Hester, K. B. (1980b). *Wide-eyed detectives.* River Forest, IL: Laidlaw.

English, L. (1993). Evidence for deductive reasoning: Implicit versus explicit recognition of syllogistic structure. *British Journal of Developmental Psychology, 11,* 391–409.

Ennis, R. H., & Millman, J. (1982). *Cornell critical thinking test.* Champaign, IL: Illinois Thinking Project, University of Illinois.

Entwisle, D. R., Forsyth, D. F., & Muuss, R. (1964). The syntactic-paradigmatic shift in children's word associations. *Journal of Verbal Learning and Verbal Behavior, 3,* 19–29.

Erftmier, T., & Dyson, A. H. (1986). "Oh, ppbbt!": Differences between the oral and written persuasive strategies of school-aged children. *Discourse Processes, 9,* 91–114.

Evans, M. A., & Gamble, D. L. (1988). Attribute saliency and metaphor interpretation in school-age children. *Journal of Child Language, 15,* 435–449.

Fay, L., Ross, R. R., & LaPray, M. (1981). *Rand McNally reading program, Level 6: Red rock ranch.* Chicago: Rand McNally.

Feifel, H., & Lorge, I. (1950). Qualitative differences in the vocabulary responses of children. *Journal of Educational Psychology, 41,* 1–18.

Feuerstein, R. (1979). *The dynamic assessment of retarded performers: The learning potential assessment device, theory, instruments, and techniques.* Baltimore, MD: University Park Press.

Feynman, R. P. (1985). *"Surely you're joking, Mr. Feynman": Adventures of a curious character.* NY: Norton.

Finley, G. E., & Humphreys, C. A. (1974). Naive psychology and the development of persuasive appeals in girls. *Canadian Journal of Behavioral Science, 6,* 75–80.

Flavell, J. H., Botkin, P. T., Fry, C. L., Wright, J. W., & Jarvis, P. E. (1968). *The development of role-taking and communication skills in children.* New York: John Wiley.

Flexner, S. B. (1987). *How to increase your word power.* Cincinnati, OH: Writer's Digest Books.

Flores d'Arcais, G. B. (1978). Levels of semantic knowledge in children's use of connectives. In A. Sinclair, R. J. Jarvella, & W. J. M. Levelt (Eds.), *The child's conception of language* (pp. 133–153). New York: Springer-Verlag.

Freeley, A. J. (1993). *Argumentation and debate: Critical thinking for reasoned decision making.* Belmont, CA: Wadsworth.

Fried-Oken, M. (1984). *The development of naming skills in normal and language deficient children.* Unpublished doctoral dissertation, Boston University, Boston.

Fromkin, V., & Rodman, R. (1988). *An introduction to language* (4th ed.). New York: Holt, Rinehart, & Winston.

Fry, E. (1972). *Reading instruction for classroom and clinic.* New York: McGraw-Hill.

Gallagher, J. M., & Wright, R. J. (1979). Piaget and the study of analogy: Structural analysis of items. In M. K. Poulsen & G. I. Lubin (Eds.), *Piagetian theory and the helping professions: Proceedings from the eighth interdisciplinary conference* (Vol. 2, pp. 100–104). Los Angeles: University of Southern California.

Gallatin, J. E. (1975). *Adolescence and individuality: A conceptual approach to adolescent psychology.* New York: Harper & Row.

Gardner, H. (1974). Metaphors and modalities: How children project polar adjectives onto diverse domains. *Child Development, 45,* 84–91.

Gardner, H., Kircher, M., Winner, E., & Perkins, D. (1975). Children's metaphoric productions and preferences. *Journal of Child Language, 2,* 125–141.

Gardner, H., Winner, E., Bechhofer, R., & Wolf, D. (1978). The development of figurative language. In K. Nelson (Ed.), *Children's language* (Vol. 1, pp. 1–38). New York: Gardner Press.

Garnett, K. (1986). Telling tales: Narratives and learning-disabled children. *Topics in Language Disorders, 6*(2), 44–56.

Garnett, K., & Fleischner, J. E. (1983). Automatization and basic fact performance of normal and learning disabled children. *Learning Disability Quarterly, 6,* 223–230.

Gates, A., & MacGinitie, W. (1978). *Gates-MacGinitie reading test.* New York: Teacher College Press.

Gentner, D. (1977). Children's performance on a spatial analogies task. *Child Development, 48,* 1034–1039.

German, D. (1986). *Test of word finding.* Allen, TX: DLM Teaching Resources.

German, D. (1990). *Test of adolescent/adult word finding.* Allen, TX: DLM Teaching Resources.

German, D. (1992). Word-finding intervention for children and adolescents. *Topics in Language Disorders, 13*(1), 33–50.

Geva, E., & Ryan, E. B. (1985). Use of conjunctions in expository texts by skilled and less skilled readers. *Journal of Reading Behavior, 17,* 331–346.

Gibbs, R. W. (1987). Linguistic factors in children's understanding of idioms. *Journal of Child Language, 14,* 569–586.

Gibbs, R. W. (1991). Semantic analyzability in children's understanding of idioms. *Journal of Speech and Hearing Research, 34,* 613–620.

Goldman, S. R., Pellegrino, J. W., Parseghian, P., & Sallis, R. (1982). Developmental and individual differences in verbal analogical reasoning. *Child Development, 53,* 550–559.

Goldstein, G. (1962). *Developmental studies in analogical reasoning.* Unpublished doctoral dissertation, University of Kansas, Lawrence, KS.

Gombert, J. E. (1992). *Metalinguistic development.* Chicago: University of Chicago Press.

Gorham, D. R. (1956). A proverbs test for clinical and experimental use. *Psychological Reports, 2,* 1–12.

Gorovitz, S., & Williams, R. G. (1969). *Philosophical analysis: An introduction to its language and techniques* (2nd ed.). New York: Random House.

Goswami, U. (1991). Analogical reasoning: What develops? A review of research and theory. *Child Development, 62,* 1–22.

Goswami, U. (1992). *Analogical reasoning in children.* Hillsdale, NJ: Erlbaum.

Goswami, U., & Brown, A. L. (1989). Melting chocolate and melting snowmen: Analogical reasoning and causal relations. *Cognition, 35,* 69–95.

Goswami, U., & Brown, A. L. (1990). Higher-order structure and relational reasoning: Contrasting analogical and thematic relations. *Cognition, 36,* 207–226.

Goulet, P., Ska, B., & Kahn, H. J. (1994). Is there a decline in picture naming with advancing age? *Journal of Speech and Hearing Research, 37,* 629–644.

Gray, W. (1967). *Gray oral reading test.* New York: Bobbs-Merrill.

Growth in mathematics (Level 8). (1978). New York: Harcourt Brace Jovanovich.

Grunwell, P. (1986). Aspects of phonological development in later childhood. In K. Durkin (Ed.), *Language development in the school years* (pp. 34–56). Cambridge, MA: Brookline.

Guilford, A. M., & Nawojczyk, D. C. (1988). Standardization of the Boston Naming Test at the kindergarten and elementary school levels. *Language, Speech, and Hearing Services in Schools, 19,* 395–400.

Guilford, J. P. (1977). *Way beyond the IQ.* Buffalo, NY: Creative Education Foundation.

Halliday, M., & Hasan, R. (1976). *Cohesion in English.* London: Longman.

Halperin, M. S. (1974). Developmental changes in the recall and recognition of categorized word lists. *Child Development, 45,* 144–151.

Hass, W. A., & Wepman, J. M. (1974). Dimensions of individual difference in the spoken syntax of school children. *Journal of Speech and Hearing Research, 17,* 455–469.

Hawkins, J., Pea, R. D., Glick, J., & Scribner, S. (1984). "Merds that laugh don't like mushrooms": Evidence for deductive reasoning by preschoolers. *Developmental Psychology, 20,* 584–594.

Henderson, J. (1995). *Did I win?* Waco, TX: WRS.

Hirsch, E. D., Kett, J. F., & Trefil, J. (1988). *The dictionary of cultural literacy.* Boston: Houghton Mifflin.

Hoffman, R. R., & Honeck, R. P. (1980). A peacock looks at its legs: Cognitive science and figurative language. In R. P. Honeck & R. R. Hoffman (Eds.), *Cognition and figurative language* (pp. 3–24). Hillsdale, NJ: Erlbaum.

Hoffner, C., Cantor, J., & Badzinski, D. M. (1990). Children's understanding of adverbs denoting degree of likelihood. *Journal of Child Language, 17,* 217–231.

Holden, M. H. (1978, February). *Proverbs, proportions, and Piaget.* Paper presented at the Annual International Interdisciplinary Conference on Piagetian Theory and the Helping Professions, Los Angeles, CA.

Hollingsed, J. C. (1958). *A study of figures of speech in intermediate grade reading.* Unpublished doctoral dissertation, Colorado State College, Fort Collins, CO.

Honeck, R. P., Sowry, B. M., & Voegtle, K. (1978). Proverbial understanding in a pictorial context. *Child Development, 49,* 327–331.

Hoyle, S. M. (1991). Children's competence in the specialized register of sportscasting. *Journal of Child Language, 18,* 435–450.

Huisingh, R., Barrett, M., Zachman, L., Blagden, C., & Orman, J. (1990). *The word test-R: elementary.* Moline, IL: LinguiSystems.

Hunt, K. W. (1965). *Grammatical structures written at three grade levels* (Research Report No. 3). Champaign, IL: National Council of Teachers of English.

Hunt, K. W. (1970). Syntactic maturity in school children and adults. *Society for Research in Child Development Monographs, 35* (Serial No. 134).

Hyde, J. P. (1982). Rat talk: The special vocabulary of some teenagers. *English Journal, 71*, 98–101.

Israel, L. (1984). Word knowledge and word retrieval: Phonological and semantic strategies. In G. P. Wallach & K. G. Butler (Eds.), *Language learning disabilities in school-age children* (pp. 230–250). Baltimore, MD: Williams & Wilkins.

Jacobs, H. R. (1987). *Teacher's guide to geometry* (2nd ed.). New York: Freeman.

Johnson, C. J. (1995). Expanding norms for narration. *Language, Speech, and Hearing Services in Schools, 26*, 326–341.

Johnson, C. J., & Anglin, J. M. (1995). Qualitative developments in the content and form of children's definitions. *Journal of Speech and Hearing Research, 38*, 612–629.

Jones, D. C. (1985). Persuasive appeals and responses to appeals among friends and acquaintances. *Child Development, 56*, 757–763.

Kagan, J., Rosman, B. L., Day, D., Albert, J., & Phillips, W. (1964). Information processing in the child: Significance of analytic and reflective attitudes. *Psychological Monographs, 78* (Whole No. 578).

Kail, R. (1984). *The development of memory in children* (2nd ed.). New York: Freeman.

Kail, R., & Hall, L. K. (1994). Processing speed, naming speed, and reading. *Developmental Psychology, 30*, 949–954.

Kail, R., & Leonard, L. B. (1986). Word-finding abilities in language-impaired children. *ASHA Monographs Number 25*.

Kail, R., & Nippold, M. A. (1984). Unconstrained retrieval from semantic memory. *Child Development, 55*, 944–951.

Kamhi, A. G. (1987, November). *Normal language development: Ages 9 through 19*. Short course presented at the Annual Convention of the American Speech-Language-Hearing Association, New Orleans, LA.

Kamhi, A. G., & Catts, H. W. (Eds.) (1989). *Reading disabilities: A developmental language perspective*. Boston: Little, Brown.

Kaplan, E., Goodglass, H., & Weintraub, S. (1976). *Boston naming test*. Unpublished test. Experimental Edition.

Kaplan, E., Goodglass, H., & Weintraub, S. (1983). *Boston naming test*. Philadelphia, PA: Lee & Febiger.

Karadsheh, R. (1991, April). *This room is a junkyard!: Children's comprehension of metaphorical language*. Paper presented at the Biennial Meeting of the Society for Research in Child Development, Seattle, WA.

Karmiloff-Smith, A. (1986). Some fundamental aspects of language development after age 5. In P. Fletcher & M. Garman (Eds.), *Language acquisition: Studies in first language development* (2nd ed., pp. 455–474). Cambridge, England: Cambridge University Press.

Katz, E. W., & Brent, S. B. (1968). Understanding connectives. *Journal of Verbal Learning and Verbal Behavior, 7*, 501–509.

Keating, D. P., & Caramazza, A. (1975). Effects of age and ability on syllogistic reasoning in early adolescence. *Developmental Psychology, 11*, 837–842.

Keil, F. (1980). Development of the ability to perceive ambiguities: Evidence for the task specificity of a linguistic skill. *Journal of Psycholinguistic Research, 9*, 219–229.

Keil, F. C. (1986). Conceptual domains and the acquisition of metaphor. *Cognitive Development, 1*, 73–96.

Kemper, S. (1984). The development of narrative skills: Explanations and entertainments. In S. A. Kuczaj (Ed.), *Discourse development: Progress in cognitive development research* (pp. 99–124). New York: Springer-Verlag.

Kernan, K. T. (1977). Semantic and expressive elaboration in children's narratives. In S. Ervin-Tripp & C. Mitchell-Kernan (Eds.), *Child Discourse* (pp. 91–102). New York: Academic Press.

Kessel, F. S. (1970). The role of syntax in children's comprehension from ages six to twelve. *Monographs of the Society for Research in Child Development, 35*(6), Serial No. 139.

Klecan-Aker, J. S., & Hedrick, D. L. (1985). A study of the syntactic language skills of normal school-age children. *Language, Speech, and Hearing Services in Schools, 16,* 187–198.

Kobasigawa, A. (1974). Utilization of retrieval cues by children in recall. *Child Development, 45,* 127–134.

Kobasigawa, A. (1977). Retrieval strategies in the development of memory. In R. Kail & J. W. Hagen (Eds.), *Perspectives in the development of memory and cognition* (pp. 177–201). Hillsdale, NJ: Erlbaum.

Kobasigawa, A., & Mason, P. L. (1982). Use of multiple cues by children in memory retrieval situations. *The Journal of General Psychology, 107,* 195–201.

Kodroff, J. K., & Roberge, J. J. (1975). Developmental analysis of the conditional reasoning abilities of primary-grade children. *Developmental Psychology, 11,* 21–28.

Kogan, N., & Chadrow, M. (1986). Children's comprehension of metaphor in the pictorial and verbal modality. *International Journal of Behavioral Development, 9,* 285–295.

Kogan, N., Connor, K., Gross, A., & Fava, D. (1980). Understanding visual metaphor: Developmental and individual differences. *Monographs of the Society for Research in Child Development, 45* (Serial No. 183). Chicago: University of Chicago Press.

Kolson, C. (1960). *The vocabularies of kindergarten children.* Pittsburgh, PA: University of Pittsburgh Press.

Kubicka, D. (1992). Comprehension of standard metaphorical similes by adolescents. *Polish Psychological Bulletin, 23,* 47–61.

Kucera, H., & Francis, W. (1967). *Computational analysis of present day American English.* Providence, RI: Brown University Press.

Kuhn, D. (1977). Conditional reasoning in children. *Developmental Psychology, 13,* 342–353.

Laing, A. (1939). The sense of humour in childhood and adolescence. *British Journal of Educational Psychology, 9,* 201.

Langacker, R. W. (1973). *Language and its structure: Some fundamental linguistic concepts* (2nd ed.). New York: Harcourt Brace Jovanovich.

Lazar, R. T., Warr-Leeper, G. A., Nicholson, C. B., & Johnson, S. (1989). Elementary school teachers' use of multiple meaning expressions. *Language, Speech, and Hearing Services in Schools, 20,* 420–430.

Leadholm, B. J., & Miller, J. F. (1992). *Language sample analysis: The Wisconsin guide.* Madison, WI: Wisconsin Department of Public Instruction.

Lenneberg, E. H. (1967). *Biological foundations of language.* New York: John Wiley.

Leona, M. H. (1978). An examination of adolescent clique language in a suburban secondary school. *Adolescence, 13,* 495–502.

Levinson, P. J., & Carpenter, R. L. (1974). An analysis of analogical reasoning in children. *Child Development, 45,* 857–861.

Levorato, M. C., & Cacciari, C. (1992). Children's comprehension and production of idioms: The role of context and familiarity. *Journal of Child Language, 19,* 415–433.

Lewis, M. M. (1963). *Language, thought, and personality in infancy and childhood.* London: Harrap.

Liles, B. Z. (1987). Episode organization and cohesive conjunctives in narratives of children with and without language disorder. *Journal of Speech and Hearing Research, 30,* 185–196.

Liles, B. Z. (1993). Narrative discourse in children with language disorders and children with normal language: A critical review of the literature. *Journal of Speech and Hearing Research, 36,* 868–882.

Lindquist, E. F., & Hieronymus, A. N. (1956). *Iowa tests of basic skills.* Boston: Houghton Mifflin.

Lippman, M. Z. (1971). Correlates of contrast word associations: Developmental trends. *Journal of Verbal Learning and Verbal Behavior, 10,* 392–399.

Litowitz, B. (1977). Learning to make definitions. *Journal of Child Language, 4,* 289–304.

Loban, W. (1976). *Language development: Kindergarten through grade twelve.* (Research Report No. 18). Urbana, IL: National Council of Teachers of English.

Lodge, D. N., & Leach, E. A. (1975). Children's acquisition of idioms in the English language. *Journal of Speech and Hearing Research, 18,* 521–529.

Lorge, I., & Thorndike, R. L. (1957). *Lorge-Thorndike intelligence tests.* Boston: Houghton Mifflin.

Lutzer, V. D. (1988). Comprehension of proverbs by average children and children with learning disorders. *Journal of Learning Disabilities, 21,* 104–108.

Lutzer, V. D. (1991). Gender differences in preschoolers' ability to interpret common metaphors. *Journal of Creative Behavior, 25,* 69–74.

MacKay, D. G., & Bever, T. G. (1967). In search of ambiguity. *Perception and Psychophysics, 2,* 193–201.

MacLachlan, B. G., & Chapman, R. S. (1988). Communication breakdowns in normal and language learning-disabled children's conversation and narration. *Journal of Speech and Hearing Disorders, 53,* 2–7.

Madden, R., Gardner, E. R., Rudman, H. C., Karlsen, B., & Merwin, J. C. (1973). *Stanford Achievement Test.* NY: Harcourt Brace Jovanovich.

Makau, J. M. (1990). *Reasoning and communication: Thinking critically about arguments.* Belmont, CA: Wadsworth.

Malgady, R. G. (1977). Children's interpretation and appreciation of similes. *Child Development, 48,* 1734–1738.

Mandler, J. M., & Johnson, N. S. (1977). Remembrance of things parsed: Story structure and recall. *Cognitive Psychology, 9,* 111–151.

Markovits, H. (1995). Conditional reasoning with false premises: Fantasy and information retrieval. *British Journal of Developmental Psychology, 13,* 1–11.

Markovits, H., Schleifer, M., & Fortier, L. (1989). Development of elementary deductive reasoning in young children. *Developmental Psychology, 25,* 787–793.

Markowitz, J., & Franz, S. K. (1988). The development of defining style. *International Journal of Lexicography, 1,* 253–267.

Mason, J. M., Kniseley, E., & Kendall, J. (1979). Effects of polysemous words on sentence comprehension. *Reading Research Quarterly, 15,* 49–65.

Masten, A. S. (1986). Humor and competence in school-aged children. *Child Development, 57,* 461–473.

May, A. B. (1979). All the angles of idiom instruction. *The Reading Teacher, 32,* 680–682.

McCartney, K. A., & Nelson, K. (1981). Children's use of scripts in story recall. *Discourse Processes, 4,* 59–70.

McCay, M. A. (1993). *Rachel Carson.* New York: Twayne.

McClure, E., & Geva, E. (1983). The development of the cohesive use of adversative conjunctions in discourse. *Discourse Processes, 6*, 411–432.

McClure, E., & Steffensen, M. (1985). A study of the use of conjunctions across grades and ethnic groups. *Research in the Teaching of English, 19*, 217–236.

McCutchen, D., & Perfetti, C. A. (1982). Coherence and connectedness in the development of discourse production. *Text, 2*, 113–139.

McDonnell, H., Nakadate, N. E., Pfordresher, J., & Shoemate, T. E. (1979). *England in literature.* Glenview, IL: Scott, Foresman & Company.

McDowell, J. H. (1985). Verbal dueling. In T. A. van Dijk (Ed.), *Handbook of discourse analysis, Volume 3: Discourse and dialogue* (pp. 203–211) London, England: Academic Press.

McGhee, P. E. (1979). *Humor: Its origin and development.* San Francisco: Freeman.

McGhee-Bidlack, B. (1991). The development of noun definitions: A metalinguistic analysis. *Journal of Child Language, 18*, 417–434.

McKeon, R. (Ed). (1941). *The basic works of Aristotle.* New York: Random House

McNeil, D. (1970). *The acquisition of language: The study of developmental psycholinguistics.* New York: Harper & Row.

Mentis, M. (1991). Topic management in the discourse of normal and language impaired children. *Journal of Childhood Communication Disorders, 14*, 45–66.

Mentis, M. (1994). Topic management in discourse: Assessment and intervention. *Topics in Language Disorders, 14*, 29–54.

Menyuk, P. (1977). *Language and maturation.* Cambridge, MA: MIT Press.

Mieder, W. (1993). *Proverbs are never out of season: Popular wisdom in the modern age.* New York: Oxford University Press.

Mieder, W., Kingsbury, S. A., & Harder, K. B. (1992). *A dictionary of American proverbs.* New York: Oxford University Press.

Milianti, F. J., & Cullinan, W. L. (1974). Effects of age and word frequency on object recognition and naming in children. *Journal of Speech and Hearing Research, 17*, 373–385.

Miller, G. A. (1979). Images and models, similes and metaphors. In A. Ortony (Ed.), *Metaphor and thought* (pp. 202–250). Cambridge, England: Cambridge University Press.

Miller, G. A., & Gildea, P. M. (1987). How children learn words. *Scientific American, 257*, 94–99.

Miller, J. F., Freiberg, C., Rolland, M., & Reeves, M. (1992). Implementing computerized language sample analysis in the public school. *Topics in Language Disorders, 12*(2), 69–82.

Milosky, L. M. (1994). Nonliteral language abilities: Seeing the forest for the trees. In G. P. Wallach & K. G. Butler (Eds.), *Language learning disabilities in school-age children and adolescents: Some principles and applications* (pp. 275–303). New York: Macmillan.

Morgan, D. L., & Guilford, A. M. (1984). *Adolescent language screening test.* Tulsa, OK: Modern Education Corporation.

Morris, N. T., & Crump, W. D. (1982). Syntactic and vocabulary development in the written language of learning disabled and non-disabled students at four age levels. *Learning Disability Quarterly, 5*, 163–172.

Muus, L. A., & Hoag, L. A. (1980, November). *Cognition and the detection of linguistic ambiguity by adolescents.* Paper presented at the Annual Convention of the American Speech-Language-Hearing Association, Detroit, MI.

Nagy, W. E., Diakidoy, I. N., & Anderson, R. C. (1993). The acquisition of morphology: Learning the contribution of suffixes to the meanings of derivatives. *Journal of Reading Behavior, 25*, 155–170.

Nagy, W. E., & Herman, P. A. (1987). Breadth and depth of vocabulary knowledge: Implications for acquisition and instruction. In M. G. McKeown & M. E. Curtis (Eds.), *The nature of vocabulary acquisition* (pp. 19–35). Hillsdale, NJ: Erlbaum.

Nagy, W. E., Herman, P. A., & Anderson, R. C. (1985). Learning words from context. *Reading Research Quarterly, 22*, 233–253.

National Educational Development Tests (1984). Chicago: Science Research Associates.

Nelsen, E. A., & Rosenbaum, E. (1972). Language patterns within the youth subculture: Development of slang vocabularies. *Merrill-Palmer Quarterly, 18*, 273–285.

Nelson, K. (1974). Variations in children's concepts by age and category. *Child Development, 45*, 577–584.

Nelson, K. (1977). The syntagmatic-paradigmatic shift revisited: A review of research and theory. *Psychological Bulletin, 84*, 93–116.

Nelson, K. (1978). Semantic development and the development of semantic memory. In K. Nelson (Ed.), *Children's language*, (Vol. I, pp. 39–80). New York: Gardner Press.

Nelson, N. W. (1988). Reading and writing. In M. A. Nippold (Ed.), *Later language development: Ages nine through nineteen* (pp. 97–125). Austin, TX: PRO-ED.

Nelson, N. W. (1993). *Childhood language disorders in context: Infancy through adolescence.* New York: Macmillan.

Nelson, N. W., & Gillespie, L. L. (1991). *Analogies for thinking and talking.* Tucson, AZ: Communication Skill Builders.

Newcomer, P. L., & Hammill, D. D. (1988). *Test of language development-2: primary.* Austin, TX: PRO-ED.

Nippold, M. A. (Ed.) (1988). *Later language development: Ages nine through nineteen.* Austin, TX: PRO-ED.

Nippold, M. A. (1990). *Idioms in textbooks for kindergarten through eighth grade students.* Unpublished manuscript, University of Oregon, Eugene.

Nippold, M. A. (1994). Third-order verbal analogical reasoning: A developmental study of children and adolescents. *Contemporary Educational Psychology, 19*, 101–107.

Nippold, M. A., Cuyler, J. S., & Braunbeck-Price, R. (1988). Explanation of ambiguous advertisements: A developmental study with children and adolescents. *Journal of Speech and Hearing Research, 31*, 466–474.

Nippold, M. A., & Haq, F. S. (1996). Proverb comprehension in youth: The role of concreteness and familiarity. *Journal of Speech and Hearing Research, 39*, 166–176.

Nippold, M. A., Hegel, S. L., Uhden, L. D., & Bustamante, S. (1997a). *Development of proverb comprehension in adolescents: Implications for instruction.* Manuscript submitted for publication.

Nippold, M. A., Leonard, L. B., & Kail, R. (1984). Syntactic and conceptual factors in children's understanding of metaphors. *Journal of Speech and Hearing Research, 27*, 197–205.

Nippold, M. A., & Martin, S. T. (1989). Idiom interpretation in isolation versus context: A developmental study with adolescents. *Journal of Speech and Hearing Research, 32*, 59–66.

Nippold, M. A., Martin, S. A., & Erskine, B. J. (1988). Proverb comprehension in context: A developmental study with children and adolescents. *Journal of Speech and Hearing Research, 31*, 19–28.

Nippold, M. A., & Rudzinski, M. (1993). Familiarity and transparency in idiom explanation: A developmental study of children and adolescents. *Journal of Speech and Hearing Research, 36*, 728–737.

Nippold, M. A., Schwarz, I. E., & Undlin, R. A. (1992). Use and understanding of adverbial conjuncts *Journal of Speech and Hearing Research, 35*, 108–118.

Nippold, M. A., & Sullivan, M. P. (1987). Verbal and perceptual analogical reasoning and proportiona metaphor comprehension in young children. *Journal of Speech and Hearing Research, 30*, 367–376

Nippold, M. A., & Taylor, C. L. (1995). Idiom understanding in youth: Further examination of familiarity and transparency. *Journal of Speech and Hearing Research*, 38, 426–433.

Nippold, M. A., Taylor, C. L., & Baker, J. M. (1996c). Idiom understanding in Australian youth: A cross-cultural comparison. *Journal of Speech and Hearing Research*, 39, 442–447.

Nippold, M. A., Uhden, L. D., & Schwarz, I. E. (1997b). Proverb explanation through the lifespan: A developmental study of adolescents and adults. *Journal of Speech, Language, and Hearing Research*, 40, 245–253.

Obler, L. K. (1993). Language beyond childhood. In J. Berko Gleason (Ed.), *The development of language* (3rd ed., pp. 421–3449). New York: Macmillan.

O'Brien, T. C., & Shapiro, B. J. (1968). The development of logical thinking in children. *American Educational Research Journal*, 5, 531–542.

O'Donnell, R., Griffin, W., & Norris, R. (1967). *Syntax of kindergarten and elementary school children: A transformational analysis* (Research Report No. 8). Champaign, IL: National Council of Teachers of English.

Olson, D. R., & Astington, J. W. (1986a). Children's acquisition of metalinguistic and metacognitive verbs. In W. Demopoulos & A. Marras (Eds.), *Language learning and concept acquisition: Foundational issues* (pp. 184–199). Norwood, NJ: Ablex.

Olson, D. R., & Astington, J. W. (1986b, October). *Talking about text: How literacy contributes to thought.* Paper presented at the Boston University Conference on Language Development, Boston, MA.

Ortony, A. (1979). The role of similarity in similes and metaphors. In A. Ortony (Ed.), *Metaphor and thought* (pp. 186–201). Cambridge, England: Cambridge University Press.

Ortony, A., Schallert, D. L., Reynolds, R. E., & Antos, S. J. (1978). Interpreting metaphors and idioms: Some effects of context on comprehension. *Journal of Verbal Learning and Verbal Behavior*, 7, 465–477.

Ortony, A., Turner, T. J., & Larson-Shapiro, N. (1985). Cultural and instructional influences on figurative language comprehension by inner city children. *Research in the Teaching of English*, 19, 25–36.

Otis, A. S., & Lennon, R. T. (1967). *Otis-Lennon mental ability test.* New York: Harcourt, Brace, and World.

Page, J. L., & Stewart, S. R. (1985). Story grammar skills in school-age children. *Topics in Language Disorders*, 5(2), 16–30.

Paivio, A. (1979). Psychological processes in the comprehension of metaphor. In A. Ortony (Ed.), *Metaphor and thought* (pp. 150–171). Cambridge, England: Cambridge University Press.

Palermo, D. S., & Molfese, D. L. (1972). Language acquisition from age five onward. *Psychological Bulletin*, 78, 409–428.

Paris, S. G. (1978). Memory organization during children's repeated recall. *Developmental Psychology*, 14, 99–106.

Pearson, B. Z. (1990). The comprehension of metaphor by preschool children. *Journal of Child Language*, 17, 185–203.

Perera, K. (1986). Language acquisition and writing. In P. Fletcher & M. Garman (Eds.), *Language acquisition: Studies in first language acquisition* (2nd ed.) (pp. 494–519). Cambridge: Cambridge University Press.

Perera, K. (1992). Reading and writing skills in the National Curriculum. In P. Fletcher & D. Hall (Eds.), *Specific speech and language disorders in children: Correlates, characteristics, and outcomes* (pp. 183–193). London, England: Whurr.

Piaget, J. (1926). *The language and thought of the child.* New York: Harcourt, Brace.

Piaget, J., Montangero, J., & Billeter, J. B. (1977). La formation des correlats. In J. Piaget (Ed.), *Recherches sur l'abstraction reflechissante: L'abstraction des relations logico-arithmetiques* (pp. 115–129). Paris, France: Presses Universitaires de France.

Piche, G. L., Rubin, D. L., & Michlin, M. L. (1978). Age and social class in children's use of persuasive communicative appeals. *Child Development, 49*, 773–780.

Pinker, S. (1994). *The language instinct: How the mind creates language.* New York: William Morrow.

Polanski, V. G. (1989). Spontaneous production of figures in writing of students: Grades four, eight, twelve and third year in college. *Educational Research Quarterly, 13*, 47–55.

Pollio, M. R., & Pickens, J. D. (1980). The developmental structure of figurative competence. In R. R. Honeck & R. R. Hoffman (Eds.), *Cognition and figurative language* (pp. 311–340). Hillsdale, NJ: Erlbaum.

Pollio, M. R., & Pollio, H. R. (1974). The development of figurative language in school children. *Journal of Psycholinguistic Research, 3*, 185–201.

Pollio, M. R., & Pollio, H. R. (1979). A test of metaphoric comprehension and some preliminary data. *Journal of Child Language, 6*, 111–120.

Preece, A. (1987). The range of narrative forms conversationally produced by young children. *Journal of Child Language, 14*, 353–373.

Prentice, N. M., & Fathman, R. E. (1975). Joking riddles: A developmental index of children's humor. *Developmental Psychology, 11*, 210–216.

Prinz, P. M. (1983). The development of idiomatic meaning in children. *Language and Speech, 26*, 263–272.

Prutting, C. A. (1983). Scientific inquiry and communicative disorders: An emerging paradigm across six decades. In T. M. Gallagher & C. A. Prutting (Eds.), *Pragmatic assessment and intervention issues in language* (pp. 247–266). San Diego, CA: College-Hill Press.

Quirk, R., & Greenbaum, S. (1973). *A concise grammar of contemporary English.* New York: Harcourt Brace Jovanovich.

Ransohoff, R. (1975). Some observations on humor and laughter in young adolescent girls. *Journal of Youth and Adolescence, 4*, 155–170.

Raven, J. C. (1960). *Guide to the standard progressive matrices.* London: Lewis.

Rawlins, W. K. (1992). *Friendship matters: Communication, dialectics, and the life course.* New York: Aldine De Gruyter.

Redfern, W. (1984). *Puns.* New York: Blackwell.

Reed, V. A. (1986). An introduction to language. In V. A. Reed (Ed.), *An introduction to children with language disorders* (pp. 3–22). New York: Macmillan.

Resnick, D. A. (1982). A developmental study of proverb comprehension. *Journal of Psycholinguistic Research, 11*, 521–538.

Reston, J. (1985, February 19). A useful book of Russian proverbs. *The Register-Guard*, p. 15A, Eugene, Oregon.

Reynolds, R. E., & Ortony, A. (1980). Some issues in the measurement of children's comprehension of metaphorical language. *Child Development, 51*, 1110–1119.

Richardson, C., & Church, J. (1959). A developmental analysis of proverb interpretations. *Journal of Genetic Psychology, 94*, 169–179.

Ridout, R., & Witting, C. (1969). *English proverbs explained.* London, England: Pan Books.

Riegel, K. F., Riegel, R. M., Quarterman, C. J., & Smith, H. E. (1968). Developmental differences in word meaning and semantic structure. *Human Development, 11*, 92–106.

Rinsland, H. D. (1945). *A basic vocabulary of elementary school children.* New York: Macmillan.

Ritter, E. M. (1979). Social perspective-taking ability, cognitive complexity and listener-adapted communication in early and late adolescence. *Communication Monographs, 46*, 40–51.

Roberge, J. J., & Flexer, B. B. (1979). Further examination of formal operational reasoning abilities. *Child Development, 50,* 478–484.

Roberge, J. J., & Flexer, B. B. (1980). Control of variables and propositional reasoning in early adolescence. *The Journal of General Psychology, 103,* 3–12.

Roberge, J. J., & Paulus, D. H. (1971). Developmental patterns for children's class and conditional reasoning abilities. *Developmental Psychology, 4,* 191–200.

Robertson, J. E. (1968). Pupil understanding of connectives in reading. *Reading Research Quarterly, 3,* 387–417.

Romero, D. (1994). Making sense of slang when your kids are doing the talking. *Corvallis Gazette Times,* p. C2, Corvallis, Oregon.

Rosenbek, J. C., LaPointe, L. L., & Wertz, R. T. (1989). *Aphasia: A clinical approach.* Boston, MA: Little, Brown.

Roth, F. P., & Spekman, N. J. (1986). Narrative discourse: Spontaneously generated stories of learning-disabled and normally achieving students. *Journal of Speech and Hearing Disorders, 51,* 8–23.

Rudel, R. G., Denckla, M. B., & Broman, M. (1981). The effect of varying stimulus context on word-finding ability: Dyslexia further differentiated from other learning disabilities. *Brain and Language, 13,* 130–144.

Rudel, R. G., Denckla, M. B., Broman, M., & Hirsch, S. (1980). Word-finding as a function of stimulus context: Children compared with aphasic adults. *Brain and Language, 10,* 111–119.

Savage, D. J., & Fallis, S. L. (1988). *Story reformulation as a measure of oral language performance.* Unpublished master's thesis, University of Western Ontario, London, Ontario, Canada.

Sawyer, W. W. (1982). *Prelude to mathematics.* NY: Dover.

Schaefer, C. E. (1975). The importance of measuring metaphorical thinking in children. *Gifted Child Quarterly, 19,* 140–148.

Schecter, B., & Broughton, J. (1991). Developmental relationships between psychological metaphors and concepts of life and consciousness. *Metaphor and Symbolic Activity, 6,* 119–143.

Scheibe, C., & Condry, J. (1987, April). *Learning to distinguish fantasy from reality: Children's beliefs about Santa Claus and other fantasy figures.* Poster session presented at the Biennial Meeting of the Society for Research in Child Development, Baltimore, MD.

Schober-Peterson, D., & Johnson, C. J. (1993). The performance of eight-to-ten-year-olds on measures of conversational skillfulness. *First Language, 13,* 249–269.

Schwartz, G., & Merten, D. (1967). The language of adolescence: An anthropological approach to the youth culture. *The American Journal of Sociology, 72,* 453–468.

Scott, C. M. (1984). Adverbial connectivity in conversations of children 6 to 12. *Journal of Child Language, 11,* 423–452.

Scott, C. M. (1988a). Producing complex sentences. *Topics in Language Disorders, 8,* 44–62.

Scott, C. M. (1988b). Spoken and written syntax. In M. A. Nippold (Ed.), *Later language development: Ages nine through nineteen* (pp. 49–95). Austin, TX: PRO-ED.

Scott, C. M. (1989). Learning to write: Context, form, and process. In A. G. Kamhi & H. W. Catts (Eds.), *Reading disabilities: A developmental language perspective* (pp. 261–302). Boston: Little, Brown.

Scott, C. M. (1994). A discourse continuum for school-age students: Impact of modality and genre. In G. P. Wallach & K. G. Butler (Eds.), *Language learning disabilities in school-age children and adolescents: Some principles and applications* (pp. 219–252). New York: Macmillan.

Scott, C. M., & Erwin, D. L. (1992). Descriptive assessment of writing: Process and products. In W. A. Secord & J. S. Damico (Eds.), *Best practices in school speech-language pathology: Descriptive/nonstandardized language assessment* (pp. 87–97). San Antonio, TX: Psychological Corporation.

Scott, C. M., & Rush, D. (1985). Teaching adverbial connectivity: Implications from current research. *Child Language Teaching and Therapy, 1*, 264–280.

Scott, C. M., & Stokes, S. L. (1995). Measures of syntax in school-age children and adolescents. *Language, Speech, and Hearing Services in Schools, 26*, 309–319.

Scoville, R. P., & Gordon, A. M. (1980). Children's understanding of factive presuppositions: An experiment and a review. *Journal of Child Language, 7*, 381–399.

Selman, R. L., Beardslee, W., Schultz, L. H., Krupa, M., & Podorefsky, D. (1986). Assessing adolescent interpersonal negotiation strategies: Toward the integration of structural and functional models. *Developmental Psychology, 22*, 450–459.

Selman, R. L., Schorin, M. Z., Stone, C. R., & Phelps, E. (1983). A naturalistic study of children's social understanding. *Developmental Psychology, 19*, 82–102.

Semel, E. M., & Wiig, E. H. (1980). *Clinical evaluation of language functions.* Columbus, OH: Merrill.

Semel, E. M., Wiig, E. H., & Secord, W. (1987). *Clinical evaluation of language fundamentals-revised.* San Antonio, TX: Psychological Corporation.

Shapiro, B. J., & O'Brien, T. C. (1970). Logical thinking in children ages six through thirteen. *Child Development, 41*, 823–829.

Shepard, W. O. (1970). Word association and definition in middle childhood. *Developmental Psychology, 3*, 412.

Shultz, T. R. (1974). Development of the appreciation of riddles. *Child Development, 45*, 100–105.

Shultz, T. R., & Horibe, F. (1974). Development of the appreciation of verbal jokes. *Developmental Psychology, 10*, 13–20.

Shultz, T. R., & Pilon, R. (1973). Development of the ability to detect linguistic ambiguity. *Child Development, 44*, 728–733.

Silberstein, L., Gardner, H., Phelps, E., & Winner, E. (1982). Autumn leaves and old photographs: The development of metaphor preferences. *Journal of Experimental Child Psychology, 34*, 135–150.

Siltanen, S. A. (1981). *Apple noses and popsicle toeses: A developmental investigation of metaphorical comprehension.* Unpublished doctoral dissertation, Ohio State University, Columbus, OH.

Siltanen, S. A. (1989). Effects of three levels of context on children's metaphor comprehension. *Journal of Genetic Psychology, 150*, 197–215.

Sinatra, R., & Dowd, C. A. (1991). Using syntactic and semantic clues to learn vocabulary. *Journal of Reading, 35*, 224–229.

Smith, C. B., & Wardhaugh, R. (1980). *Dreams and decisions.* New York: Macmillan.

Smith, J. W. A. (1976). Children's emphasis of metaphor: A Piagetian interpretation. *Language and Speech, 19*, 236–243.

Snow, C., Cancini, H., Gonzalez, P., & Shriberg, E. (1989). Giving formal definitions: An oral language correlate of school literacy. In D. Bloome (Ed.), *Classrooms and literacy* (pp. 233–249). Norwood, NJ: Ablex.

Snow, C. E. (1990). The development of definitional skill. *Journal of Child Language, 17*, 697–710.

Snyder, L. S., & Downey, D. M. (1991). The language-reading relationship in normal and reading-disabled children. *Journal of Speech and Hearing Research, 34*, 129–140.

Spector, C. C. (1996). Children's comprehension of idioms in the context of humor. *Language, Speech, and Hearing Services in Schools, 27*, 307–313.

Stein, N. L., & Glenn, C. G. (1979). An analysis of story comprehension in elementary school children. In R. O. Freedle (Ed.), *New directions in discourse processing* (Vol. 2, pp. 53–120). Norwood, NJ: Ablex.

Sternberg, R. J. (1979). Developmental patterns in the encoding and combination of logical connectives. *Journal of Experimental Child Psychology, 28,* 469–498.

Sternberg, R. J. (1980). The development of linear syllogistic reasoning. *Journal of Experimental Child Psychology, 29,* 340–356.

Sternberg, R. J. (1982). Reasoning, problem solving, and intelligence. In R. J. Sternberg (Ed.), *Handbook of human intelligence* (pp. 225–307). Cambridge, England: Cambridge University Press.

Sternberg, R. J. (1987). Most vocabulary is learned from context. In M. G. McKeown & M. E. Curtis (Eds.), *The nature of vocabulary acquisition* (pp. 89–105). Hillsdale, NJ: Erlbaum.

Sternberg, R. J. & Downing, C. J. (1982). The development of higher-order reasoning in adolescents. *Child Development, 53,* 209–221.

Sternberg, R. J., & Nigro, G. (1980). Developmental patterns in the solution of verbal analogies. *Child Development, 51,* 27–38.

Stitch, T. G. (1979). Educational uses of metaphor. In A. Ortony (Ed.), *Metaphor and thought* (pp. 474–485). Cambridge, England: Cambridge University Press.

Storck, P. A., & Looft, W. R. (1973). Qualitative analysis of vocabulary responses from persons aged six to sixty-six plus. *Journal of Educational Psychology, 65,* 192–197.

Strand, K. E., & Fraser, B. (1979). *The comprehension of verbal idioms by young children.* Unpublished paper, Boston University, School of Education.

Swartz, K., & Hall, A. E. (1972). Development of relational concepts and word definition in children five through eleven. *Child Development, 43,* 239–244.

Taplin, J. E., Staudenmayer, H., & Taddonio, J. L. (1974). Developmental changes in conditional reasoning: Linguistic or logical? *Journal of Experimental Child Psychology, 17,* 360–373.

Thorndike, E., & Lorge, I. (1944). *The teacher's word book of 30,000 words.* New York: Columbia University Press.

Thorndike, R., & Hagen, E. (1971). *Cognitive abilities test.* Boston: Houghton Mifflin.

Thorndike, R. L., Hagen, E. P., & Sattler, J. M. (1986). *Stanford-Binet intelligence scale* (4th ed.). Chicago, IL: Riverside.

Thorum, A. (1980). *Fullerton language test for adolescents.* Palo Alto, CA: Consulting Psychologists Press.

van Kleeck, A. (1984). Metalinguistic skills: Cutting across spoken and written language and problem-solving abilities. In G. P. Wallach and K. G. Butler (Eds.), *Language learning disabilities in school-age children* (pp. 128–153). Baltimore, MD: Williams & Wilkins.

van Kleeck, A. (1994). Metalinguistic development. In G. P. Wallach & K. G. Butler (Eds.), *Language learning disabilities in school-age children and adolescents: Some principles and applications* (pp. 53–98). New York: Macmillan.

Vosniadou, S. (1987). Children and metaphors. *Child Development, 58,* 870–885.

Vosniadou, S., & Ortony, A. (1983). The emergence of the literal-metaphorical anomalous distinction in young children. *Child Development, 54,* 154–161.

Vosniadou, S., Ortony, A., Reynolds, R. E., & Wilson, P. T. (1984). Sources of difficulty in the young child's understanding of metaphorical language. *Child Development, 55,* 1588–1606.

Waggoner, J. E., Messe, M. J., & Palermo, D. S. (1985). Grasping the meaning of metaphor: Story recall and comprehension. *Child Development, 56,* 1156–1166.

Waggoner, J. E., & Palermo, D. S. (1989). Betty is a bouncing bubble: Children's comprehension of emotion-descriptive metaphors. *Developmental Psychology, 25,* 152–163.

Wagner, S., Winner, E., Cicchetti, D., & Gardner, H. (1981). "Metaphorical" mapping in human infants. *Child Development, 52,* 728–731.

Wallace, G., & Hammill, D. D. (1994). *Comprehensive receptive and expressive vocabulary test*. Austin, TX: PRO-ED.

Watson, R. (1985). Towards a theory of definition. *Journal of Child Language, 12*, 181–197.

Watson, R. (1995). Relevance and definition. *Journal of Child Language, 22*, 211–222.

Watts, A. R. (1944). *The language and mental development of children* (pp. 195–217). London: Harrap.

Weaver, P. A., & Dickinson, D. K. (1982). Scratching below the surface structure: Exploring the usefulness of story grammars. *Discourse Processes, 5*, 225–243.

Wechsler, D. (1991). *Wechsler intelligence scale for children* (3rd ed.). San Antonio, TX: Psychological Corporation.

Wehren, A., De Lisi, R., & Arnold, M. (1981). The development of noun definition. *Journal of Child Language, 8*, 165–175.

Welch, B. Y., & Bennett, R. A. (1981a). *Introduction to Literature*. Lexington, MA: Ginn.

Welch, B. Y., & Bennett, R. A. (1981b). *Teacher's handbook for introduction to literature: Grade 7*. Lexington, MA: Ginn.

Westby, C. E. (1984). Development of narrative language abilities. In G. P. Wallach & K. G. Butler (Eds.), *Language learning disabilities in school-age children* (pp. 103–127). Baltimore: Williams & Wilkins.

White, T. G., Power, M. A., & White, S. (1989). Morphological analysis: Implications for teaching and understanding vocabulary growth. *Reading Research Quarterly, 24*, 283–304.

Wiegel-Crump, C. A., & Dennis, M. (1986). Development of word-finding. *Brain and Language, 27*, 1–23.

Wiig, E. H., Gilbert, M. F., & Christian, S. H. (1978). Developmental sequences in perception and interpretation of ambiguous sentences. *Perceptual and Motor Skills, 46*, 959–969.

Wiig, E. H., & Secord, W. (1989). *Test of language competence: Expanded edition*. San Antonio, TX: Psychological Corporation.

Wiig, E. H., & Secord, W. (1991). *Test of word knowledge*. San Antonio, TX: Psychological Corporation.

Wilson, J. A. (1975). Developmental and social interaction in categories of word-definition. *British Journal of Educational Psychology, 45*, 268–278.

Windsor, J. (1994). Children's comprehension and production of derivational suffixes. *Journal of Speech and Hearing Research, 37*, 408–417.

Wing, C. S., & Scholnick, E. K. (1981). Children's comprehension of pragmatic concepts expressed in 'because,' 'although,' 'if,' and 'unless.' *Journal of Child Language, 8*, 347–365.

Winner, E. (1979). New names for old things: The emergence of metaphoric language. *Journal of Child Language, 6*, 469–491.

Winner, E. (1988). *The point of words: Children's understanding of metaphor and irony*. Cambridge, MA: Harvard University Press.

Winner, E., Engel, M., & Gardner, H. (1980a). Misunderstanding metaphor: What's the problem? *Journal of Experimental Child Psychology, 30*, 22–32.

Winner, E., McCarthy, M., & Gardner, H. (1980b). The ontogenesis of metaphor. In R. P. Honeck & R. R. Hoffman (Eds.), *Cognition and figurative language* (pp. 341–361). Hillsdale, NJ: Erlbaum.

Winner, E., McCarthy, M., Kleinman, S., & Gardner, H. (1979). First metaphors. In D. Wolf (Ed.), *Early symbolization: New directions for child development* (pp. 29–41). San Francisco, CA: Jossey-Bass.

Winner, E., Rosenstiel, A., & Gardner, H. (1976). The development of metaphoric understanding. *Developmental Psychology, 12*, 289–297.

Wolf, M. (1984). Naming, reading and the dyslexias. *Annals of Dyslexia, 34*, 87–115.

Wolf, M., Bally, H., & Morris, R. (1986). Automaticity, retrieval processes, and reading: A longitudinal study in average and impaired readers. *Child Development, 57*, 988–1000.

Wolf, M., & Goodglass, H. (1986). Dyslexia, dysnomia, and lexical retrieval: A longitudinal investigation. *Brain and Language, 28*, 154–168.

Wolf, M., & Segal, D. (1992). Word finding and reading in the developmental dyslexias. *Topics in Language Disorders, 13*(1), 51–65.

Wolfenstein, M. (1978). *Children's humor: A psychological analysis.* Bloomington, IN: Indiana University Press.

Wolman, R. N., & Barker, E. N. (1965). A developmental study of word definitions. *Journal of Genetic Psychology, 107*, 159–166.

Wood, J. R., Weinstein, E. A., & Parker, R. (1967). Children's interpersonal tactics. *Sociological Inquiry, 37*, 129–130.

Wysocki, K., & Jenkins, J. R. (1987). Deriving word meanings through morphological generalization. *Reading Research Quarterly, 22*, 66–81.

Zachman, L., Huisingh, R., Barrett, M., Orman, J., & Blagden, C. (1989). *The word test: Adolescent.* Moline, IL: LinguiSystems.

Zigler, E., Levine, J., & Gould, L. (1966). Cognitive processes in the development of children's appreciation of humor. *Child Development, 37*, 507–518.

Author Index

Subject Index

ABOUT THE AUTHOR

Marilyn A. Nippold, PhD, is director of graduate studies for Communication Disorders and Sciences at the University of Oregon. A former public school speech–language pathologist, she obtained her bachelor's degree from the University of California Los Angeles (Philosophy), her master's degree from California State University Long Beach (Communicative Disorders), and her doctorate from Purdue University (Audiology & Speech Sciences), in West Lafayette, Indiana. She has worked at the University of Oregon since 1982, teaching undergraduate and graduate courses and conducting research in the areas of later language development, language disorders in youth, and stuttering.

Notes

Notes

Notes

Notes

Notes

Notes

Notes